W9-BAA-133

What Others Are Saying About This Book

"This book is required reading for turning your centers into high performing strategic assets. You cannot achieve excellence in your centers until you clearly understand this book's content."

TODD ARNOLD

Group Vice President, Customer Service, Duke Energy

"Brad Cleveland writes as he speaks at conferences — engagingly and with passion about the global contact centre industry…"

MICHAEL STOCK

Customer Contact Association (CCA) International Board Director and Head of Business and Partnerships, Marketing Communications and Audiences, BBC

"Whether you are a seasoned customer service professional or new to the contact center industry, *Call Center Management on Fast Forward* is a 'must-read' to learn the keys to providing real value to your customers and organization."

LISA SUSIN

Director, Michigan Customer Care Center, Blue Cross Blue Shield of Michigan

"ICMI has transformed Contact Centre Management into a precise science, giving it structure and modularity, which supports, applicability irrespective of size, environment or regional context."

SANDRA DE ZOYSA

Head of Customer Service & Contact Centre, Dialog Telekom, Sri Lanka

"From cost center to profit center? Brad Cleveland leads the way; again and again."

HENK VERBOOY

Chief Editor, CCM Magazine, *The Netherlands*

"As a new call center director, the first edition of *Call Center Management on Fast Forward* was my roadmap. Simply put, this new expanded edition is — once again — a 'must-read' to understand the basic challenges in a modern call center."

MICHELLE FOLLETTE

Director, Portland Customer Contact Center, PacifiCorp

"This book is a classic. It's a must-read for the call center professionals who wish to improve their service quality, achieve process efficiency and reduce operational cost."

LI JIAN

Director, Customer Service Center, Bank of China

"Get it! Read it! Highlight it! Keep it on top of your desk! Read it again and again and again! Share the knowledge with everyone who needs to understand and value the contact center as 'front door to the customer.'"

PHYLLIS BATSON

Vice President, Customer Contact, Exelon – Energy Delivery

"You will learn essential formulas for call center management from reading this book. Furthermore, you will have a definite chance of upgrading your understanding of call center management from Brad's worldwide consulting, speech and intensive research experiences contained in this book."

KJ CHEONG

Director of CIRC, Korea

"Well done, easy to read and recommended content for any contact center employee."

BOOK BOOKER

Senior Vice President, SunTrust Online Business and Technology Solutions, SunTrust Banks, Inc.

"This volume provides a comprehensive overview of how to build a successful call center career... these are the building blocks of knowledge and key insights that anyone in call centers needs — and can — relate to!"

BRETT FRAZER

Regional Customer Service Manager, Customer Service and Support, Asia Pacific Region, Microsoft

"Brad and the ICMI team continue to stay ahead of the curve with the principles of call center management. As the industry evolves, it is critical to have a source that call center management leaders can turn to... this new edition hits the mark."

DEE KOHLER

Director, Customer Service & Membership, Blue Cross Blue Shield Nebraska

"Recommended for all call centre professionals… this book provides clear, easy-to-understand insight into a complex subject."

MALLIKARJUNA RAO

Assistant Vice President – Service Delivery, Idea Cellular Ltd., India

"This new version provides current customer management strategies that capture the essence of effectively serving today's more discerning and ever more demanding customer!"

DOMINICK KEENAGHAN

President, INSIGHTS, Dubai

"This book continues to be the one that I hand out regularly. It is an easy read with great depth for those new to contact centers, and a handy resource for those who are more experienced."

KATHERINE GREGG

Group Manager – Contact Center Consulting, Intuit

"This book is an essential tool for every call centre manager. These principles promote the professionalism of our entire industry."

ANN-MARIE STAGG

Chair, Call Centre Management Association (U.K.) and Head of Customer Contact Centres, Co-operative Financial Services

"Whether you're a small or large call center, this is the 'Complete Guide' to call center management. Learn key ingredients to building a successful call center or refresh your mind on maintaining the right mix for success."

LEE BARONA

Director, Call Center, American Diabetes Association

"This is an outstanding book that provides the necessary tools for managers to effectively manage their day-to-day operations and understand the strategy behind the tasks… invaluable for the new manager of a call center, as well as a seasoned manager striving to increase the value of the call center operation…"

JEAN A. KOSTELANSKY

Director, Physician Services, Northwestern Memorial Hospital

▶▶Brad Cleveland

▶▶Call Center Management On Fast Forward

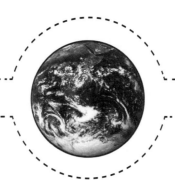

▶▶Succeeding in Today's Dynamic Customer Contact Environment

Updated and Expanded Edition

▶▶Brad Cleveland

▶▶Call Center Management On Fast Forward

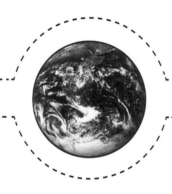

▶▶Succeeding in Today's Dynamic Customer Contact Environment

CMP
United Business Media

Updated and Expanded Edition

Published by:
ICMI Press
An imprint of ICMI, a division of CMP Media LLC
Post Office Box 6177
Annapolis, Maryland 21401 USA
www.icmi.com

To Kirsten. Thank you for your never-ending love and encouragement.

BRAD

Table of Contents

Acknowledgements

A few people have asked me how long it took to write this book. Candidly, I don't quite know the answer. The heads-down writing part took perhaps three or four months. However, it was spread over many more months than that, as blocks of time here and there — in the office, on airplanes and at the kitchen table in the wee hours of the morning. The tougher estimate, of course, is the amount of time it took to acquire the content — e.g., to do the research, gather different angles and observe these principles in action. That answer — many years.

And so, a related and equally difficult question is who gets credit for contributing to the book. I feel so grateful and fortunate to have had so many people contribute in so many ways.

Julia Mayben was my co-author for the first edition — she researched facts, clarified passages, pieced together chapters emailed from hither and yon, and served as project manager. Although she has since moved onto other ventures — writing about boating on the Atlantic Seaboard — her work in the first edition helped make this new version possible. She has my wishes for fair skies and steady breezes.

I also want to thank Susan Hash, who served as editor and project manager, and Ellen Herndon who did the design work; Susan and Ellen are among the most capable professionals with whom I've ever worked. I also want to thank Greg Levin for his work in reviewing and proofing the book, as well as providing a number of the case studies through his work for ICMI's monthly publications.

Others also deserve much credit. Jay Minnucci and Dan Rickwalder made significant contributions to several new sections; Jay was also enormously helpful in reviewing numbers and calculations, as was Tiffany LaReau. Keith Dawson and Joe Fleischer, through their work for *Call Center Magazine*, contributed to Chapters 12 and 16, respectively. Lori Bocklund of Strategic Contact provided expertise and insight into Chapter 16. Mary Murcott's fabulous book, *Driving Peak Sales Performance in Call Centers*, was the basis for a sidebar in Chapter 12. Ted Hopton contributed several key cases, and Debbie Harne reviewed the book to ensure alignment with ICMI educational courses. Linda Harden, who was so instrumental in making the first edition possible, also reviewed this new edition for readability and clarity. Jean Bave-Kerwin, Kelly Brickley, Rebecca Gibson, Laura Grimes, Cliff Hurst, Tim Montgomery, George Nichols, Daniel Ord, Rose Polchin, Marilyn Saulnier, Becky Simpson, Laurie Solomon, Lesley Vereen and other current and past ICMI consultants, associates and course instructors have contributed in many ways to ICMI content and, in turn, helped to shape this book.

ICMI's management team — Philip Chapnick (VP of our group), Ruthann Fisher (Group Director) and Linda Harden (Director of Operations) gave me the running room and encouragement necessary to get this project done. And so many others who are part of the ICMI team helped make this possible, by covering for me, helping with priorities and providing encouragement — thank you!

I'd also like to thank those who provided review comments and testimonials: Todd Arnold, Lee Barona, Phyllis Batson, Book Booker, KJ Cheong, Sandra De Zoysa, Michelle Follette, Brett Frazer, Katherine Gregg, Li Jian, Dominick Keenaghan, Dee Kohler, Jean A. Kostelansky, Mallikarjuna Rao, Ann-Marie Stagg, Michael Stock, Lisa Susin, and Henk Verbooy. Thanks again to each of you!

I owe much gratitude to Gordon F. MacPherson, Jr. (see Foreword), who founded ICMI Inc. in the mid-1980s. He presented the world's first comprehensive seminar on the subject more than two decades ago, and created many of the tools and methodologies that today are used world-wide. Though he retired in 1997, his work still influences the profession — he's a pioneer and a friend, and this book wouldn't be the same without his work.

I'd like to extend a special thanks to my parents, Doug and Annie Cleveland, who have encouraged and prayed for me since day one. My father was instrumental in developing my early interest in technology and communications (I remember when we built a telephone for a third grade project, right down to the carbon and wiring).

Most of all, I want to thank my two favorite people: my wife Kirsten and daughter Grace, who have helped and encouraged me every step of the way. I love you both more than words can express!

Brad Cleveland
Annapolis, Maryland USA
bradc@icmi.com

Foreword

Call Center Management on Fast Forward: Succeeding in Today's Dynamic Customer Contact Environment is a clear voice with an unconfusing message: To successfully lead and manage, you need a good understanding of the unique call center environment and an effective planning and management framework.

This message was true when telephone operators used cord switchboards and when inbound agents at catalog companies used pen and paper to capture order information. It is just as true in this new century, as call center managers deal with new contact channels, Internet-based services, virtual call centers, and quality and performance issues that impact the entire organization. And it will continue to be true in the future as call centers increasingly heed the demands of customers to provide a continuously improving and expanding array of choices for how those customers will be served.

This book outlines principles that you can use and trust. They are not passing fads. For example, service level and queuing theory are not abstract concepts; they are material facts that can be learned. The behavior of humans relating to queuing is sometimes fickle and difficult to predict, but the resources it will take to consistently achieve a specific level of service is a matter of mathematics. And the underpinnings of quality and customer satisfaction are well-known. A comprehension of service level, queuing and quality makes it easy to understand customer contact processes in any industry and rationalizes key decisions and crucially important budgets.

The truly wise understand that rapid and lasting learning comes from choosing well your instructors and texts. The best will not waste your time or go off on tangents. They will present their information in a way that makes it easy to learn and retain.

So... you must be truly wise because you have this book in your hands. Brad Cleveland has made a career of learning everything vital to effective call center management and presenting it with sparkle and conviction. He has paid the price in time, effort and miles to learn what's really happening, and he is the acknowledged leader in this field.

Brad and the ICMI team have put together a book that belongs on the shelf of every call center manager — as well as every senior level executive who oversees customer service operations. Turn the page now for the good stuff. You'll see what I mean!

Gordon F. MacPherson, Jr.

*Gordon MacPherson, Jr. was founder and first president of ICMI (now part of CMP's International Customer Management Institute). One of the industry's most influential thinkers, Gordon launched the first newsletter for call center managers (*Service Level Newsletter, *now* Call Center Management Review*), as well as the first seminar series on call center management. Gordon's formative work helped to shape many of the terms and practices in use worldwide today. He is now retired, and lives in Annapolis, Md.*

Introduction

The first edition of *Call Center Management on Fast Forward* was introduced in 1997. Sales soon surpassed our highest expectations, and we were excited and amazed to see the book reach so many corners of the world. It quickly became evident that it was benefiting from a much larger trend, as organizations everywhere were building their customer contact services and reaching out for management practices that could help. While we made small revisions along the way, we decided that nine years and 18 printings later, it was high time for a major revision.

As I worked on this new edition, two seemingly contradictory observations kept coming to mind. One is *how much* the call center environment has changed in the past decade. No surprise there, I'm sure. Management practices, processes, technologies, customer expectations and even (or especially) the call center's role in the organization have all substantially evolved. But the other thought that I couldn't shake was *how little* things had changed. After all, the fundamental principles of good management still apply — they always will.

So… which view was more correct? There were urgent and practical implications to finding the right answer — after all, I was *supposed to be* working on an update. And yet, chapter after chapter — especially in the early weeks of the project — I found myself staring at a cursor blinking over text I was loath to change.

Then it hit me… both views are correct! The bedrock principles and fundamentals will always be with us — and understanding and applying them leads to new discoveries and opens new frontiers. I pondered other examples. A talented artist with a solid understanding of color, texture, depth and design can create beautiful new paintings that challenge conventional practices. An ever-deeper grasp of the fundamentals of flight has enabled engineers to move us beyond biplanes and into the space age. Exciting new discoveries in medicine are based largely on what has come before.

With this liberating revelation, I was off to the races. Rather than tamper with what didn't need changing, the challenge became one of filling in gaps, adding where necessary and rounding out the story. In the process, I became more and more excited about the important role customer contact services play in today's economy, and how much more they will change in coming years.

So, what's different about this new edition? There are all-new chapters — on building a customer access strategy (Chapter 2), establishing performance objectives (Chapter 12) and designing an effective organization (Chapter 15) — and every chapter has been expanded to reflect current trends and developments. But if you read an earlier version of the book, you'll also find much familiar territory. All of the basics from the first edition are here — i.e., the factors of caller tolerance, customer expectations, the planning process, the immutable laws and, in general, the principles of effective management. It's my hope that this book will be truly helpful to you as you build your organization's customer contact services, and that you will use it often.

Many times during this project, my four-year-old daughter, Grace, would climb onto my knee and ask me, "Daddy, is your book done yet?" I can finally say yes — yes, it's done! But I can't help but think that, as a profession, we're just getting started.

Brad Cleveland
Annapolis, Maryland
bradc@icmi.com

Part One:
The Vibrant Customer Contact Environment

CHAPTER 1:
Familiar Challenges, New Opportunities

CHAPTER 2:
The Blueprint — A Customer Access Strategy

CHAPTER 3:
Driving Forces in Customer Contact Centers

To succeed in today's call center, you must understand the new environment: More types of contacts, increasing complexity and heightened customer expectations. But to those who make the effort to acquire the right professional skills and knowledge, leadership and management opportunities are significant.

CHAPTER 1:
Familiar Challenges, New Opportunities

The future ain't what it used to be.

YOGI BERRA

It all started about a century ago. The early 1900s were abuzz with progress. Steam-driven locomotives could whisk you across a continent in a matter of days. Henry Ford's horseless carriages — automobiles, as the French called them — could take you across town in a fraction of an hour. And in 1903, two brothers from Dayton, Ohio, Wilbur and Orville Wright, built a machine that could fly — an invention that was quickly improved upon by others, to the point that the British established the first airmail route in 1911. Speed was becoming a potent economic and social currency.

It was against this backdrop that popular use of the telephone — invented in 1876 — really began to take off. As fast as an airplane could fly between two points, the telephone could "get you there" even faster. "By the wondrous agency of electricity, speech flashes through space and, swift as lightning, bears tidings of good and evil," wrote French artist Puvis de Chavannes in a caption to one of his famous murals.

Historian John Brooks described the impact of the telephone on life in the first decade of the 1900s this way: "In city and country alike, the telephone was creating a new habit of mind — a habit of tenseness and alertness, of demanding and expecting immediate results, whether in business, love or other forms of social interaction."

But fast-growing demand in both transportation and communication services — they have fed, not displaced, each other from the beginning — was creating enormous new challenges. Whether it was roads, rails, runways or relay circuits, the pressure was on to get capacity in place.

The First Call Centers?

As the subscriber base grew, telephone companies were contending with a particularly vexing resource-planning problem. Automated central offices hadn't yet been invented, and so human operators were required to establish connections for callers. One big question was, how many telephone operators are necessary? Too few, and service levels would be unacceptable to callers. But too many would be inefficient for telephone companies and would drive up costs for subscribers. Further complicating the issue: Calls arrived randomly, driven by the myriad motivations individual callers had for placing the calls. It was one thing to get physical roads, telephone networks and rail systems in place. But it was a different challenge altogether to get dynamic calling demand accurately matched up with the correct number of human operators — day in, day out, morning, noon and night. And service that was slow or unavailable was simply unacceptable to a public that had thoroughly embraced this new means of communication.

In the years that followed, many bright people would grapple with these and related resource management challenges. One of the first was A.K. Erlang, an engineer with the Copenhagen Telephone Company in Denmark, who, in 1917, developed the queuing formula Erlang C. The formula is still widely used today in call centers for calculating staffing requirements. Others who followed Erlang focused on developing disciplined forecasting techniques, scheduling methodologies and system reporting parameters. The advances continued.

Ring of Familiarity?

A century later — even as speed and innovation have reached levels unimaginable to our predecessors of just 10 decades ago — there are unmistakable similarities. We are abuzz with innovation — from 550-seat airplanes to broadband wireless services. Speed is a powerful economic force. Capacity issues still challenge us. And Brooks' description of the early 1900s is just as fitting today — probably more so: Communication technologies have fed a habit of demanding and expecting immediate results.

If you manage a modern call center, there is a particularly familiar ring to the challenges the early telephone switchboard centers faced. Accurately matching resources to demand in a dynamic, always-changing environment is an ever-present challenge. Forecasting the workload, getting the right people and other resources in place at the right times, developing accurate budgets, meeting customer demands — these continue to be key objectives.

A Definition for Call Center Management

ICMI has developed a definition of call center management that has been published numerous times: "Call center management is the art of having the right number of properly skilled people and supporting resources in place at the right times to handle an accurately forecasted workload, at service level and with quality."

This definition can be boiled down to two major objectives: 1) Get the right resources in the right places at the right times; and 2) do the right things. Or more succinctly, provide service level with quality.

> Call center management is the art of having the right number of properly skilled people and supporting resources in place at the right times to handle an accurately forecasted workload, at service level and with quality.

THE RIGHT RESOURCES IN THE RIGHT PLACES AT THE RIGHT TIMES...

The ability for call centers to accomplish these objectives didn't happen overnight. In terms of meeting service level objectives, the call center industry has evolved through three primary stages:

1. SEAT-OF-THE-PANTS MANAGEMENT — very little consideration of service level in planning.

2. SERVICE LEVEL AWARENESS — an effort to maintain service level as contacts arrive, but only a vague correlation to service level in planning.

3. CORRELATING SERVICE LEVEL TO THE ORGANIZATION'S MISSION — choose an appropriate service level and tie resources to achieving it.

Individual organizations have evolved through the same general stages, and many now have linked service level to quality and their overall mission. To do so, you need an overall plan that defines how you will interact with

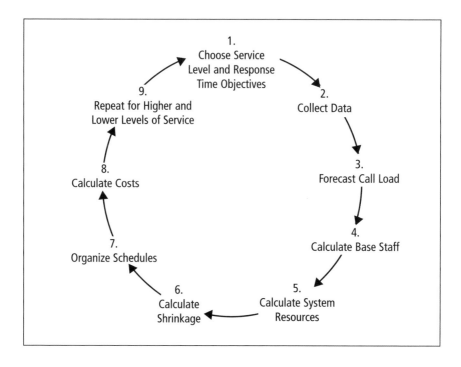

customers — we'll look at the importance of developing and maintaining a "customer access strategy" in Chapter 2. Then, you will need a systematic planning and management process, which can be summarized in nine steps:

1. CHOOSE SERVICE LEVEL AND RESPONSE TIME OBJECTIVES. These two major objectives set parameters for the two major types of contacts: Those that must be handled when they arrive (requiring a service level objective), and those that can be handled at a later time (requiring a response time objective). Service level takes the form of "X percent of calls answered in Y seconds," e.g., 90 percent of calls will be answered within 20 seconds. Response time is defined as "100 percent of contacts handled within N days/hours/minutes," e.g., all customer email will be responded to within 24 hours. Service level and response time objectives must be understood, taken seriously and adequately funded. We'll look at them in detail in Chapter 4.

2. COLLECT DATA. Today's call center systems are important sources of planning data, telling you how many contacts you're getting, where they are going, how long they last, what the arrival patterns are, and how the call mix is changing. But you also need information from a myriad of other sources, such as what marketing is up to, how customer preferences are changing, competitive activity that may impact your workload, and relevant developments in the economy. We'll discuss this important step in Chapter 5.

3. FORECAST CALL LOAD. Call load includes three components: average talk time, average after-call work (wrap-up) and volume. A good forecast predicts all three components accurately for future time periods, usually down to a half-hour. Forecasts must include all types of contacts — telephone calls, email, chat, Web-based contacts and others. We'll discuss forecasting in Chapter 6.

4. CALCULATE BASE STAFF. Most call center managers use Erlang C or variations of it to calculate staffing requirements. Erlang C is the formula used in virtually all workforce management software systems. But capabilities such as skills-based routing and complex network environments present challenges that may require computer simulation and modeling. We'll explore these issues in Chapter 7.

5. CALCULATE SYSTEM RESOURCES. Staffing and system resource issues are inextricably associated and must be calculated together. We will summarize this step in Chapter 7.

6. CALCULATE SHRINKAGE. Rostered staff factor and shrinkage are terms that relate to an important step in planning: You've got to be realistic and account for breaks, absenteeism, training, non-phone work and all of the other things that keep agents from handling customer contacts. We'll take a look at this important step in Chapter 8.

7. ORGANIZE SCHEDULES. Schedules are essentially forecasts of who needs to be where and when. They should lead to getting the right people in the right places at the right times. We will discuss this process in Chapter 8.

8. CALCULATE COSTS. This step projects costs for the resources required to meet service and quality objectives. We will cover cost issues throughout Parts Two, Three and Four.

9. REPEAT FOR HIGHER AND LOWER LEVELS OF SERVICE. Preparing budgets around different levels of service provides an understanding of cost trade-offs, which is invaluable in budgeting decisions. We will discuss this step in Chapter 10.

DOING THE RIGHT THINGS...

The best-managed call centers do a good job of resource planning and management, and have built processes that are systematic, collaborative and accurate. But of course, meeting your service level and response time objectives is just an enabler — the game then comes down to what you do once those contacts reach the right places.

Doing the right things means creating real value for your customers and for your organization. Customer contact centers have the potential to create value on three distinct levels:

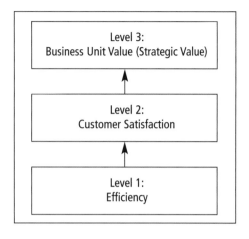

LEVEL 1: EFFICIENCY. Because call centers pool information, people and technology resources, they are a highly efficient means of delivering service. Disciplined planning, accurate staffing and schedules, and effective real-time management complement and further the call center's inherent efficiencies. These subjects are covered in Parts Two and Three of the book.

LEVEL 2: CUSTOMER SATISFACTION. In recent years, research has begun to reveal the powerful connection between high levels of satisfaction and profitability. Even in non-commercial environments, such as government agencies or non-profit organizations, high levels of customer satisfaction bring many returns to the organization. One of the call center's major objectives should be to ensure that customers' views end up as often as possible in the "top box" on customer satisfaction surveys.

LEVEL 3: BUSINESS UNIT VALUE (STRATEGIC VALUE). Contact after contact, hour after hour, day after day, the call center captures information that can literally transform an organization — e.g., intelligence that helps other departments improve quality, further research and development, focus marketing campaigns, detect potential legal or publicity problems, and provide input on how to improve self-service systems.

Many organizations are focused primarily on the first level of value — efficiency. But you can't focus on efficiency alone and be very efficient. Delivering strategic value requires measures, objectives and processes that support organizationwide contributions. It is essential to take inventory of the call center's job roles, processes, objectives and technologies and design and align them to deliver maximum value on all three levels. This subject will be covered throughout Parts Four and Five of the book.

Have the Rules Changed?

Today's always-on, connected world is changing the nature of how products and services are sold, delivered and supported. Interactions enabled by the Internet, wireless capabilities and multimedia technologies are fueling new customer demands, and creating new opportunities for those organizations that are prepared — and enormous problems and headaches for those that are falling behind. Many managers are justifiably wondering, where are the changes taking us?

Effective step-by-step planning and management is as important as ever in the emerging customer contact environment.

In fact, many inside the industry have challenged the term "call center" because call centers do more than handle telephone calls. Further, the word "center" doesn't accurately depict the many multisite environments, nor the growing number of organizations that have teleworking programs. Call center has evolved into an umbrella term that can refer to sales and service centers, technical support functions, information lines, emergency hotlines and other types of environments. (I use the terms "call," "contact," "transaction" and "interaction" interchangeably throughout the book. The words "caller" and "customer" are used interchangeably, as well. See further discussion on terms in Chapter 2.)

So, what about call center planning and management? Have the rules changed? Should the planning process change? At a basic level, no. Let's say that customers browsing your Web site can click a button, be connected to the call center and receive immediate live assistance — a contact type that will become more common with the proliferation of broadband services and voice over internet (VoIP) capabilities. To manage that environment, you first choose an appropriate service level (Step 1). You then establish processes for collecting data related to these contacts (Step 2). Next, you forecast the load (Step 3), and calculate staff and system resources required (Steps 4 and 5). After that, you account for shrinkage and organize schedules (Steps 7 and 8). You then analyze costs and compare them to other service levels (Steps 8 and 9). All the while, you'd be developing services and processes that boost customer satisfaction and create value for other business units.

Or, how about communicating with customers who one day may be using hand-held video devices? Will that change things? Beyond the need for agents to look and dress the part, management issues will be very familiar. The principles of getting the right people and supporting resources in the right places at the right times, doing the right things will never become obsolete. Effective step-by-step planning and management is as important as ever in the emerging customer contact environment.

So... how is call center management changing? There are new contact channels to manage. Customers demand service that is ever faster, more intuitive, more effective. As self-service capabilities become more prevalent and robust, contacts requiring agents' assistance are more complex. Senior managers are demanding better returns on these investments. And the stakes for your organization will be higher than ever. Call it call center management on fast forward!

If you learn the principles covered in this book, your skills and knowledge will be in high demand — and you'll be ready for whatever the future brings.

PROFESSIONAL SKILLS

- Leadership and management
- Communication — writing, speaking and interpersonal
- Project management
- Performance assessments
- Quantitative analysis

From the Back Room to the Boardroom

Well-run customer contact operations have become a major factor in customer retention, competitiveness and the ability for organizations to adapt to changing markets. To call center managers who successfully meet the challenges, the opportunities for advancement are as significant as ever. Call center management — once in the category of "mystical arts" or a backroom function — is emerging as a thriving, global profession.

> **KNOWLEDGE REQUIREMENTS**
>
> - Customer behavior
> - Random call arrival
> - Forecasting
> - Queuing theory
> - Staffing and scheduling
> - Systems and software
> - Organizational behavior
> - Ergonomics and workplace environment
> - Industry vocabulary

An important step to meeting the challenges ahead is to recognize that you are in a bona fide profession that is constantly advancing. Treat it as such. That means staying in tune with the growing body of industry knowledge. It means continual personal growth and development. It requires developing a network of other professionals and resources that you can count on. In short, you have to pay the price in time and effort.

Whatever your background or level of experience, I hope that this book helps you in that effort. Thanks for coming along!

CHAPTER 2:
The Blueprint — A Customer Access Strategy

You've got to think about the big things while you're doing small things, so that all the small things go in the right direction.

ALVIN TOFFLER

It could be that your organization has thousands of agents working across multiple sites. Or maybe you're just getting started — you've got seven people handling contacts in an environment that's still managed rather informally. Or you may not have a call center at all — you're kicking the tires on the idea and asking lots of questions: Does your organization need one? What would it do? How would it operate?

Wherever you are in the development process, you need a high-level plan — a customer access strategy — to guide direction and decisions. As a part of that effort, you will need to review your customers' expectations often to ensure that your plan reflects their needs and realities.

What Is a Call Center?

A prerequisite to developing an effective customer access strategy is to decide that you need a call center — or, in some cases, to acknowledge that you *may already have* a call center but haven't recognized it as such. To hurdle this initial step, it's worthwhile to review what a call center is and does,

13

and to identify the characteristics that define all call centers.

ICMI defines call center as: "A coordinated system of people, processes, technologies and strategies that provides access to organizational resources through appropriate channels of communication to enable interactions that create value for the customer and organization." Yes, it's an involved definition — but call centers are involved operations.

It's often easier to explain what a call center does than to try to define it. And diverse examples are everywhere. I recall receiving a newsletter from Anne Arundel Medical Center (AAMC) in Annapolis, Md. — the hospital serving the area where I live — highlighting its "consumer health line." The center is staffed by local registered nurses and other healthcare professionals. According to the article, the service is available 24x7, and anyone in the community can call for help with anything — from assessing medical symptoms and recommended courses of action, to getting physician referrals, resolving insurance questions and signing up for local wellness classes.

The center is advertised as "the only full-service telehealth line in the country" — a statement others providing similar services would likely dispute. But I doubt that the hospital, which has an excellent reputation, is trying to inflate claims — I think they're just eager to highlight the comprehensive services the center provides and encourage people to use them.

It's a great idea, and a valuable resource to the community and the hospital. You can imagine the rationale that the management team must have thought through before the launch: Customers have thousands of questions. They call different departments looking for answers, often reaching the wrong places. The professionals in those areas don't have the time, training or know-how to handle many of the inquiries that they get. In many cases, the employees fielding the contacts don't know where to send callers for the information they need, so they direct them to other units or back to the switchboard.

Then someone begins to ponder a solution. *Hey... what if we create a cen-*

tralized service that is equipped to handle all of the diverse questions we get from customers? We could train agents well and give them access to all of the information they will need, from symptom-based references to class schedules. We'll hire nurses to handle the medical-related questions. And we'll put in a system for documenting each contact, logging the symptoms described and advice provided. We'll put in processes for coordinating with the rest of the organization so that information is up-to-date and accurate.

And then, one day... applause is in order... a new call center is born! And it shares the basic characteristics common to all call centers:

- Customer contacts are received and made by a group of people, not a specific person.
- Agents are cross-trained to handle a variety of contacts.
- Calls are distributed based on agent availability and/or specific skills.
- Agents have access to information on products, services, the organization's policies and other resources they will need to handle contacts.
- Reports provide managers with information on services delivered, number of contacts, service levels and other data, which can be used for forecasting, planning and process improvements.

Interestingly, there are a lot of people running call centers who don't know they are... well, running call centers. They know they get lots of contacts, and that they need the right people available at the right times or the queue gets out of control and customers quickly become unhappy. And they realize that somehow they need to predict how many contacts they are going to get, when they are going to arrive, and the agents and supporting resources needed to handle them.

One fortunate day, they will be on the Web or talking to a supplier or colleague, and they'll learn that call center management is a *bona fide profession* supported by a world of resources. They will begin to find books, conferences and professional membership organizations made up of other people who also run call centers. They will realize — with great relief and a growing sense of excitement — *they are not alone!*

WHAT SHOULD YOU CALL IT?

As organizations continue to transition centers dominated by telephone calls into multichannel operations handling email, chat, click-to-talk and other types of contacts, many have justifiably questioned the use of the term "call center." Examples of alternative terms include:

- Contact center
- Interaction center
- Customer care center
- Customer support center
- Customer communications center
- Customer services center
- Sales and service center
- Technical support center
- Help desk
- Information line

There are also terms specific to vertical industries, i.e., reservations center (travel), hotline (emergency services) and trading desk (financial services).

Although the jury is still out on which terms will emerge as front-runners in the long run, the general business press is widely using the term call center, while many inside the industry prefer contact center, customer care center or (when applicable) technical support center. However the terms evolve, there is a parallel and very positive development taking place: Business executives and consumers alike are beginning to develop a better understanding and appreciation of what these operations do and how important they are to customers and organizations.

(There's also a different ilk of managers — those who run call center-like environments but refuse to acknowledge them as call centers. "We're a help desk or a professional support line or an internal hotline," they say. "We're different." I'm not referring to those who simply reject the term "call center" — no problem there. Rather, I'm referring to those who miss out on the benefits that forecasting, staffing, scheduling and other disciplined call center management practices could yield because they purportedly don't apply. Thank goodness for those who one day decide that, whatever they call their operation, call center management principles and practices *do apply*.)

In short, call centers enable customers to access the resources they need on a real-time basis. The best deliver these services efficiently, while boosting customer satisfaction and helping to improve the larger organization's products, services and processes. But that doesn't just happen. It requires a plan — a customer access strategy.

Developing a Customer Access Strategy

A customer access strategy can be defined as "a framework — a set of standards, guidelines and processes — defining the means by which customers are enabled to access the information and services they need."

At some point in developing customer contact services, the need for an overall plan becomes obvious. Not only have management activities multiplied, the interrelated nature of decisions has implications for existing organizational structure and personnel responsibilities as well as on the allocation of resources, human and otherwise. Every decision must be viewed in terms of its impact on others and on overall results and direction.

As with corporate strategy, a customer access strategy can take many different forms. But the most effective plans cover, in one form or another, these essential components:

CUSTOMERS: This part of the plan summarizes how customers and prospective customers are segmented (e.g., by geography, purchasing behavior, demographics, volume of business or unique require-

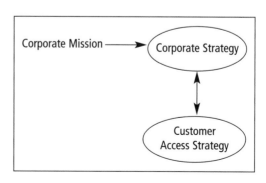

ments) and how the organization will serve each segment. Customer segmentation generally comes from the organization's marketing strategy, but given the operational realities and tradeoffs of serving different segments differently, call center managers are increasingly involved in this process. You may also want to establish guidelines for how the organization communicates with customers and ensures coordination across units (e.g., informing the call center of marketing campaigns).

> A customer access strategy is a framework — a set of standards, guidelines and processes — defining the means by which customers are enabled to access the information and services they need.

CONTACT TYPES: This step anticipates and identifies the major types of interactions that will occur — e.g., placing orders, changing orders, inquiries, technical support, etc. Each type of interaction should be analyzed for opportunities to build customer value and enhance customer satisfaction and loyalty.

ACCESS ALTERNATIVES: This step — where strategy really begins to hit home for call centers — identifies the organization's communication channels (e.g., telephone, Web, fax, email, IVR, kiosk, handhelds, face-to-face service, postal mail, etc.) along with corresponding telephone numbers, Web URLs, email addresses, fax numbers and postal addresses.

CUSTOMER ACCESS STRATEGY COMPONENTS

- Customers
- Contact types
- Access alternatives
- Hours of operation
- Service level and response time objectives
- Routing methodology
- People/technology resources required
- Information required
- Analysis and business unit collaboration
- Guidelines for deploying new services

HOURS OF OPERATION: This part of the plan identifies

appropriate hours of operation and how they may be different for different contact channels and customer segments. Generally, self-service applications will always be available, while some agent-assisted services may be available 24x7 and others have more limited hours. Decisions should be driven by cost and service considerations defined in the plan.

SERVICE LEVEL AND RESPONSE TIME OBJECTIVES: This step summarizes the organization's service level and response time objectives. Different objectives may be appropriate for different contact channels and customer segments.

ROUTING METHODOLOGY: How — by customer, type of contact and access channel — is each contact going to be routed and distributed? While these terms have inbound connotations, this also applies to outbound; e.g., when the organization originates the contacts, through which agent group or system will the contact be made?

PEOPLE/TECHNOLOGY RESOURCES REQUIRED: This step transitions from "getting the customer's contact to the right place at the right time" into "doing the right thing." Which agents or systems will be required for each customer segment and contact type?

INFORMATION REQUIRED: What information on customers, products and services will need to be accessible to agents and callers? What information should be captured during contacts? How will the organization comply with applicable privacy or reporting requirements?

ANALYSIS AND BUSINESS UNIT COLLABORATION: This step defines how the information captured and produced during contacts will be used to better understand customers and to improve products, services and processes. You may also want to summarize major performance objectives and how the call center's value and contributions will be measured.

GUIDELINES FOR DEPLOYING NEW SERVICES: Finally, the plan should outline a framework for deploying new services, including technology architecture (corporate standards and technology migration plans) and investment guidelines (priorities and plans for operational and capital expenditures). This step should also describe who will keep the customer access strategy current as services evolve — e.g., who has overall responsibility, how often the plan will be updated, and who has ownership of individual components.

Your customer access strategy will help you formulate answers to many important questions. For example:

- How should your call center be organized — e.g., how should agent groups be structured?
- What kinds of skills and knowledge will your agents, supervisors and managers need? How should your hiring and training practices support these requirements?

WHAT DOES A CUSTOMER ACCESS STRATEGY LOOK LIKE?

Customer access strategies are like business plans in the sense that some are well-documented and others exist only in pieces and in the heads of various managers. Too often, the latter is the case.

But there are standout examples of plans that are effective and up-to-date. A mobile phone company that I have worked with has a well-organized customer access strategy. It consists of a cover page that is a directory to other documents that, in turn, define customer segments, track access numbers and email addresses, document service levels and other objectives, and provide guidelines for rolling out new services. The plan includes different types of documents (spreadsheets, database files, text documents), but the directory pulls it all together. It could be printed out, but would be many pages long (primarily because it includes long lists of access numbers and related data), so they keep the files in a shared directory.

The most impressive aspect of the plan is that it lists who is responsible for keeping the overall plan current, and the individuals who have ownership over various components; e.g., marketing (customer segments), telecommunications (access numbers) and others. Each document has an "updated on __" date. The plan is current, and they don't make major decisions without referring to it.

- What system capabilities best support your strategy? Do you have what you need inhouse or will you need to build, buy or contract for required technologies?
- What kind of processes best support your plans? Where should they be refined or restructured?
- Is it feasible or advisable to outsource some or all of your call center services? (If so, the customer access strategy is still the responsibility of the client organization.) What capabilities must the outsourcer have to support your requirements?
- Can call center strategy help shape the organization's strategy (e.g., by helping to differentiate the organization's services)? Are the organization's overall strategy, call center strategy and the realities of budgets and resources in alignment?

Make It Unique!

I'm often asked for a list of "best practices" related to various components of the customer access strategy: What access channels should be opened up? How many agent groups should there be? How many menu selections in the IVR? The fact is, beyond applying the sound management principles we'll be looking at throughout the book, these decisions are yours to make.

Your customer access strategy should be a reflection of your organization's unique brand. Southwest Airlines — known as a leading low-cost carrier — doesn't use IVR menus; after hearing an upfront announcement that lower fares may be available on Southwest.com, all calls go to a common group. Of course, most airlines use lots of menus to offload calls that can be automated (i.e., flight arrival and departure times) and to get them to specific agent groups. But the management team at Southwest believes that keeping things simple for customers is an extension of their brand and culture. *Lesson: It's OK to depart from accepted practices when that makes sense for your organization.*

Another example of a unique customer access strategy is Centrelink Call, set up by the government of Australia. Centerlink Call is a virtual call center consisting of 27 sites with around 4,000 agents who handle calls for a wide range of government agencies and services. It makes sense: Why duplicate recruiting and hiring, training, technologies, network services, workstations and other processes and services across every agency? *Lesson: A thoughtful customer access strategy can transform your organization, even one as large and involved as a national government.*

Your customer access strategy should be a reflection of your organization's unqiue brand.

Internet businesses are opening up a variety of new access alternatives. For example, Sears.com has a click-to-call feature in the "personal kitchen advisor" and "personal laundry advisor" sections of its Web site where customers can enter their phone number in a field and indicate whether they would like to be called right now, or in one minute, five minutes or an hour. Amazon.com, Hermes.com and a growing number of other online retailers are providing similar services, and it will likely only be a matter of time before various click-to-call services are commonplace. *Lesson: Innovative access alternatives are pushing the boundaries of technology and furthering customer expectations.*

Many companies have personalized their services and systems. For example, 1-800-FLOWERS and 1-800-LOVEBOAT (Princess Cruises) are hard to forget. Amtrak's speech recognition system — "Julie" — books thousands of reservations a day. Gardener's Supply Company hires agents who love to garden and even has a garden outside the call center building (their customer service tagline is "Gardener to gardener… how can we help you?"). Yes, your hiring practices and culture are extensions of your customer access strategy! *Lesson: Your customer access strategy can help give your company pizzazz and personality.*

Of course, creating an effective and appropriate customer access strategy depends on a good understanding of your customers. Who are your customers? What do they expect? How are their expectations changing?

Evolving Customer Expectations

Customer expectations are constantly evolving because improvements in service shift customer demands. While customers initially appreciate better services, they quickly get used to, expect and demand them. Further, the experiences that customers have with any organization — not just yours or others in your vertical industry — help to shape their expectations and demands. In short, service leaders in any sector are raising the bar for *every organization.*

Fortunately, zeroing in on customer expectations is not the hit-or-miss proposition it may seem. ICMI has followed this issue since the early 1990s, and we've found 10 customer expectations that consistently emerge from customer feedback and surveys.

The real challenge, of course, is in defining what these expectations

10 KEY CUSTOMER EXPECTATIONS

1. Be accessible
2. Treat me courteously
3. Be responsive to what I need and want
4. Do what I ask promptly
5. Provide well-trained and informed employees
6. Tell me what to expect
7. Meet your commitments and keep your promises
8. Do it right the first time
9. Follow up
10. Be socially responsible and ethical

mean. Fifteen years ago, *being accessible* meant having a call center, a toll-free number and well-trained, well-equipped agents. Today, multiple channels of access, 24x7 operations and one-stop, once-and-done contacts have become well-established practices. Appropriate service level and response time standards, easy-to-use self-service capabilities, and the ability to reach the right agents through the desired channels are also important aspects of accessibility. And technologies continue to evolve: Advances in Web-based services, mobile devices and telematics (vehicle-based navigation and communication systems) are examples of developments that are furthering the meaning of accessibility.

While *courtesy* used to refer primarily to the way agents handled calls, the definition today is much more systems- and process-dependent. Don't make customers repeat the same information. Don't transfer them around. And don't make them go over their account history again. Simple steps can go a long way, such as programming IVR menus that are intuitive to use and that allow callers to opt out. Another issue we see in customer surveys: "Put your phone number where I can find it when I need it!" Listing appropriate phone numbers, URLs and email addresses on your Web site, as well as on billing statements, product manuals, etc., conveys that you care and are committed to delivering high levels of service.

Definitions of *responsiveness and promptness* are also evolving. Consider email response times, which have seen significant revisions in recent years — from several days to 24 hours to a matter of hours in many organizations. Some organizations are staffing for email contacts similar to phone calls and are handling them as they arrive. Customers also expect all contact channels to be integrated and work seamlessly — e.g., changes a customer makes to an account online will be reflected in the records that agents can access.

Another common expectation — *provide well-trained and informed employees* — continues to challenge many organizations. With multiple channels of contact and better-informed consumers, this is as important as ever. Leading call centers are making monumental efforts to change recruiting and hiring practices, educate agents and managers, and implement the necessary tools and processes.

Tell me what to expect. Meet your commitments and keep your promises. Do it right the first time. Follow up. These issues are inextricably interrelated and require that people, processes and technologies work in sync. For example, automated replies to email messages can help to establish response time expectations. Complementing the automated replies are forecasts, schedules, tools and training that ensure contacts reach the right agents at the right times and are handled appropriately. Similarly, commitments that call center agents make must be backed up by people, processes and technologies across departments to ensure that orders, deliveries, account changes, etc., are handled as promised. Consumers seem to live by the mantra "trust, but verify" — they'll trust your organization if you fulfill your end of the bargain.

Be socially responsible and ethical. Lapses, or even perceived lapses, in ethics or social responsibility quickly make the rounds in networked, digital communities. Watchdog groups have established numerous Web sites and blogs, and consumers can monitor activities and quickly sound alarms. Corporate ethics and responsibility concern the entire organization, but the call center as a hub of communication tends to be at the center of these issues, which can develop quickly.

In short, knowing your customers and anticipating their expectations is essential to developing an effective customer access strategy. Yes, it's a challenge. But the positive news is that evolving customer expectations present an enormous opportunity for organizations to differentiate themselves from competitors in a global economy where products and services can otherwise be quickly copied.

How do you make the most of changing customer expectations and ensure that they are being built into your plans and direction? The following are some important rules of the road:

- First, ensure that your management team thoroughly understands the 10 basic customer expectations. Post them prominently. And work considerations of them into all decisions, large and small. (I know of one organization that had its managers literally memorize the list.)

- Don't guess at what your direction should be. Rather than create services based on what your executive team "believes" customers expect, get your information from the source. Ensure that your customer surveys are frequent and detailed enough to provide the specifics related to each of the 10 areas — and how you're measuring up to them.

- Build crossfunctional teams to ensure that the organization is addressing these issues. The call center cannot single-handedly exceed expectations. It takes the organization's combined information, support, processes, products and services to do that. (This reality underscores the call center's potential to disseminate customer input and intelligence throughout the organization, a subject that will be covered in Chapter 13.)

- Finally, ensure that these expectations form the context in which you develop your customer access strategy. They should drive everything from how you segment customers to what channels you make available, service level objectives, hours of operation — right through the list.

Clearly, developing an effective customer access strategy that springs from your customers' expectations is not something you throw together during a weekend retreat. It takes leadership, persistence and participation from across the organization. It's hard work and, in many ways, detailed work. But the payoffs are compelling. From a customer's perspective, a good strategy will result in simplified access, consistent services, ease of use and a high degree of convenience and satisfaction. From the organization's perspective, the benefits translate into lower overall costs, increased capacity, higher customer retention and a framework that guides developments.

Points to Remember

- Call centers in today's environment must be accessible, handle increasingly complex contacts, meet customer expectations, support organizationwide initiatives and deliver a healthy return on investments.

- Meeting these challenges requires an effective customer access strategy, which is a blueprint that guides call center developments and decisions. Your customer access strategy should be appropriate for your organization and customers, and should reflect your organization's unique brand and personality.

- Customer expectations are constantly evolving because improvements in service shift customer demands and because the experiences that customers have with any organization influences their expectations.

- Ten customer expectations consistently emerge from customer feedback and surveys. Defining what these expectations mean and building a customer access strategy around them is an important and ongoing process.

CHAPTER 3:
Driving Forces in Customer Contact Centers

Calls bunch up!

GORDON F. MACPHERSON, JR.

N ewcomers to call centers are often surprised at how different they are compared with other types of customer service and support environments.

"The workload is volatile."

"Timing is so critical."

"I think callers sometimes picture us sitting around in the break room!"

Indeed, call centers operate in a unique environment. The workload *does* change from moment to moment. And when callers can't see the queue, they often become impatient much more quickly than in settings where they can "see" the line and the progress they are making.

In any center that handles at least some inbound contacts (versus all outbound), three major forces are at work: random or peaked call arrival; callers' perception of the queue, be it visible or invisible to them; and caller tolerance. These "driving forces" help explain why the call center environment is so unique.

> **THREE DRIVING FORCES**
>
> - Call Arrival: Random or Peaked?
> - The Queue: Visible or Invisible?
> - The Seven Factors of Caller Tolerance

29

Understanding them is a prerequisite to making good decisions on everything from staffing and scheduling requirements to establishing the right performance objectives.

Call Arrival — Random or Peaked?

If you've spent more than just a few minutes in a call center, you've discovered a dominant fact of life: contacts arrive *as they please.* They certainly do not arrive in anything resembling an even, orderly flow.

RANDOM ARRIVAL

Calls arrive randomly in most call centers most of the time. Take a look at a monitor or a readerboard on the wall. Watch the dynamics. In comes a call. Then one, two more… there's another. And two, three, four more… Exactly when calls arrive from moment to moment is the result of decisions made by callers who are motivated by a myriad of individual needs and conditions. Put another way, *calls bunch up!*

The figure illustrates two possible scenarios of how 50 calls might arrive. The input for the chart came from a statistical table of random numbers.

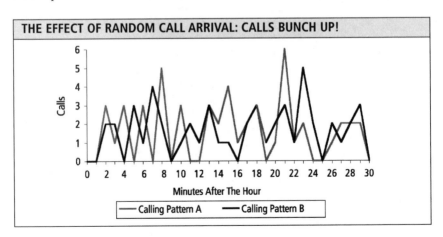

However, there is an important distinction between random call arrival and predictable call arrival patterns. Virtually all call centers — even those of the more volatile type, such as emergency services centers — have distinctive calling patterns, which are usually detectable down to at least a half-hour. You can predict that you will get around, say, 240 calls next Tuesday between 11 a.m. and 11:30 a.m. What you can't predict with any precision is how many of those calls are going to arrive in the first minute, the second minute and so forth.

Consider another example. If you manage an ice cream stand, you can, with some analysis and practice, predict the number of customers and sales based on day of week, time of day, promotions, etc. Saturday afternoons during the summer months will be busy, but traffic will be light on midweek mornings. You could also predict the traffic before and after promotions that you run and events in the community, such as baseball games. But you wouldn't be able to predict the moment-by-moment arrival of customers.

WHAT INCREMENT (INTERVAL) SHOULD YOU USE FOR PLANNING?

Given variations in the workload throughout the day, call center forecasts and resource calculations must be based on specific increments, not daily averages. (Increments, also called intervals, are the smallest units of time reflected in reports.) Typical reporting increments include:

30 minutes. Thirty-minute increments are common because they provide an adequate level of detail and accuracy for many call centers without burying them in unnecessary detail.

15 minutes. Large call centers (e.g., those approaching or exceeding 100 agents in an agent group) often pick up additional accuracy by planning around 15-minute increments.

60 minutes. Call centers that handle long calls (e.g., when average call length approaches or exceeds 30 minutes) often establish report increments and staff calculations around hours.

10 minutes or less. Peaked traffic, which is a surge beyond random variation within a half hour, requires reports and staffing calculations at five- or 10-minute increments.

There are several important implications to random call arrival. First, staffing must be calculated by using either a queuing formula that takes random call arrival into account or a computer simulation program that accurately models this phenomenon. Other approaches almost always lead to inaccurate staffing calculations. And unfortunately, it's not just staffing that will be off. Because staffing impacts the load the network and systems must carry, miscalculated staff inherently leads to miscalculated system and network resources.

Second, call centers that handle inbound contacts operate in a "demand-chasing" environment. At any given time, there are either more calls than staff to handle them or more staff than calls. That means call centers must augment good forecasting and staff-planning with real-time management. A solid understanding of random arrival is necessary to avoid overreacting to normal variation in traffic arrival and underreacting to bona fide trends.

Third, performance objectives and standards must take random call arrival into account. For example, a standard of "N widgets per day" may make sense in a traditional assembly line setting, but it doesn't work in an environment where the workload arrives randomly. Unless the queue is always backed up and service is lousy, your agents will spend a portion of their day just waiting for calls to arrive.

SMOOTH AND PEAKED TRAFFIC

In addition to random or "normal" traffic, there are two other general types of traffic in the telecommunications world: "smooth" and "peaked." Telecommunications traffic engineers have assigned statistical "variance-to-mean" ratios to designate each type of traffic, but essentially the patterns for each look like those in the figure, "Three Types of Traffic Arrival."

Smooth traffic is virtually nonexistent in call centers handling incoming contacts, but can apply in outbound environments. For example, a group of people may be assigned to make outbound calls, one after another, for

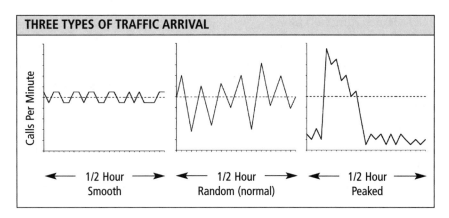

the duration of their shift. In that case, staffing requirements can be based on a units-of-output approach common in many manufacturing and service settings, and the number of trunks (telephone circuits) required will be equal to the number of agents placing the calls.

Another type of call arrival — peaked traffic — is a reality in some call centers. Many of us use the term "peak" in a general sense when referring to call traffic: What's your peak time of year? Peak day of the week? Peak time of day? But the term "peaked traffic" specifically refers to a surge of traffic beyond random variation. It is a spike within a short period of time.

Television and radio ads will often generate peaked traffic. For example, QVC (QVC, Inc.) gets a surge of calls when new products are advertised on its home-shopping channel. Service bureaus that handle everything from charitable donations to self-improvement programs get peaked traffic when those television or radio ads are aired, as do mobile phone providers when they send SMS messages to a large portion of their subscribers. And because of the proliferation of always-on Internet services, email promotions that are sent in batches can also generate an initial surge of contacts (as well as traffic that will arrive in subsequent hours and days). The (typically) large centers that handle peaked traffic can go from zero to hundreds of calls a minute, almost instantly.

It is important to correctly distinguish between random and peaked traffic. When catalog companies send out thousands of new catalogs by mail, they begin getting calls associated with the mail drop. But that's not peaked call arrival. It's random arrival, but at a much higher level than recent history. Similarly, a utility that has a power outage will get a lot of calls until the problem is fixed. But other than the few minutes following the outage, calls will arrive randomly, albeit at a much higher level than usual.

The key question is this: Is there a surge of calls that come and go within less than a half-hour? If the surge lasts longer than a half-hour, it's probably random call arrival.

RANDOMLY ARRIVING PEAKED TRAFFIC?

Some call centers experience call arrival that is a hybrid between random and peaked traffic. Emergency services centers will get calls immediately following a traffic accident. In the past, call volume for a single event would amount to a handful of calls. Now, with the widespread use of mobile telephones, they often get flooded with calls reporting the same accident. And many call centers are learning that news in a wired world travels fast — news stories, blogs, press releases and world events can quickly generate calls. These are examples of "randomly arriving peaked traffic."

The distinction between random and peaked traffic is important. To correctly calculate staffing needs (Chapter 7), you need to know what type of traffic you're going to get. Traffic arrival type also helps dictate what type of real-time management strategies you deploy, which will be covered in Chapter 11.

The Queue: Visible or Invisible?

Queue comes from *cue*, an old French word that means "line of waiting people." Queues are a fact of life in most call centers. After all, answering every call immediately would be about as practical for many call centers as it would be for airlines to check in every passenger immediately. But an important difference between a call center and the lines at an airline counter, grocery store or sports arena is that callers usually can't see how long the queue is and the progress they are making in it.

The top row of faces in the figure "Visible or Invisible Queue," reflects a queue that the customers can see. Few would choose to wait in line so, as they enter the queue, the first face represents them. As they move forward, the subsequent faces illustrate their progress. The final face reflects the fact that they "made it." They are at the counter, hearing the sweet words, "How may I help you?"

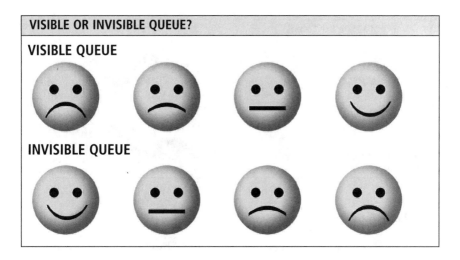

The second row of faces represents a setting where customers are ignorant of the queue they are entering. "Ignorance is bliss," and expectations are initially high. But after some amount of waiting, say 10 or 15 seconds of ringing, they begin to doubt that they are going to get right through (second face). The third face illustrates the transition from doubt to mild frustration. By now, they have probably heard the first delay announcement and it confirms that they are in a queue.

The fourth face represents callers who, from their perspective, have waited *too long*. Often, the first thing they do when they reach an agent is tell him or her about the miserable experience they just had. That's a bad situation because it lengthens call-handling time, which will back up the queue even more... and will cause even more callers to unload on your agents once their calls are answered.

There's another phenomenon that kicks in here. Callers who have waited a long time in queue tend to "dig in their heels" as they attempt to squeeze all the value out of the call that they can. Callers seeking technical support are a classic example: "Geesh, I waited this long to get through, I'd better go over a few more things while I have you."

FRANK & ERNEST ® by Bob Thaves

"...PLEASE CONTINUE TO HOLD. YOUR CALL IS IMPORTANT TO US. ... BUT YOUR TIME ISN'T."

Reprinted with permission.

VISIBLE QUEUE

Software company WordPerfect (now owned by Corel Corporation) pioneered the "visible queue" in the mid-1980s. They set up their system to enable live "queue jockeys" to make announcements of expected hold times to incoming callers. They could also play music and deliver announcements to keep callers entertained and informed while they waited in queue:

Thank you for calling WordPerfect. If you're calling for assistance with Version 2, there are nine of you in queue, and if you just joined us, it looks like the wait is just over three minutes. If you are calling for Version 3, there are 18 callers in queue. But we've got more staff there this morning, and it looks like your wait will be about two minutes. Now, here's Kenny G, from his latest album...

WordPerfect discovered that callers who abandon a visible queue do so at the beginning. Callers who decide to wait generally do so until they reach an agent.

Many call center managers keep a diligent eye on how many callers abandon. But *when* callers abandon is an important consideration, as well. If they are abandoning early on because they are making an informed choice, that's a different story than waiting for what seems like forever in an invisible queue, then hanging up in frustration.

What the queue jockey never said, but what was implicit in the message, was something like:

Thanks for calling. If you're going to abandon, would you kindly do so now, before you get frustrated, drive up our costs and clog up the queue only to abandon before we get to you anyway...

Other software companies, including Microsoft, followed WordPerfect's lead. The feedback from callers was overwhelmingly positive. But having real-time, live queue jockeys is impractical for most organizations. Accordingly, automatic call distributors (ACDs) that could "tell time" began to appear in the early 1990s. With this capability, the ACD can analyze real-time variables, make predictions and announce expected wait times to callers as they arrive.

It's a great feature... but there's a catch. These systems provide fairly accurate predictions in reasonably straightforward environments, especially in large agent groups. However, if you are using any form of complex, contingency-based routing, the system can outsmart itself. Some callers have found themselves actually moving backward in queue as arriving priority callers are moved to the front of the line. By all means, if the feature isn't accurate in your environment, don't use it! This is a challenge that system designers have yet to fully conquer.

There has been quite a bit of debate and study over the years around the question of how callers react to visible versus invisible queues. But I think that the debate misses the real point: Given the choice, callers want to know what's happening!

Someday, we'll probably look back on the days when we, as callers, entered queues we knew nothing about. With the emergence of new wireless and Internet-based technologies, predicted wait times may even be graphically displayed on customers' computers or hand-held devices. Watch for more developments in coming years. (System announcements will be discussed further in Chapter 11.)

Seven Factors Affecting Caller Tolerance

Another important driving force is "caller tolerance." There are seven factors that affect caller tolerance. They influence everything from how long callers will wait in queue to how many will abandon, how many will retry if they get busy signals, and how they will react to automation, such as an interactive voice response (IVR) system. These factors, identified by ICMI research almost two decades ago, also affect how callers perceive the service the call center is providing.

1. DEGREE OF MOTIVATION. How important is the call to callers? What are the consequences to them of not getting through? How badly do they need or want the product or service? Callers experiencing a power outage will usually wait longer to reach their utility than those with billing questions.

2. AVAILABILITY OF SUBSTITUTES. Even though they are highly motivated to make the call, callers who encounter difficulties may abandon if they know of another way to satisfy their need. Web services, IVR applications, walking down the street to a retail location, reading the manual — all are examples of potential substitutes. If callers are highly motivated and have no substitutes, they will retry many times if they get busies, and will generally wait a long time in queue. Even though they do not abandon, they still might be very unhappy about the experience.

THE SEVEN FACTORS OF CALLER TOLERANCE

1. Degree of motivation
2. Availability of substitutes
3. Competition's service level
4. Level of expectations
5. Time available
6. Who's paying for the call
7. Human behavior

3. COMPETITION'S SERVICE LEVEL. If it's easier for callers to use competitive services or if they have a tough time reaching you, they may go elsewhere. (You'll need to consider whether competition is available in a practical sense. For example, if you are a bank and a customer has a problem with an online payment, a competitive bank is not going to be able to help in that case — although if the problem is difficult to get resolved, the customer may decide to switch banks.) It's also important to consider the availability of substitutes and that a call center is often its own competition — callers may dial other numbers available, or they may choose incorrect routing selections in the IVR menu just to reach an agent... any agent... more quickly. The result is transferred calls, inflated reports and longer handling times.

4. LEVEL OF EXPECTATIONS. The experiences callers have had with the call center and the reputation that the organization or industry has for service (or the level of service being promoted) have a direct bearing on tolerance. As discussed in Chapter 2, the experiences that customers have had with any organization — including those in completely different industries than yours — have a bearing on their expectations.

5. TIME AVAILABLE. How much time do callers have to accomplish the call? Doctors who call insurance providers have a well-deserved reputation for not tolerating even a modest wait (or what most of us would perceive to be a modest wait), while retirees calling the same companies may have more time or inclination to talk. Further, the widespread use of mobile phones has created many small windows of time callers have to reach you — e.g., before boarding a flight or in between meetings, when long waits to reach an agent are unworkable and frustrating.

6. WHO'S PAYING FOR THE CALL? Callers are usually more tolerant when they are not paying for the call. In many cases, this is not the substantial issue it used to be when long-distance rates were more expensive. Even if the call center doesn't provide toll-free service, a growing percentage of callers have calling packages associated with mobile and fixed lines that are priced by blocks of time, not distance (although some customers may still be paying for the call, e.g., if they are beyond their usage allotment). In the event they are paying for the call, they are less tolerant than ever of waiting in queue.

7. HUMAN BEHAVIOR. The weather, the customer's mood and the day's news all have some bearing on caller tolerance.

These seven factors are not static. They are constantly changing. Even so, it is important to have a general understanding of the factors affecting your callers' tolerance. Important questions to consider include:

- How motivated are your customers?
- What type of customer is least motivated? Why?
- What type of customer is most motivated? Why?
- What substitutes to contacting you do they have?
- Which substitutes would you want them to use?
- Which substitutes would you not want them to use?
- What are their expectations?
- What level of service are others in the industry providing?
- Who pays for the contacts?
- How might your customers' lifestyles influence their tolerance?
- All things considered, how high is their tolerance level?

Putting Abandonment in Perspective

In many call centers, abandonment rate is viewed as a key measure of how adequately the call center is staffed. I often get questions like, what is an acceptable rate of abandonment? What is abandonment in such and such an industry? Are there any studies on how long callers will wait? What should our service level be to keep abandonment under X percent?

The usual assumptions are: a) There must be industry "standards" for abandonment; and b) abandonment is a good indicator of call center performance. But neither is true.

For one thing, abandonment is tough to forecast accurately, at least on a consistent basis. To do so would require predicting the impact of the seven factors of caller tolerance. But because the conditions that drive them are constantly changing, there are an almost unlimited number of variables that can impact abandonment.

Further, abandonment can be a misleading measure of call center performance. The conventional wisdom is that longer queues translate into higher abandonment. But the seven factors can help to explain apparent paradoxes:

- When financial markets swing significantly, mutual funds and others in the financial sector get a surge of calls. Even though service level may drop, abandonment also often goes down because customers have a higher degree of motivation — and are willing to wait longer, if necessary.

A CASE STUDY IN CALLER TOLERANCE

To celebrate its 10th anniversary since privatization, British Airways launched an international phone promotion in February 1997 that drew millions of callers. The contest offered callers the chance to win virtually free tickets to fly roundtrip on the Concorde, British Airway's legendary (and now retired) supersonic jet, if they were among the first 100 callers to reach the center once the promotion officially began.

The airline designated its Newcastle, England, call center to handle all calls during the promotion and doubled its staff. With a great deal of pomp and circumstance, the contest was kicked off on a Tuesday at 10 p.m. To minimize the use of annoying busy signals, British Airways used a recorded message that gave callers information about the promotion and thanked them for calling. As expected, most callers who got the announcement kept trying to get through; those who reached the queue were willing to wait and abandonment was negligible. Just 25 minutes after the contest began — and over 20 million call attempts later — the promotion was over.

Source: *Call Center Management Review*

CAN YOU ELIMINATE ANY WAIT FOR CALLERS?

One way to eliminate abandonment would be to eliminate the queue. Realistically, though, answering all calls immediately would be highly impractical for most. The reason is the call center version of the law of diminishing returns: When successive individual agents are assigned to a given call load, marginal improvements in service level that can be attributed to each additional agent will eventually decline (see Chapter 9). The table below illustrates this phenomenon.

Input: 500 calls in half-hour; 3.5-minute average handling time		
Agents	**Percent of calls answered immediately**	**Percent of calls answered within 20 seconds**
59	10%	16%
60	24%	35%
61	36%	50%
62	47%	62%
63	56%	72%
64	64%	79%
65	70%	84%
66	76%	88%
67	81%	92%
68	85%	94%
69	88%	96%
70	91%	97%
71	93%	98%
72	94%	98%
73	96%	99%
74	97%	99%
75	98%	100%

There are emerging "virtual queue" or "virtual hold" technologies (e.g., from Virtual Hold Technology, LLC) that enable callers to hang up and receive a return call without losing their place in queue. For callers, this capability prevents the need to leave a voicemail or to wait on hold. For agents, there's little difference between an inbound call or a callback — the system places outbound calls and delivers connected calls to agents much like inbound calls. How well this approach works depends on the willingness and availability of callers to take callbacks and the resource capacity of the center to handle the calls. It's not for everyone, but organizations such as Atmos Energy, BellSouth and Comcast Cable are reporting drops in abandonment and boosts in caller satisfaction. While there's no getting around the laws of nature — the realities of matching resources with demand still exist — this can be a creative and more palatable form of waiting.

- When airlines and resorts advertise significant price specials, callers are generally willing to wait longer. Service level may drop because of heavy response to the promotions, but abandonment will likely be minimal.

- If callers encounter busy signals before they get into the queue, they will almost always wait longer if necessary. The psychology is, "At least I've made it into the system. I'd better hang in there."

While these may be obvious examples, what about the more subtle day-to-day shifts in caller tolerance? It can be baffling. Sometimes, when people have to wait a long time, they wait. Other times, when service level is really good, abandonment is higher than expected. If you don't believe it, graph out service level versus abandonment by half-hour for a few typical days. You are not likely to see an exact correlation.

(I've had a few managers and researchers contact me after the first edition of *Call Center Management on Fast Forward* was published, insisting that abandonment *can* be predicted much of the time. Some are doing excellent work with mathematical tools that correlate abandonment to causal factors, and I think these efforts are useful — as long as abandonment does not become the basis for resource planning nor a replacement for more stable performance measures.)

Organizations that maintain high levels of service — e.g., catalog companies or mutual funds committed to providing good service levels — see abandonment rates of generally no more than 1 percent or 2 percent. No organization has zero abandonment for long — not unless they are answering every call immediately (something even emergency service centers don't always do). Most call centers have a queue at least part of the time. And any time there is a queue, there is opportunity for callers to abandon.

In the final analysis, you can't control how callers will react or the myriad circumstances that influence their behavior. But you can control how accessible you are — how many agents are plugged in and ready, and how many telephone circuits are available. Concentrate on accurately matching resources with workload — the subject of the next five chapters — and abandonment will take care of itself.

Points to Remember

- Call centers handling inbound contacts will either have random or peaked traffic arrival. Outbound call centers often control outbound dialing, resulting in a workload that is smoother. The type of workload — smooth, random or peaked — will dictate the staffing calculations you should use.

- Callers behave differently, depending on whether the queue is visible or invisible. If possible, callers prefer to know the status of the queue.

- There are seven factors that affect caller tolerance, and the impact of these factors is constantly changing.

- You cannot directly control abandonment, but you can control how accessible you are. Concentrate on accurately matching resources with workload, and abandonment will take care of itself.

Part Two:
A Planning and Management Framework

CHAPTER 4:
Accessibility, a Core Value

CHAPTER 5:
Acquiring Necessary Data

CHAPTER 6:
Forecasting the Center's Workload

CHAPTER 7:
Determining Base Staff and Trunks Required

CHAPTER 8:
Successful Scheduling

To effectively manage a contact center, you need a solid planning and management framework. Forecasting, staffing and scheduling activities should be collaborative, focused on customer needs and expectations, and built on appropriate service level and response time objectives.

CHAPTER 4:
Accessibility, a Core Value

"Your call is important to us..."

TYPICAL DELAY ANNOUNCEMENT

The principle of accessibility is at the heart of effective call center management. Without service level objectives, the answers to many important questions would be left to chance. How long will customers have to wait in queue? What is the optimum level of staff and supporting resources? How busy are your agents going to be? Are you prepared to handle the response to marketing campaigns? What are your costs going to be?

Service level ties the resources you need to the results you want to achieve. It measures the degree to which you're getting contacts "in the front door" and to agents. It is a stable target for planning and budgeting. It is a unifying concept, and it is concrete.

Service level is tried-and-true in call centers worldwide for contacts that must be handled when they arrive. Inbound phone calls are a common example, and services such as Web chat, click-to-talk, walk-in customers and video calls (though not common yet) also fit into this category. Consequently, service level will remain an important objective in future generations of call centers.

Most call centers are also responsible for contacts that belong in a second category — those that don't have to be handled at the time they arrive. Examples include most email messages, many types of outbound calls,

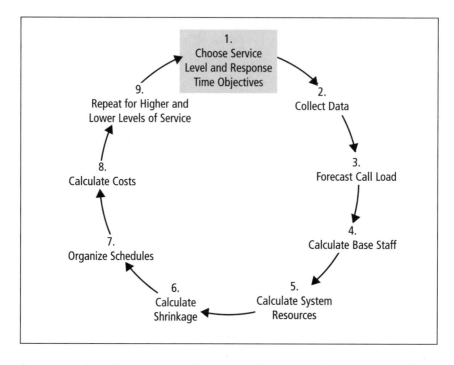

faxes, postal mail, customer voicemail and (eventually) videomail. These transactions allow larger windows of time and more flexibility in terms of when the center can respond. It is important to have concrete "response time" objectives for these interactions and ensure that they are met through disciplined resource planning and management.

Service Level and Response Time Defined

The term service level is often used to refer to an organization's overall responsiveness to customer contacts. (I, too, often use it to refer in a general sense to accessibility.) But, when applied to resource calculations, service level has a specific definition: "X percent of all contacts answered in Y seconds," e.g., 90 percent of calls answered within 20 seconds.

There are various alternative terms in use. Service level is sometimes referred to as telephone service factor, or TSF. Some call it grade of service

(GOS), although I don't prefer that term because it can be confused with the same term to denote the degree of blocking on a group of trunks. It can also be called accessibility and service standard.

Service level is not average speed of answer, X percent of

> **TWO MAJOR CATEGORIES OF CONTACTS**
>
> • Those that must be handled when they arrive. Performance objective: *Service Level*
> • Those that can be handled at a later time. Performance objective: *Response Time*

calls answered (which is the inverse of abandonment — e.g., a 97 percent answer rate would inherently mean a 3 percent abandonment rate) or longest delayed call. When applied to staff requirements, I will stick to the definition and use of service level as it's covered in this chapter.

Response time is the related objective for contacts that don't have to be handled when they arrive, and is defined as "100 percent response within N days/hours/minutes," e.g., handling customer email messages within 24 hours. Response time can be referred to as speed of reply or even "service level" (not to be confused with the specific definition of service level). Throughout the book, I will use response time in the specific sense described here, to refer to the level of service assigned to contacts that can be handled at a later time.

Differentiating between service level and response time is essential because base staff calculations vary for these two major categories of contacts. Service level is used in situations with randomly arriving traffic and requires Erlang C or computer simulation for determining staff requirements. Response time contacts can be held for later processing and can rely on more common methods of staff planning. (We'll discuss staff calculations in Chapter 7.)

There is a point at which response time objectives become service level objectives. For example, some organizations have upped their response time objectives for email from 24 hours to "within the same hour." Some

	Use Service Level	Use Response Time
Inbound telephone calls	X	
Outbound telephone calls*		X
Email*		X
Text-chat	X	
Web call-me-now	X	
Web click-to-talk	X	
Fax		X
Postal mail		X
Video calls	X	
Walk-in customers	X	
*These contacts use response time *if* they can be deferred.		

are going even further and handling email messages as they arrive — just as they do inbound calls. For targets of less than an hour, service level, not response time, becomes the defining objective and base-staff requirements should be calculated using a service level methodology (see Chapter 7).

Understanding and Using Service Level Objectives

Why service level and not percent answered, percent abandoned, average speed of answer or other alternatives? Because "X percent answered in Y seconds" gives the clearest indication of what customers experience when they attempt to reach the organization. And as we'll see in more detail in later chapters, service level is the most stable measurement of the queue.

Average speed of answer (ASA) is a close cousin of service level and is derived from the same set of data. But a big downside to using ASA is that it is often misinterpreted. Most of us tend to assume that the average lies somewhere in the middle of a set of data, or that average represents a "typical experience." Not so with ASA. It is mathematically correct, but does not represent what happens to individual callers.

ASA has its uses so don't throw it out. For example, ASA is an important

AVERAGE SPEED OF ANSWER IS MISLEADING!

Average speed of answer (ASA) reflects the amount of time callers spend in queue, waiting to reach agents. It's available from virtually any ACD. It's widely used and reported — and it's misleading.

ASA is mathematically sound, no problem there. The problem is in interpretation. Let's say you expect 250 calls in a given half-hour and anticipate an average handling time of 3.5 minutes. If you want to achieve an ASA of between 10 and 15 seconds, you'll need 34 agents, which will produce an ASA of 12.7 seconds (these calculations are based on Erlang C, covered in Chapter 7).

But the following illustration gives the waiting times for individual calls in this scenario. Notice what happens. Sixty-five callers will wait five seconds or longer. In the next five seconds, seven of those callers reach agents, so 58 callers are still waiting 10 seconds or longer. In the next five seconds, six more callers will reach agents, leaving 52 callers waiting 15 seconds or more. And so forth. There's still a caller waiting at three minutes.

	Number of Calls Still Waiting This Many Seconds:												
	Immediate Answer	<5	10	15	20	30	40	50	60	90	120	180	240
Calls	185	65	58	52	46	37	29	23	18	9	5	1	0
Scenario: 250 calls in half-hour 34 agents required	3.5-minute average handling time ASA predicted to be 12.7 seconds												

So, the call center reports an ASA of 12.7 seconds and everything's dandy—other than for an unhappy caller or two who say they waited "several minutes" to get through. C'mon, ASA is less than 15 seconds! Surely no one waited over 30 seconds, tops! Take a deeper look, though, and the real story becomes clearer.

variable when calculating trunk load (discussed in Chapter 7). Further, if service level is so bad that zero percent of calls are answered within Y seconds, ASA is a practical alternative to service level. But service level is usually a more reliable and more telling measure of what callers experience — you know exactly what happens to the percentage of callers you define. If you do use ASA reports, just

> **SERVICE LEVEL:**
>
> - Provides a link between resources and results
> - Impacts customer goodwill
> - Impacts levels of lost calls
> - Impacts agent burnout and errors
> - Focuses planning and budgets

remember, ASA is not a bell-shaped curve — longest waits are far beyond what those numbers suggest, and it's important to know what is really happening.

What about abandoned calls? As discussed in Chapter 3, looking solely at abandonment rates as a measure of whether staffing levels were appropriate can be highly misleading. The point is not to ignore abandonment — a high abandonment rate is probably a symptom of significant staffing problems. But a low abandonment doesn't necessarily mean everything is fine. Further, if abandonment is beyond acceptable, what are you going to do? You are going to look at when it's out of whack, and why. You will likely run smack into a low service level. When service level is appropriate, abandonment tends to take care of itself.

All of this brings up an important point: Different callers have different experiences with your call center, even if they are part of the same set of data measured by service level, ASA and other reports. Why? Random call arrival. Because of this reality, you will need an understanding of what happens to different callers. At a high level, service level is the single best measure of these experiences. In later chapters, we'll also look at other measures that will fill the gaps.

How Systems Calculate Service Level

There are a number of alternative methods your call center systems may use to calculate service level. With many, you can specify the calculation you prefer. In any case, you need to know which is being used since each handles abandoned calls somewhat differently. Here are the most common formulas for calculating service level:

1. (CALLS ANSWERED IN Y SECONDS + CALLS ABANDONED IN Y SECONDS) ÷ (TOTAL CALLS ANSWERED + TOTAL CALLS ABANDONED). This calculation takes all calls into consideration and is generally a good alternative. Calls that abandon before the objective positively affect service level.

2. CALLS ANSWERED IN Y SECONDS ÷ TOTAL CALLS ANSWERED. This alternative only considers answered calls and, therefore, is not a good reflection of all activity. Abandonment is entirely ignored. I do not recommend this calculation.

3. CALLS ANSWERED IN Y SECONDS ÷ (TOTAL CALLS ANSWERED + TOTAL CALLS ABANDONED). This alternative tends to be the least popular among call center managers because all calls that abandon negatively affect service level, even those that abandon before the objective. This measure is appropriate in situations where callers enter a queue after they hear a delay announcement.

4. CALLS ANSWERED IN Y SECONDS ÷ (TOTAL CALLS ANSWERED + CALLS ABANDONED AFTER Y SECONDS). With this calculation, abandoned calls only impact service level negatively if they happen after the Y seconds specified. Calls that abandon before the objective do not affect service level. Consequently, this is a way to avoid getting "penalized" by callers who abandon quickly without ignoring abandoned calls altogether. This is an acceptable approach.

Giving Service Level Teeth

For service level to have meaning, it must be interpreted in light of blockage, or calls that aren't getting through. Any time a portion of callers are getting busies, whether the busies are generated by the system or are a result of a limited number of staff and trunks during a busy time of day, the reports only tell you what is happening to the calls that get through. In fact, you can make reports such as service level and average speed of answer look as good as you want them to by limiting the number of calls that get through.

You must also view service level over an appropriate timeframe. Daily service level reports often conceal important information. Service level can take a big hit in the morning, but if you have staff handling every call immediately much of the afternoon, the daily report will look OK. The level of service from callers' perspectives is a different story.

Further, managers who are held accountable for daily reports may have an incentive to manage inappropriately. If the morning was rough, they may keep agents on the phones through the afternoon when the call load drops, just to make the reports look better. That's a waste of valuable time and resources, and it doesn't help callers who encountered poor service earlier in the day.

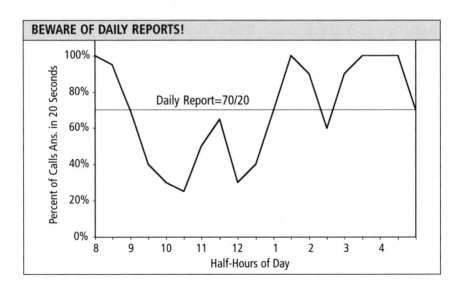

If daily reports are potentially misleading, monthly averages for service level are virtually meaningless. They simply don't reflect the day-by-day, half-hour-by-half-hour realities. Monthly reports that aggregate data remain an all-too-common way to summarize activity to senior management (we'll look at better alternatives in Chapter 10).

Choosing Service Level Objectives

The number of staff you need to handle contacts and the schedules you produce should flow from your service level objective. Imagine that, in a half-hour period, you're going to receive 50 calls that last an average of three minutes. If you have only two people to answer the calls, the delay time for most callers will be long, and you'll probably have high abandonment. As you add people, delay times will drop.

How many people should you add? Enough to reduce the queue to an acceptable level for you and your callers. In other words, the answer to that question becomes your service level target, and you won't be able to achieve your target without the correct level of resources.

WHY THERE IS NO "INDUSTRY STANDARD" SERVICE LEVEL

The optimum service level is affected by:
- The value of a call
- Labor costs
- Telecommunications costs
- The seven factors of caller tolerance
- The organization's desire to differentiate products or services by the level of service provided

There is generally no "industry standard" service level that you can hang your hat on. (There are some exceptions — e.g., service levels for utilities may be regulated.) The optimum service level is affected by a host of factors, including the value of the call, fully loaded labor costs, trunk costs and caller tolerances. An industry standard would have to be based on all call centers having the same values for these things.

The correct service level for you is the one that:

- Meets customers' needs and expectations
- Keeps abandonment at an acceptable level
- Minimizes agent burnout and errors
- Minimizes expenses
- Maximizes revenue
- Is agreed upon and supported by senior management

From a practical sense, no one service level would fit all situations affecting how long callers will wait. Consider the factors of caller tolerance. How motivated are callers to reach you? What is the availability of substitutes for calling you? What is your competition's service level? What are your callers' expectations based on their past experiences? How much time do they have? What are the conditions at the locations from where they are calling?

There are essentially five approaches you can use to determine your service level objective, though all require some subjectivity and judgment.

One is to choose a "middle-of-the-road" service level objective, such as 80 percent answered in 20 seconds. The 80/20 objective was once published in ACD manuals as an "industry standard." In reality, it never was, but many early call centers used this target. 80/20 is still fairly common because for many call centers it is a reasonable balance between callers' expectations and the practicality of having enough staff to meet the objective. But it may or may not be right for you.

ALTERNATIVES FOR CHOOSING A SERVICE LEVEL OBJECTIVE

- Follow the crowd
- Relate to competition
- Minimize abandonment
- Conduct a customer survey
- Combined approach

Another popular method for choosing a service level objective is to benchmark competitors or organizations similar to yours, or to use industry surveys that relay what others are doing. Whatever the approach, keep in mind that the results reported by others and what they are actually achieving may be two very different things. I once worked with three different insurance companies with the same stated service level objective — 80 percent answered in 30 seconds. But the results they were achieving were very different.

EXAMPLE SERVICE LEVEL OBJECTIVES	
General Comparisons	**Service levels (X percent answer / Y seconds)**
Emergency services	100/0
Service level objectives that are "high"	90/20, 85/15, 90/15
Service level objectives that are "moderate"	80/20, 80/30, 90/60
Service level objectives that are "modest"	70/60, 80/120, 80/300

A third approach is to choose a service level objective by essentially asking, how low can you go without losing callers? This assumes that a higher level of service means lower abandonment and vice versa. One big flaw with this approach is that it assumes that as long as callers don't abandon, service is acceptable. But that is not always the case. Further, as discussed in Chapter 3, abandonment is not static. It will fluctuate as the seven factors of caller tolerance change. As a result, abandonment is difficult to forecast, and choosing a service level around abandonment is building on the proverbial foundation of "shifting sand."

Incremental revenue analysis is a variation of this approach and is a more formal methodology to determine the potential impact of abandonment on overall costs. This approach has been traditionally applied in revenue-generating environments (such as reservation centers and catalog companies) where calls have a measurable value. It's much tougher to use in call centers where the value of calls is difficult to measure, such as customer service centers and help desks.

INCREMENTAL REVENUE ANALYSIS (EXAMPLE ONLY)*

Talk Time: 180 sec	After-Call Work: 30 sec		Half-Hour's Calls=200**			Rostered Staff Factor=1.3					
Agents on Phone	Rostered Staff (Agents x 1.3)	Calls Ans. In 20 Sec.	% Lost Calls (Assumed)	% Calls Lost Forever (Assumed)	Trunk Hours	Eventual Calls Handled (Hr.)	Gross Revenue Avg. Call $22.25	Labor Cost $15/Hr.	Toll-free Trunk Cost: .05/Min.	Net Revenue	$ Increm. Revenue
25	32.5	45%	26.0%	7.80%	29.1	369	$8,210	$488	$87	$7,635	—
26	33.8	62%	12.5%	3.75%	24.3	385	$8,566	$507	$73	$7,986	$351
27	35.1	74%	6.5%	1.95%	22.3	392	$8,722	$527	$67	$8,128	$142
28	36.4	83%	3.5%	1.05%	21.3	396	$8,811	$546	$64	$8,201	$73
29 ▲ Optimum	37.7	89%	2.0%	0.60%	20.8	398	$8,856	$566	$62	$8,228	$27
30	39.0	93%	1.5%	0.45%	20.5	398	$8,856	$585	$62	$8,209	-$19

*Rounding variations will produce slightly different results.

**To compare hourly costs, this example assumes call load and staff requirements will repeat (be the same) in the second half-hour.

To use this approach, you attach a cost to abandoned calls and make assumptions around how many calls you would lose for various service levels. The theory is you should continue to add agents and trunks as long as they produce positive incremental (marginal, additional) revenue (value) after paying for their own costs.

Incremental revenue analysis can be valuable when used in conjunction with other approaches, as long as the assumptions are understood and communicated to others in the budgeting process. Nevertheless, don't let the scientific look of this approach be misleading — it requires some pretty serious guesswork.

A fourth method for choosing service level is to conduct a customer survey. This involves analyzing the seven factors of caller tolerance.

While it's always a good idea to know what your callers expect, random call arrival means that different callers have different experiences with your call center. Even for a relatively modest service level such as 80 percent answered in 60 seconds, more than half of the callers will get an immediate answer. Some, though, will wait in queue for three to five minutes (assuming no overflow or other contingency). As a result, many in that set of callers would say that your service level is great, while a handful would tell you that it is poor.

Some managers use a variation of a typical customer survey. They have taken samples of individual callers and then compared the responses to actual wait times of those calls. The results are interesting. In many customer service environments, waits of up to 60 to 90 seconds are generally OK with callers. But beyond about 90 seconds, callers' view of reality can become rather skewed, and their moods can sour. Those who wait three minutes in queue may say they waited four or five. Those who wait five minutes will often tell you they waited something like eight or 10 minutes. Of course, answers will vary based on the type of organization and the seven factors affecting caller tolerance. But the issue remains: At some point, perception deteriorates beyond reality.

THE QUICK VERSION OF CHOOSING A SERVICE LEVEL OBJECTIVE

Sometimes I hear, "OK, the analysis is fine, but let's get to the point: What should our service level objective be?"

Fair enough. If you're in a competitive industry (e.g., shipping, catalog, mutual funds) and want to be on the high end of the scale, 90/20 is fairly common. Others go for 85/15 or 90/15. If you hit these targets fairly consistently, your abandonment rate will likely be around 1 percent or 2 percent.

Going for the middle of the road? 80/20 is common. That's what a lot of banks, insurance companies and travel reservation centers shoot for. 80/30 and 90/60 are other popular mid-range service levels. Hit these objectives, and you'll generally see abandonment rates of 3 percent or 4 percent.

Want a service level that is more modest? 70/60 or 80/120 or even 80/300 are targets more common with technical support centers and government organizations. Abandonment can range up to 10 percent, 15 percent or higher. But hold your judgment — some of these organizations do a great job of hitting these objectives consistently, a lesson many with more lofty goals could use.

Of course, just throwing out numbers like this can be dangerous. There are exceptions to the norm in any industry — e.g., technical support operations that charge for support usually maintain comparably high service levels. Also, interpret these numbers with common sense. If you are an emergency services center, you will target 100/0. On the other end of the scale, there are centers for which 80/300 is a dream. I once worked with a center that was blocking over 70 percent of its calls, yet still losing a large portion of those that got through due to excruciatingly long waits (yes, they've since improved performance!).

Finally, remember that it's not just how high your objectives are, but how consistently you hit them. If your service level objective is 90/20, but you base your performance on daily or monthly summaries, you might be getting walloped mid-mornings when a lot of your customers are calling. If you really want to see how you're doing and what realistic targets might be, produce some service level graphs like those shown in Chapter 8.

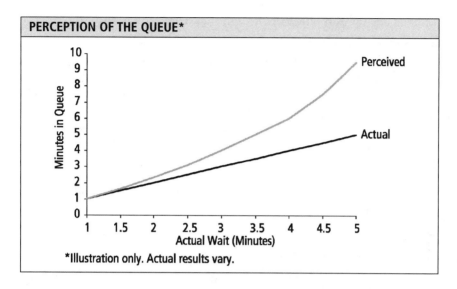

PERCEPTION OF THE QUEUE*

Perceived

Actual

Minutes in Queue

Actual Wait (Minutes)

*Illustration only. Actual results vary.

A fifth — and overall best — approach to choosing service level is an iterative process that combines all of these methods. See where you are, run some calculations, look at what others are doing, and assess what callers are saying and how they are reacting. In that sense, choosing a service level happens further down the line in the planning process. You need a forecast in order to calculate staff, schedules, etc. So this step initially has to happen in parallel with others.

Whichever combination of methods you choose, you will have more success managing your call center just by having a service level target on which to base your planning. Showing senior management what kind of service can be bought for a specific amount of funding is an excellent way to involve them in this decision and to get their buy-in from the beginning.

Realistic Targets, Taken Seriously

If your operation is chronically missing your target, it may be an indication of a fundamental misconception about the importance of service level. You'll need to focus on a service level objective that your center can realistically achieve. Once you know your center's true capabilities, you must be able to back up your objectives with the right amount of resources. Service level should not be a "goal," something that is nice to strive for. An airline doesn't have the "goal" of reaching Hawaii when it takes off from L.A. It's a concrete objective, supported by adequate resources (fuel, pilots, navigation equipment, etc.).

Why don't some call centers get the resources they need? Sometimes it's because the money isn't available. Or maybe management at the top believes that it's possible to achieve the service level target with the current level of resources, thinking all that is needed is a little improvement in efficiency. Or maybe the call center manager has failed to educate senior management on the link between service level and budget.

SERVICE LEVEL OBJECTIVES SHOULD BE:

- Realistic
- Understood
- Taken seriously
- Adequately funded

Service levels that are impossible to hit are particularly difficult for managers whose job success and salary are tied to meeting the objectives. When senior management hands down an objective without backing it up with adequate resources, these managers are set up for failure.

Part of taking a service level objective seriously means getting the buy-in of everyone who is involved in achieving it. To reach your target, agents, supervisors, managers and those with supporting roles should know what the service level objective is, why it was set where it is, and whether or not it is being met. A value system that people do not understand will have little or no impact.

A call center that is serious about service level objectives will ensure that hitting them is a priority. There may be times when your service level drops because you have assigned people to catch up on a backlog of important non-phone work, like customer correspondence or research. Further, these activities can turn into inbound calls if they aren't handled within customers' expected timeframes. Consequently, to maintain a consistent and appropriate service level, you will also need to establish reasonable response time objectives.

Understanding and Using Response Time Objectives

Response time is the equivalent of service level for contacts that don't have to be handled when they arrive. Response time, like service level, becomes the critical link between the resources you need and the results you want to achieve.

VARIATIONS ON RESPONSE TIME

There are three types of response, including:

AUTOMATED REPLY: This is a system-generated response that automatically sends a reply to the customer acknowledging that an email they sent was received and informing them of when to expect a response. This establishes appropriate expectations and minimizes telephone calls or other additional contacts inquiring about the status of the original message.

AGENT-ASSISTED RESPONSE: This refers to the response the customer receives when the transaction is actually handled by an agent. The time that elapses between the customer's original message and the call center's response is measured as "response time."

RESOLUTION: This is a measure of when the problem or issue is actually resolved and is used in environments where the call center's initial response may not fully resolve the issue. For example, in a technical support environment additional research may be necessary; the problem is "resolved" when the matter is handled to completion and the case is closed.

Additionally, there are two primary types of response time — scheduled and rolling. Scheduled response time, like a dry-cleaning service, is geared around blocks of time. For example, you may commit to handle all messages received up to noon by 4 p.m., and to respond to messages received between noon and 5 p.m. by 10 a.m. the next morning.

Rolling response time is hinged on the specific times each message arrives. Strictly applied, if you establish a four-hour response time, a customer who sends a message at 9:03 a.m. should get a response by no later than 1:03 p.m., and one who sends a message at 9:12 a.m. should receive a response by no later than 1:12 p.m.

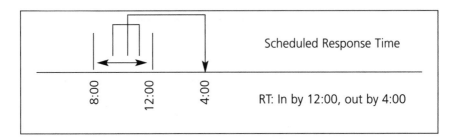

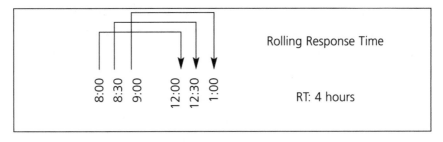

CHOOSING RESPONSE TIME OBJECTIVES

Choosing response time objectives involves considering many of the same questions you analyzed when choosing an appropriate service level; e.g., the seven factors affecting customer tolerance.

Today, many call centers are establishing straightforward, 24-hour scheduled response time objectives, but some in more competitive environments are targeting rolling response times of four hours or even one hour or less. A small but growing number of call centers are handling email messages like telephone calls, handling them as they arrive or soon thereafter, in which case service level rather than response time objectives apply.

EXAMPLE RESPONSE TIME OBJECTIVES		
	Low End of Range	**High End of Range**
Customer email	48 to 72 hours	Less than one hour*
Fax	Three days	Three hours
Voicemail	Next day	Within one hour
Letter by mail	One to two weeks	Same-day turnaround
*According to ICMI surveys, 24-hour response time objectives are common for email, but there is a wide disparity between low-end and high-end targets. We expect objectives to tighten across most call centers as they improve in coming years.		

An important step in establishing response time objectives is to relay to customers what your objectives are. That means telling them upfront what they can expect. Otherwise, what started out as a fax or email may turn into a phone call: "I'm calling to check up on an email I sent to you. I haven't heard from you yet, and am wondering..."

INTERNAL COMMUNICATIONS

In some cases, meeting response time objectives for customers requires various internal resources to be available in a timely manner. Don't leave this to chance — create a plan with your group that establishes agreed-upon internal service level and response time standards.

For example, the agreement should stipulate levels of priorities and appropriate responses for internal email — i.e., urgent messages (requiring an immediate response), routine messages (requiring a response time of, say, the same day) and informational messages only (requiring no response).

Instant messaging is also becoming a pervasive and valuable tool for internal communications. But you'll need to talk through expectations and get agreement on when and how it will best be used. Ditto for internal phone calls, voicemail messages and other channels of communication. Coming up with an agreement — even just an informal one — will go a long way toward meeting customer expectations and preventing unnecessary stress among colleagues.

As we will discuss in Chapter 13, one useful way to identify the resources required to handle a transaction is to chart the handling process step by step. This will identify weak links in the process and help to identify where internal standards are necessary, ensuring that customers are getting the response time promised.

© Randy Glasbergen

"At this time, we'd like to remind you to eat and drink at regular intervals. Thank you for continuing to hold."

Reprinted with permission.

The Link to Quality

When you talk about being accessible, someone is bound to bring up an important point: You can achieve your service level objectives regularly and, at the same time, be creating waste, extra work and low quality.

Sure, you can rush through those calls in queue, and service level will improve while quality suffers. You can have fast service even though your agents misunderstand customer requests, enter data incorrectly, relay the wrong information to customers, make them mad, miss opportunities to capture valuable feedback, and unnecessarily cause repeat contacts.

But longer term, service level and quality are inextricably associated with, and complementary to, each other. You cannot have one without the other. What if data is not entered correctly? What if the caller does not have confidence the call was handled correctly? What if you did not capture useful information from the transaction? These problems contribute to repeat calls, escalation of calls and complaints to higher management. The problems also entail callbacks and rework, further reducing service level.

Just as service level and quality are linked, so, too, are quality and response time. For example, if customers don't receive a reply to an email as quickly as expected, or don't receive the correct or expected response, they may send another. This can be the start of a similar cycle.

A poor service level will steal away productivity. As service deteriorates, more and more callers will express their frustration when their calls are answered. Your agents will have to spend valuable time apologizing — and this means they will not be able to answer as many calls as they would if service was better. Your costs will go up.

But that is just the beginning. Calls also get longer because agents will eventually pace themselves differently. If they can't get a "breather" between calls because the "in-between" time no longer exists, they may start taking their breathers while they're on calls as a survival mechanism. When service level initially starts to slip, agents often try to clear up the queue. If this proves to be a futile effort, they eventually settle in for the long term. Call-handling time goes up. If this condition continues, employee morale will sink. Turnover and burnout will go up. So will recruitment and training costs.

Somewhere along the way, quality begins to suffer, which has a further negative impact on service level. When your agents are overworked due to constant congestion in the queue, they become less accurate and can become less "customer-friendly." Callers are telling them in no uncertain terms about the tough time they had getting through. And agents make more mistakes. These mistakes contribute to repeat calls, unnecessary service calls, escalation of calls and complaints to higher management, callbacks, etc. — all of which drive service level down further.

Service level against quality? Nope. Service level and quality go hand in hand. In the end, they must be viewed in the context of a much larger objective: customer satisfaction and strategic value. Consider the positive impact on the organization's workload when the call center helps manufacturing pinpoint quality problems, enables marketing to develop focused campaigns, or helps IT design better self-service systems. The call center has the potential to positively impact the entire organization's workload, productivity and quality. (We'll look at these issues in greater detail in Chapter 13.)

The call center has the potential to positively impact the entire organization's workload, productivity and quality.

Service level and response time objectives are enablers — nothing happens unless contacts get to the right places at the right times. In the chapters to follow, we will cover the planning steps required to meet the service level and response time objectives you have established. These activities will include forecasting, staffing, scheduling and budgeting. But none of these later steps are possible without first establishing appropriate targets.

Points to Remember

- Service level is the performance objective for contacts that must be handled when they arrive (e.g., inbound calls). Response time is the performance objective for contacts that can be handled at a later time (e.g., customer email).
- Staffing, trunking, scheduling and budgeting are all hinged upon your service level and response time objectives.
- Choosing service level and response time objectives is not an exact science, and you may need to adjust your targets when you determine required resources and calculate costs later in the planning process.

- Service level and response time objectives are not at odds with quality. Good quality improves service levels by minimizing repeat calls and waste and rework. And good service levels create the environment in which quality can thrive.

CHAPTER 5:
Acquiring Necessary Data

We're drowning in information and starving for knowledge.
RUTHERFORD D. ROGERS

Collecting the data you need for effective call center management is a critical — and often undervalued — activity in the planning process. To many, collecting data sounds... well, mechanical. A humdrum step on the

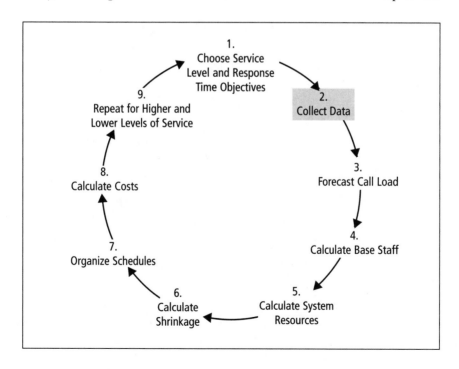

path to bigger and better things.

But, too often, inaccurate forecasts, variable quality and unpredictable costs stem from a lack of good information. Acquiring the data that you need will take you to distant corners of your organization and into the farthest reaches of the external environment. It's one of the most involved, politically charged and outwardly focused aspects of successfully managing a customer contact center.

Sources of Data

The information necessary for effective planning and management comes from many different sources. Consider the systems, departments and external sources of information that a call center for, say, a financial services organization would turn to (listed in no specific order):

- Customer information systems
- ACD systems
- Email servers
- Imaging servers
- Fax servers
- Dialers
- Web servers
- Quality monitoring/recording systems
- Analytics and performance management systems
- IVR/voice processing systems
- Workforce management systems
- Telecommunications network
- Vendors/suppliers
- Marketing department
- Legal department
- Upper management
- Human resources department

- Employees
- Customers
- Product development
- Regulatory bodies
- Economic reports
- Competition
- Media

Lots of information! Call center systems alone crank out reports with a vengeance. In fact, it's all too easy to get buried in information. And data does little good unless it becomes usable, actionable knowledge.

In today's world, the external environment changes rapidly, many organizations have become more nimble, and past history is not as good a predictor of future activity as it once was. This is why having more data from more systems hasn't inherently translated into better-managed centers — and why human know-how and experience is as important as ever in managing these information-intensive environments.

Past history is not as good a predictor of future activity as it once was. This is why having more data from more systems hasn't inherently translated into better-managed centers — and why human know-how and experience is as important as ever.

Diverse Requirements

For an appreciation of the diverse information requirements in today's customer contact environment, consider how job titles and responsibilities are evolving. As recently as a decade ago, "call center manager" was the usual title for those who ran call centers. Often, the same person or team (depending on the size of the center) would do the recruiting, hiring, coaching, training, systems troubleshooting — and about everything else that goes into running a call center. Forward-thinking managers would make time to do basic forecasting, staffing and scheduling. "Be proactive, not reactive" was the oft-repeated management admonition.

The process for acquiring, interpreting and using data has become as important as the data itself.

Today, many additional job roles and responsibilities have emerged — each requiring different types of information from different sources. In larger centers, job roles can include forecasting analysts, training managers, quality specialists, knowledge managers, reporting analysts, finance managers, traffic controllers, coaching and monitoring supervisors, real-time coordinators and professionals with a host of other titles and positions. If you run a small call center, you probably wear many of these hats — but they are increasingly specialized hats, nonetheless!

Given the need for specialized roles, along with the numerous variables affecting the call center's workload, it's easy to understand why many organizations that were previously successful at developing accurate forecasts and plans are now finding these requirements more challenging.

The process for acquiring, interpreting and using the data has become as important as the data itself. Those who view the data collection step as little more than a rote, mechanical process are in trouble from the start.

Building Cross-Functional Processes

Identifying the information you need begins with a good customer access strategy (see Chapter 2). Your customer access strategy will help to define such things as customer segmentation, agent group structure (pooled versus skills-based routing), service level goals and the information needed for specific contact types. These issues will, in turn, help reveal specific data requirements.

Many call centers have charged a person or a group of people with essential planning responsibilities, i.e., forecasting, staffing and scheduling. As a part of their job, they are given the task of collecting information required for these activities. But if they don't get the cross-functional input they need, they are set up for failure. The organizations that do the best job of planning have developed cross-functional teams that are an integral part of the planning and management process.

Cross-functional planning groups can take many forms. For example, Georgia Power, which has been rated one of the top utilities for customer satisfaction, set up an agent liaison team to facilitate information exchange between the call center and other departments. Typical tasks for an agent liaison include participating in meetings in other areas, reporting call center activities and exploring ways to achieve overall goals. At fast-growing Mountain America Credit Union, the call center implemented a similar initiative with their "Public Relations" team — made up entirely of call center

FACTORS AFFECTING CALL CENTER WORKLOADS

- Revenue growth (or decline)
- Mergers and acquisitions
- Marketing activities
- Changes in customer segmentations
- Competitor activities
- Ecommerce developments
- Technology changes (internal and external)
- Web site revisions (content or structure)
- Laws and regulations
- Customer experience levels
- Agent experience levels
- New product rollouts
- Customer relationship initiatives
- Reengineering or restructuring efforts
- Quality improvement initiatives
- Publicity
- New suppliers and business partners
- Human resources policies
- Cost-cutting or growth initiatives
- Economic developments
- Media activities

agents who update other areas on call center activities and stay abreast of objectives in other areas to ensure that cross-functional projects and processes are successful. Retailer and catalog company Eddie Bauer pioneered an interdepartmental forecasting team some years ago that directly involves representatives from marketing and other business units in the forecasting process; many organizations have established similar integrated planning initiatives.

Additionally, customer "listening posts" — which often consist of a regular (e.g., weekly) meeting with representatives from departments throughout the organization who review customer input and implications for projects and processes — have become popular. And given the many diverse aspects of good planning, some organizations have established a dedicated planning manager position whose primary function is to enhance cross-functional communication within the organization, and to use the shared information to drive better forecasts and plans. Whatever the specific approach, better cross-functional communication depends on a commitment from the call center management team to reach out and better

IDENTIFYING THE INFORMATION YOU NEED

A great way to identify gaps in getting and using the data you'll need for resource planning is to create a flow chart of the nine-step planning process and the data required for each step. The chart should identify:

- The information you need for each step
- The form it should take
- Where it comes from
- Who or what produces it
- When you need it
- How and when it fits into the planning process

This exercise will identify missing links in your data collection activities and lead to ideas for developing a more integrated, collaborative approach. For best results, you'll need to update the chart fairly regularly (e.g., semi-annually).

understand other areas.

Success in collaboration goes well beyond attending meetings, of course — it extends to building relationships which ensure that key information will be shared in a timely manner. And as many have found firsthand, these efforts tend to build the call center's stature across the organization — which, in turn, facilitates essential support from other areas.

These activities are especially critical if a service bureau is handling some or all of the customer contacts. High-quality, cost-effective services are absolutely dependant on good cross-functional, cross-organizational planning.

Better Tools

New developments in call center reporting are creating opportunities for more closely integrating call center activities, getting a handle on what callers are experiencing, and anticipating key trends. But good results don't happen just because new information is available. The mandate for call center managers is to identify both the opportunities and the potential problems that information-generating systems present, and to develop appropriate plans and guidance.

One of the key benefits of ACD, workforce management, quality monitoring, customer information and other systems prevalent in call centers

has always been their ability to produce reports — lots of them. But, until recently, reporting was system-specific and based primarily on parameters defined by the suppliers.

Today's systems are characterized by open standards and interfaces that allow reporting and integration across a network. In many cases, anyone who is tied into the organization's information systems can view, extract, print and store real-time and historical call center performance information (as allowed by system administrators). This trend has been enormously helpful in raising the call center's profile internally, especially where call center management teams have actively identified information that would be helpful to colleagues across the organization, and have enabled them to access and understand it.

Most systems also have the capability to export data to a variety of formats. This allows anyone with some programming ability to develop custom reports that combine information from multiple systems. The result has been reports and analysis that give a much more "three-dimensional" view of contacts — i.e., you can correlate call management details such as call types, average handling time, quality scores and calling trends to customer demographics, marketing campaigns, sales, customer satisfaction, buying histories and other relevant information.

Another highly useful development is the ability to model and test different scenarios. Examples include:

- IVR and ACD programming modules are often represented graphically, and even managers with limited programming know-how can design and test alternative call-handling routines.
- Workforce management systems have greatly improved in their ability to model and test alternative staffing, scheduling and budget scenarios.
- Quality monitoring, analytics and performance management tools can use what were disparate historical observations and identify causal factors, trends and probable outcomes given different sets of variables.

These forward-looking capabilities are major improvements over relying primarily on historical reports to identify problems and improvement opportunities.

Old Reporting Environment	New Reporting Environment
Proprietary	Exportable to other formats and systems
Defined by system manufacturers	User-definable
Limited data storage	Large storage capacity
System-specific	Integrated reports from a variety of systems
Limited graphing	Expansive graphing capabilities
Limited number of users	Accessible across the network and (in many cases) remotely

New Responsibilities

Emerging information capabilities are creating challenges that necessitate informed and active leadership. For example, the rapid market penetration of call center systems has brought computer and communications monitoring technologies to tens of thousands of organizations — but it's still somewhat uncommon for the use of these capabilities to be preceded by training on how to establish appropriate policies and practices. In many cases, first- and second-level supervisors have been left to implement technologies with potentially enormous legal, quality and productivity implications. And within organizations with multiple sites, policies and practices often differ between locations.

A related challenge is the uneasiness some callers feel about the sheer quantity of information that is being captured, shared, integrated with other data, and used for management and marketing purposes. And employees can feel much the same — "the computer watches me all the time — it never blinks." These issues require sound and up-to-date policies on data protection, monitoring practices and good communication with all involved. (See Chapter 14 for more on monitoring and related issues.)

Some managers have also assumed — perhaps in part due to overly aggressive promises from some supplier representatives — that new systems can practically "run the business." And yet, an understanding of underlying processes and a supporting culture are necessary for these capabilities to reach their potential. For example, workforce management systems don't coordinate with marketing, define agent preferences or develop good scheduling strategies. Quality monitoring systems can't define quality or strategic value for your operation. Real-time management information can't compel agents to want to be in the right places at the right times. The rich information provided by reporting, analytics and performance management systems doesn't inherently bring business units together to create better products, services and customer experiences.

In short, using information effectively is as challenging as ever. Ensuring that those in your center are getting and judiciously using the right information at the right times for the right purposes is a key leadership responsibility and an important enabler to running an effective customer contact operation.

Revisit and Refine This Step

This is a planning step that you'll need to continually reassess and improve. Don't leave it to chance! Regularly revisit the issue of how you are using information and why. Which information is relevant? How do you want the information formatted and presented? Who should see what? How will the information be used?

And remember to keep your eye on the prize. The purpose of information is to support key activities of the call center that, in turn, support the principles and mission of the organization. To that end, we'll look at the specific information you'll need in chapters to follow.

Points to Remember

- The data required for call center planning and management comes from numerous internal and external sources.
- Acquiring and using the data you need should be a collaborative, cross-functional effort.
- Develop a flowchart of the data and information required for each of the nine planning steps; this will help to identify weak or missing links and point to collaboration opportunities.
- Continually review and improve your information systems and processes to ensure that they are supporting your most important objectives.

CHAPTER 6:
Forecasting the Center's Workload

My interest is in the future because I am going to spend the rest of my life there.
C.F. KETTERING

Matching resources with the workload is a critical step in managing a call center effectively. This responsibility goes to the heart of call center management: "Having the right number of properly skilled people and supporting resources in place at the right times *to handle an accurately forecasted workload,* at service level and with quality."

Here's the scoop: If the forecast is not reasonably accurate, the rest of the planning process will be off the mark. The forecast is the basis for determining staffing needs and requirements for other resources, such as how many workstations are required and how many lines are necessary. It provides the foundation for:

- Calculating base staff required to meet your service level and response time objectives
- Calculating trunking and system requirements
- Minimizing abandoned and blocked calls
- Organizing accurate, workable schedules
- Predicting future staffing and network costs
- Meeting customer expectations
- Establishing an environment in which quality service can be provided

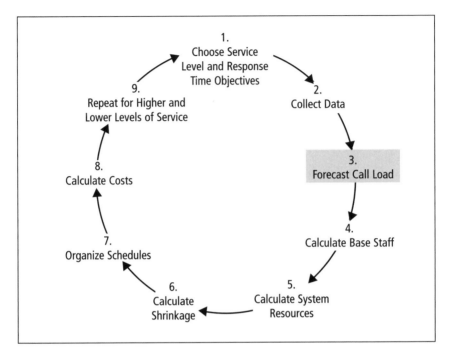

Art and Science

Forecasting is the proverbial mix of art and science. It begins with predicting how many contacts you are going to get in a future period, usually a year. To do that, you look at historical data to determine patterns that reflect when people call, and you consider possible trends that will affect call patterns. You then take that information and break it into the contacts that will be coming to you in different months, weeks of the month, days of the week, and half-hours of the day — or even five minutes of the half-hour, if you are forecasting peaked traffic. Next, you factor in the handling times of the interactions. Finally, you modify results based on conditions not reflected in historical data.

In the call center environment, longer-term forecasts look out a year and beyond. They are used to estimate future annual budgets, establish long-term hiring plans and define future system needs. Shorter-term forecasts project workload out to three months. They are necessary for organizing and adjusting scheduling requirements, anticipating seasonal staffing needs, planning for holidays, and determining imminent hiring requirements. Weekly, daily and intraday forecasts are short-term tactical forecasts used to tighten up schedules and adjust priorities around current conditions and near-term events.

How far out you forecast will depend on the purpose of the forecast. Regardless, the basic principles and concepts are similar.

Essential Data

The basic historical data you need for forecasting includes how many contacts you have received in the past, when they arrived and how long they took to handle. Four key terms reflect this activity:

- TALK TIME is everything from "hello" to "goodbye." In other words, it's the time callers are connected with agents. Anything that happens during talk time — such as putting the caller on hold to make an outbound call, confer with a supervisor or access an internal help desk — should be included in this measurement.
- AFTER-CALL WORK TIME (also referred to as "wrap-up" or "not ready") is the time agents spend completing transactions after saying goodbye to callers. Legitimate after-call work should immediately follow talk time.

IMPORTANT DEFINITIONS

Talk Time: Everything from "hello" to "goodbye."

After-Call Work (Wrap-up): Work that is necessitated by and immediately follows an inbound contact.

Average Handling Time: Average talk time + average after-call work.

Call Load: Volume x (average talk time + average after-call work)

- **AVERAGE HANDLING TIME** (AHT) is average talk time plus average after-call work.
- **CALL LOAD** is the volume of contacts coupled with how long they last. More specifically, it is volume x (average talk time + average after-call work), for a given period of time.

CLEAN THE DATA!

It's critical to "clean" the data you use to forecast future resource requirements. Too often, we see managers take data from systems and use it for forecasting and planning without giving it a second thought. But what if the IVR was down for an hour yesterday? What if an essential reporting system malfunctioned? What about other variables that will — or will not — repeat and that need to be accounted for in the numbers? In these cases, appropriate adjustments that reflect what's likely to continue will ensure that you are building forecasts on a solid foundation.

OFFERED CALLS

The historical data you use in forecasting should reflect "offered calls" discounted for multiple attempts from individual callers. Offered calls include all of the attempts your callers make to reach you. There are three possibilities for offered calls: They can get busy signals; they can be answered by the system, but abandon before reaching an agent; or they can successfully reach an agent.

There has been a lot of debate around the term "offered call." Some define it as a call that reaches the ACD. Many ACDs utilize that definition, and have report columns labeled "offered calls" that reflect answered calls (those that reach agents) and abandoned calls. However, the traditional definition of offered call — and the one I'll stick with here — is any attempt a caller makes to reach you, even if they never reach the ACD (e.g., they get a busy signal in the network).

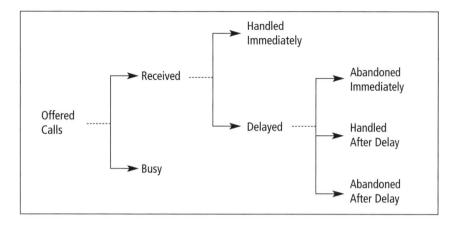

ABANDONED CALLS

Acquiring data on abandoned calls is usually straightforward. Virtually every ACD provides reports on abandonments down to specific increments of time. The seven factors of caller tolerance (see Chapter 3) will influence how long of a queue callers will tolerate, how many will abandon and how many will call back if they abandon.

Many managers count abandoned calls "one for one." The usual logic is that the forecast is based on half-hour data and callers who abandon are not likely to call back within the half-hour. To the degree that callers who abandon do, in fact, call back and get through to agents, they will be counted more than once in the data. Consequently, some managers use either "educated guesses" or, in some cases, hard data made possible by automatic number identification (ANI) reports (alternatively referred to as calling line identification — CLI) to discount a portion of the abandoned calls.

Without good data, you run the risk of discounting calls too deeply, which will lead to forecasts that underestimate demand. Consequently, we generally recommend that you include most abandoned calls in the data (i.e., 70 percent or more), unless you have specific reports or surveys you can use as a guide. This may lead to forecasts that overstate demand; however, forecasts that underestimate the workload will likely lead to insufficient staffing and abandoned calls — which will perpetuate the problem.

BUSY SIGNALS

Busy signals are far less common today than they were even five years ago. But when they happen, they create havoc in reports. The age-old question is, for every 100 busy signals, was that 100 people who tried to reach you once, or one persistent soul who tried 100 times? Of course, the answer is usually somewhere in-between. Studies have shown that even when callers have other options, they will generally retry at least once or twice when they get a busy signal. So busy signals should almost always be discounted. The question is, how much?

Callers will encounter busy signals either when you don't have enough physical capacity to handle the calls or when you've programmed your ACD system to reject calls from entering the queue if the wait backs up beyond a threshold you define. Consequently, data on busy signals may come from your ACD, local telephone company, long-distance provider or all of the above.

Virtually all ACDs have a report called "all trunks busy" (ATB). This will tell you how much of the time and how many times all of the trunks in a specific group were 100 percent occupied. But it won't tell you how many attempts callers made to reach you when all trunks were busy, nor how many callers were represented by those attempts.

If you have an ACD that can dynamically generate busy signals based on real-time circumstances, it will likely provide a report on how many calls received busies. Likewise, you can often obtain basic reports from your local and long-distance providers that give data on how many times busies were generated, for specific time periods. However, these basic reports won't tell you how many *individuals* are represented by those attempts, unless you can capture callers' numbers and run a sort to identify multiple attempts.

Some network carriers provide more advanced reports that can solve the retrial mystery. These reports provide actual retrial rates (average number of attempts per individual caller), down to the specific days or increments of time that you specify.

Alternatives to retrial reports can include customer surveys, answering all calls for a short period (even if by voicemail) to determine true demand and variations of judgment (guessing). Naturally, it's best to have hard data. But whatever information is available, be sure to question the rules of thumb, which generally state that callers will retry an average of three to five times. Like abandoned calls, retries are determined by the seven factors affecting caller tolerance — and three to five attempts may be off the mark for your scenarios.

Whatever the level of reports you can get, your forecast should, as accurately as possible, reflect the number of individuals attempting to reach you. If you count every busy signal and abandoned call, the forecast will overestimate true demand. If you ignore busy signals and abandoned calls, your forecast will underestimate demand.

WHAT ABOUT IVRS AND ROUTING CONTINGENCIES?

Many call centers use interactive voice response units (IVRs) to provide customers with self-service options and to help route calls. Additionally, contingency-based routing alternatives can mean that calls start out in one place and end up in another depending on real-time circumstances.

Consequently, callers may make several hops and be counted by multiple systems before reaching an agent. While it is important to predict the workload that will be handled by your network and systems so that you can engineer them correctly, you'll need a forecast *specific to each agent group* for staffing purposes. In other words, count and forecast the contacts that reach each individual agent group — whatever the path that got them there.

UNDERSTANDING AGENT GROUPS

An agent group (also called a split, gate, queue or skills group) shares a common set of skills and knowledge, handles a specified mix of contacts (e.g., service, sales, billing or technical support) and can be comprised of hundreds of agents across multiple sites. Supervisory groups and teams are often subsets of agent groups.

Agent groups are the building blocks of call center structure. If you have one group of 100 agents handling all contacts, you will have one forecast and one set of schedules. If you have 10 groups of 10 agents, you'll need 10 sets of forecasts and schedules — one for each unique agent group. In other words, planning must be specific enough to ensure that you get *the right number of properly skilled people* and supporting resources in place at the right times.

PROPORTIONS

The fundamental information you need for call-load forecasting includes the three components of call load: talk time, after-call work and volume.

From this data, proportions can be derived. If you received 1,000 calls for the day, and 60 came in between 10:00 and 10:30, that half-hour's proportion would be 6 percent or .06 (60/1,000). Proportions are used to project patterns into the future.

(Note: We'll look at forecasting in the context of typical, random call arrival throughout this chapter. In many ways, the forecasting principles are similar for both random and peaked traffic. But the one big difference is in the level of detail you will need from your reports. While half-hour reports are sufficient for random call arrival, you will need historical reports down to much more specific increments of time; e.g., five- or 10-minute segments, in order to adequately forecast and staff for peaked traffic.)

This is information your ACD and/or workforce management systems should be collecting *now and forever.* Building on this essential half-hour

	Calls	Prop.	Average Talk Time	Average Work Time	Average Hndl. Time
08:00-08:30					
08:30-09:00					
09:00-09:30					
09:30-10:00					
10:00-10:30					
10:30-11:00					
11:00-11:30					
11:30-12:00					
12:00-12:30					
12:30-13:00			The Fundamental Quantitative Information Necessary For Call-Load Forecasting		
13:00-13:30					
13:30-14:00					
14:00-14:30					
14:30-15:00					
15:00-15:30					
15:30-16:00					
16:00-16:30					
16:30-17:00					
17:00-17:30					
17:30-18:00					
Totals/Avgs					

data, you will accumulate necessary daily, weekly and monthly data. Whatever you do, don't throw data away. You'll never know when you will need information about that campaign from four years ago. "Hey, how did callers react that time we…"

REPEATING PATTERNS

Virtually all call centers handling inbound contacts notice at least three dominant patterns.

MONTH OF YEAR OR SEASONALITY. The graph, "Monthly Calls Offered," illustrates data from a financial services company. Notice that the most recent year is at a higher plane, but looks similar to the patterns in previous years. Even if your organization is going through dramatic changes, you will usually detect seasonality in your call-arrival patterns. Three years of data will provide a good reading on these patterns; if you have addition-

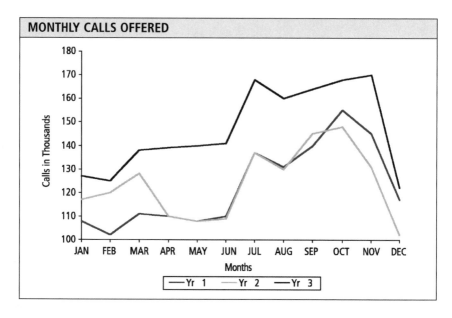

al history, even better. If you don't have three years of data, use what you have; even one year will often reflect what is likely to continue.

DAY OF WEEK. The graph, "Calls by Day of Week," is from a telecommu-

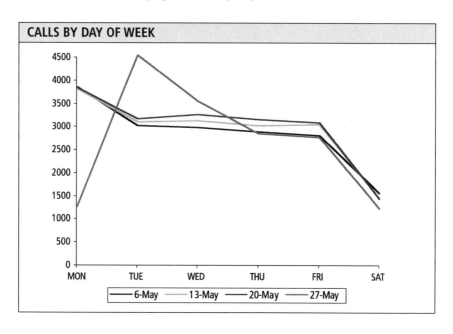

nications company. The first week reflects a holiday on a Monday. The call center was open, but, of course, callers were behaving differently than usual. Consequently, that following Tuesday gets more calls than normal, illustrating the "pent-up demand" that is common after holidays. Otherwise, the pattern is highly predictable from one week to the next. (Holiday weeks are predictable, as well, if you have some history of similar holidays.) As the example shows, as few as four or five week's worth of history can reveal this pattern.

Half-hour of day. The data for the graph, "Half-Hourly Calls Offered" is from a bank. Notice the system outage? That kind of exception from the norm tends to "stick out like a sore thumb." And it raises an important point: Exceptions need to be pulled out of the data or they will throw off predictions. A week or two's worth of data will often be enough to identify this pattern.

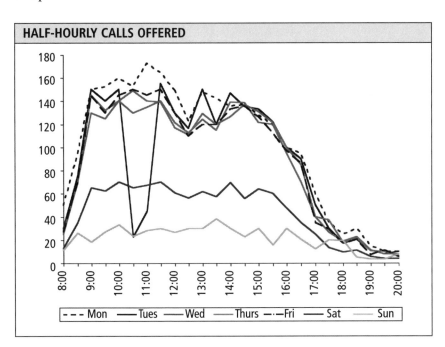

HALF-HOURLY CALLS OFFERED

- - - Mon ——Tues ——Wed —— Thurs —·—Fri —— Sat —— Sun

You may have other patterns, as well. For example, if you send out statements to your customers on the 5th and 20th of each month, you'll notice day-of-month patterns. And marketing campaigns will create their own traffic patterns.

Individuals call for a myriad of reasons, but become part of highly predictable patterns. It's pretty amazing, actually. Hey, whoever said that forecasting was boring?

So, one of the most essential steps in forecasting is to look at your data and identify the patterns that exist. Even if you are using forecasting software, it is still important to graph the "raw" patterns so you can identify exceptions.

Breaking Down a Forecast

OK, grab a cup of coffee, roll up your sleeves and let's go through a basic

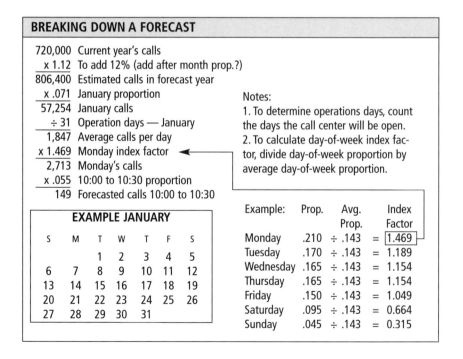

BREAKING DOWN A FORECAST

720,000	Current year's calls
x 1.12	To add 12% (add after month prop.?)
806,400	Estimated calls in forecast year
x .071	January proportion
57,254	January calls
÷ 31	Operation days — January
1,847	Average calls per day
x 1.469	Monday index factor
2,713	Monday's calls
x .055	10:00 to 10:30 proportion
149	Forecasted calls 10:00 to 10:30

Notes:
1. To determine operations days, count the days the call center will be open.
2. To calculate day-of-week index factor, divide day-of-week proportion by average day-of-week proportion.

EXAMPLE JANUARY

S	M	T	W	T	F	S
		1	2	3	4	5
6	7	8	9	10	11	12
13	14	15	16	17	18	19
20	21	22	23	24	25	26
27	28	29	30	31		

Example:	Prop.		Avg. Prop.		Index Factor
Monday	.210	÷	.143	=	1.469
Tuesday	.170	÷	.143	=	1.189
Wednesday	.165	÷	.143	=	1.154
Thursday	.165	÷	.143	=	1.154
Friday	.150	÷	.143	=	1.049
Saturday	.095	÷	.143	=	0.664
Sunday	.045	÷	.143	=	0.315

approach that illustrates how to break down a forecast. This example starts with longer-term patterns, and works its way down to specific half-hour increments. The steps involved include:

1. Obtain the number of calls received in the past 12 months; 720,000 in this example.

2. Multiply the year's calls by 1.12 to reflect 12 percent expected growth. Factoring in growth at this level assumes that transactions will increase proportionally to previous years' patterns. If growth will instead be concentrated around marketing campaigns or other events that don't necessarily happen at the same time from year to year, you should factor it in at a more specific level, such as monthly or weekly.

3. Multiply the estimated calls in the year you are forecasting by January's proportion, 7.1 percent. This percentage comes from history and is the typical proportion of the year's calls that January receives.

4. Divide the number of operation days in the month into the estimated monthly calls. This yields average calls per day. In this example, the center is open every day of the month.

5. Adjust average calls per day, using the appropriate daily index factor. The first column in the index factor calculation gives the proportion of the week's transactions that typically arrive each day. For example, Monday normally gets 21 percent of the week's traffic; Tuesday gets 17 percent and so forth.

The next column reflects the proportion of a week that an operation day represents. For example, if you're open seven days a week, each day is 1/7 or 14.3 percent of a week. If your center is open five days, each day is 1/5, or 20 percent of a week. A day in a six-day work week is 16.7 percent of the week.

The final column is the result of dividing the first column by the second column. These index factors are then multiplied against the average calls per day to estimate traffic by the specific day of week. In this example, Monday's index factor, 1.469, is multiplied against 1,847.

6. The final step is to multiply the predicted calls for each day of the week by each half-hour's proportion. In this example, the half-hour 10:00 to 10:30 will get a projected 149 calls.

This process must take a lot of time, right? Actually, once you establish a system and an approach, it won't take nearly as much time as you may think. You will get better at it with practice. And forecasting software or, at least, spreadsheets can take much of the labor out of it. But even if it does take time, forecasting is one of the most high-leverage activities in the planning process. You'll spend a lot more time "putting out fires" later on if you don't have a good forecast.

Keep in mind, this is a basic approach and there are many possible refinements — e.g., to account for calendar variations, intra-month trends or other variables — that may improve accuracy. But if you are pulling out the exceptions and working with good data, going through this type of process provides a good foundation on which to build. You will still need to blend in judgment, coordinate with marketing, etc. After all, past history doesn't always reflect what's going to happen in the future.

You may also need to incorporate other patterns into the forecast. For example, if you send out billing statements twice a month, that will generate traffic a day or two after the mail drop. But the percent increase caused by these events will also fall into predictable patterns, and you can adjust accordingly. You may need to calculate day-of-month index factors, a process similar to deriving day-of-week index factors.

HOLIDAY WEEKS

Holiday weeks will require their own index factors. But the pattern for one week with a holiday on a Monday will often be similar to another week in the year with a holiday on a Monday. Holidays that fall on various days of the week are another reason to hang on to your historical data.

HOLIDAY WEEK INDEX FACTORS

Examples of Calculating Day-of-Week Index Factors For Week With A Holiday (divide proportion by average proportion)

	Prop.	Avg. Prop.	Index Factor
Monday	0	0	0
Tuesday	.290	.167	1.737
Wednesday	.240	.167	1.437
Thursday	.175	.167	1.048
Friday	.155	.167	0.928
Saturday	.095	.167	0.569
Sunday	.045	.167	0.269

INTRADAY FORECASTS

Intraday or intraweek forecasts are quick and easy to produce, and are often quite accurate. Typically, short-term forecasts are more accurate than long-term forecasts.

The approach works like this: At some point in the morning, say just after 10:30 a.m., you begin to realize that this is not a typical day. Your reports indicate that you have received 402 calls so far, which may be more or fewer than originally expected. Either way, you divide the usual proportion of the day's calls that you would expect by 10:30 — 18 percent in this case — into 402 (18 percent came from looking at traffic patterns on previous days and calculating half-hourly proportions). Bingo, you now know that if the trend continues, you can expect to receive 2,233 calls for the day.

Next, you can break down the revised daily forecast into the remaining half-hours by multiplying historical half-hourly proportions by 2,233. For

INTRADAY FORECASTING

402	Calls received by 10:30 a.m.
÷ .18	Usual proportion of calls by 10:30 a.m.
2,233	Revised forecast for day
x .066	3:30 - 4:00 p.m. proportion
147	Intraday forecast for 3:30 - 4:00 p.m.

example, since you would normally expect to get 6.6 percent of a day's calls between 3:30 and 4:00 p.m., you can expect 147 calls during that half-hour.

The assumption behind intraday forecasting is that the morning will set the tone for the afternoon. However, if you are a utility getting swamped with calls in the morning due to a major power outage, this will be a bad assumption. When the outage is fixed, the calls will go away. In many cases, though, intraday forecasting is a useful and accurate tool. You can use similar logic to create an intraweek forecast.

INTRAWEEK FORECASTING	
3,050	Calls received on Monday
÷ .23	Usual proportion of calls by Monday
13,261	Revised calls forecast for week
x .17	Friday's proportion
2,254	Intraweek forecast for Friday

SALES FORECASTS

Some call centers use sales forecasts to verify or improve their call load forecasts. To use this methodology, you need to know the average sales value in the call center and the conversion factor (the number of received calls that result in a sale compared to the total calls received). The conversion factor can be expressed as a whole number or as a proportion. For example, if it takes five calls on average to make a sale, then the expected number of calls would be sales times five (i.e., 5 x 1,000 = 5,000).

HOW WILL NEXT YEAR BE DIFFERENT? — SALES													
	Jan	Feb	Mar	Apr	May	June	July	Aug	Sept	Oct	Nov	Dec	Total or Avg
A. Projected Revenue	__	__	__	__	__	__	__	__	__	__	__	__	__
B. Average Sale Value	__	__	__	__	__	__	__	__	__	__	__	__	__
C. No. of Sales (A ÷ B)	__	__	__	__	__	__	__	__	__	__	__	__	__
D. Conversion Factor 1 ÷ (orders ÷ calls)	__	__	__	__	__	__	__	__	__	__	__	__	__
E. Projected Calls (C x D)	__	__	__	__	__	__	__	__	__	__	__	__	__

Alternatively, you could divide one by five to get a proportion and then divide the number of sales expected by that proportion (i.e., 1,000 ÷ .20 = 5,000).

The subject of sales forecasting is complex and you will need the input and collaboration of the marketing people in your organization. With their help, a sales forecast can provide a good sanity check to ensure that the call center is able to handle the load from marketing efforts.

DIRECT MARKETING CAMPAIGNS

Organizations that run direct marketing campaigns often utilize response rates to forecast call load. Usually there is a taper-down effect, where volume is relatively high in the initial days of a campaign and then tapers down over time.

PROJECTING CALLS FROM A DIRECT MARKETING CAMPAIGN

A. Target Audience Size _____

B. Overall Response Rate (orders ÷ target audience) _____

	Day 1	Day 2	Day 3	Day 4	Day 5	Day 6	Day 7	Day 8	Day 9	Day 10	Day 11	Day 12	Day 13	Day 14
C. Percent Orders by Day	__	__	__	__	__	__	__	__	__	__	__	__	__	__
D. Projected Orders (A x B x C)	__	__	__	__	__	__	__	__	__	__	__	__	__	__
E. Conversion Factor 1 ÷ (orders ÷ calls)	__	__	__	__	__	__	__	__	__	__	__	__	__	__
F. Number of Calls (D x E)	__	__	__	__	__	__	__	__	__	__	__	__	__	__

One of the things that makes this tricky is that there are often overlapping campaigns going on at any given time. Another is deciding what constitutes an order — is it a single call from a customer or each item ordered? You will need to decide on definitions and stick to them.

OTHER TYPES OF CONTACTS

Like telephone calls that must be handled when they arrive, other contacts — email, chat, click-to-talk, etc. — tend to have repeating and predictable volume and average handling time patterns. They also usually have a strong correlation to other forecasts, such as the inbound call load, units of sales or number of customers.

Whatever the contact channel, the same basic principles apply: Look for patterns, break them down into proportions, and use the proportions to project future traffic. You will also need to blend in the appropriate amount of judgment, as discussed in a later section.

AVERAGE HANDLING TIME

Many of us have a tendency to refer to call volume as if it's the only criteria in the workload: "How many calls did you get last year? How about yesterday? How about this morning?" Equally important, though, is average handling time, which, when coupled with volume, makes up call load. It is call load that matters. Volume alone is relatively meaningless.

As with call volume, average talk time and average after-call work usually fall into predictable, repeating patterns. Similarly, the basic forecasting approach involves utilizing historical reports along with a measure of good judgment. You begin by looking at the average handling time for a recent week, broken down by half-hour. If the week is "typical," the data represented by this pattern is what will likely continue.

It is call load that matters. Volume alone is relatively meaningless.

The graph of average handling time is from a mobile phone company. Their average handling time went up in the evenings for several reasons. First, they let agents bid on shifts based on seniority. Most agents, when given the choice, prefer to start and quit earlier in the day, so they had a

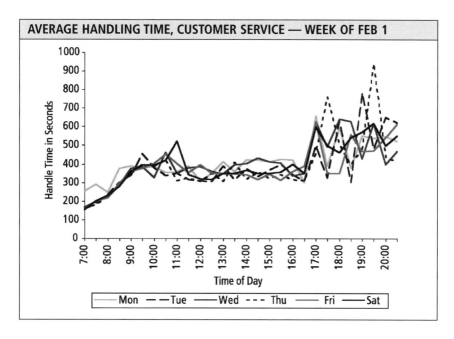

AVERAGE HANDLING TIME, CUSTOMER SERVICE — WEEK OF FEB 1

Legend: Mon — —Tue ——Wed - - - Thu —— Fri ——Sat

X-axis: Time of Day (7:00 to 20:00)

Y-axis: Handle Time in Seconds (0 to 1000)

higher concentration of new agents assigned to the evening shift. (That's not necessarily a bad approach, but it will impact average handling time and must be reflected in the forecast.)

Second, they did not have a good definition for after-call work, and much of it was getting postponed until late in the day. Third, their call mix changed throughout the day, and they got relatively longer calls in the evening.

Average handling time, like call volume, must be incorporated into planning by half-hour. Assuming the same average handling time all day for forecasting purposes will not reflect the environment accurately.

Some relatively simple analysis can go a long way toward tightening up your projections. Here are a few important prerequisites for getting this part of your forecast right:

1. LOOK FOR PATTERNS. For each answer group, identify how average talk time and average after-call work vary. You may also discover patterns by day of the week, season of the year, billing cycles and marketing campaigns.

For a deeper look at average handling time, make separate graphs for average talk time and average after-call work. This will reveal the patterns for each. You will need these reports when calculating system resources, which will be discussed in Chapter 7.

2. TRAIN YOUR AGENTS TO USE ACD MODES CONSISTENTLY. Each agent has an impact on the components of handling time (talk time and after-call work) and, therefore, on the data that will be used in forecasting and planning for future call loads. When the queue is building, it can be tempting to postpone after-call work that should be done at the time of the call. This skews reports, causes planning problems and may lead to increased errors. An important and ongoing training issue is to define ahead of time what type of work should follow calls and what type of work can wait.

3. IDENTIFY THE AVERAGE HANDLING TIME FOR DIFFERENT CALL TYPES. This presupposes that you have defined and categorized calls by type, that you are accurately tracking calls based on the categories, and that you have the reporting capability to link average handling time to the categories. A

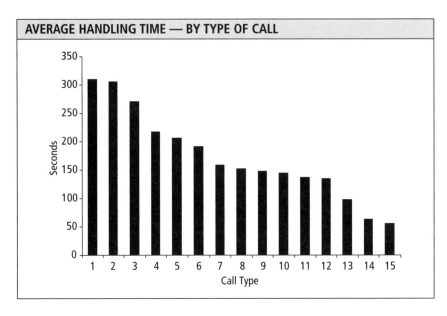

AVERAGE HANDLING TIME — BY TYPE OF CALL

Pareto chart is often the best way to represent this data.

You can use this information in a number of ways. For example, when you are forecasting an increase or decrease of a specific type of call, you will be able to project the impact on average handling time. A marketing campaign will generate certain types of calls. A new Web-based service, or calls coming through your IVR will likely reduce some types of calls agents handle (and may increase others). In each case, you'll be equipped to estimate average handling time.

4. ASSESS THE IMPACT OF NEW AGENTS AND PROCESS CHANGES. Less-experienced agents often require more time to handle calls as they learn how to deal with processes, systems and callers.

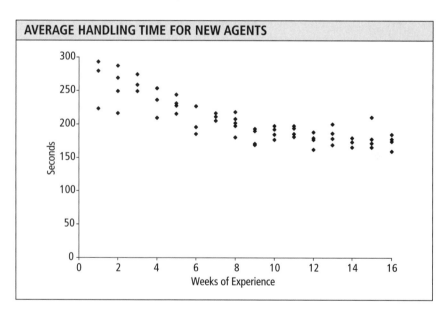

Compare average handling time to the experience levels of your agents. This will enable you to estimate the impact that new-hires have on average handling time. It will also be useful in establishing realistic expectations for them.

Beyond the Basics

The major categories of quantitative forecasting include "time-series" and "explanatory" approaches. The examples in this chapter are fairly basic, and more advanced alternatives within each category exist. I'll introduce a few of them here to give you an idea of the breadth of possibilities.

Time-series forecasting methods include simple or "naive" rules (e.g., the forecast equals last year's same month, plus 12 percent), decomposition, simple time-series and advanced-time series methods. The governing assumption behind time-series forecasting is that past data will reflect

---

SOFTWARE AND SERVICES FOR ADVANCED FORECASTING

If you're in an organization or industry going through significant changes, or if your center handles contacts generated by television commercials or overlapping direct marketing campaigns, the simple time-series and explanatory techniques used in most workforce management systems or user-defined spreadsheets may not cut it. Fortunately, there are alternatives.

For example, standalone business forecasting software packages — e.g., from providers such as SAS and ForecastPro — include a wide range of forecasting methodologies. These programs enable you to build in multiple events and variables, and produce forecasts based on different models. By comparing forecasts, you can identify the best methodology for your environment. Since one approach may work better than others for specific types of events, you can change models as circumstances dictate. You'll need an analyst or two to spearhead this effort — but more accurate forecasts (and therefore, better staffing plans and schedules) often provide a solid return on the investment.

You may also be able to access outside services. For example, ICMI's Bull's-Eye Forecasting Service provides forecasts based on advanced methodologies for centers that need transitional or ongoing help. Similar services exist in other fields (e.g., financial and sales forecasting), and will likely become more common in the call center space in coming years.

---

trends that will continue into the future. Time-series methodologies are common in workforce management software. Most time-series forecasts are reasonably accurate when projecting out three months or less.

Explanatory forecasting methods include simple regression analysis, multiple regression analysis, econometric models and multivariate methods. Explanatory forecasting essentially attempts to reveal a linkage between two or more variables. For example, if you manage an ice cream shop, you could statistically correlate the weather (e.g., outside temperature) to ice cream sales. In a call center, you might correlate a price increase to the impact on calling volumes.

Advanced time-series and explanatory forecasting methods go beyond the scope of this book. In fact, you can spend a couple of college semesters — make that a career — learning about forecasting. If you would like more information, we recommend *Principles of Forecasting — A Handbook for Researchers and Practitioners* (Jay Scott Armstrong, Editor), which includes contributions from experts on a wide range of forecasting topics and references to other useful sources.

Blending in Judgment

So far, we've looked at quantitative forecasting — in other words, how to use hard data in your forecasting process. Judgmental forecasting goes beyond purely statistical techniques and encompasses what people think is going to happen. It is in the realm of intuition, interdepartmental committees, market research and executive opinion.

Judgmental forecasting can be influenced by things like politics and personal agendas. However, some judgment is inherent in virtually all forms of forecasting. And a degree of good judgment can significantly improve accuracy. The trick is to combine quantitative and judgmental approaches effectively, and to be aware of the limitations of each.

The worksheet, "Blending in Judgment," illustrates one way of applying common sense and a logical approach to judgmental forecasting. In a cus-

BLENDING IN JUDGMENT								
	May 1	May 8	May 15	May 22	May 29	June 5	June 12	June 19
A. Projected Customers	—	—	—	—	—	—	—	—
B. Calls per Customer	—	—	—	—	—	—	—	—
C. Base Calls (A x B)	—	—	—	—	—	—	—	—
D. Activity Level Change								
1. New Customers	—	—	—	—	—	—	—	—
2. Media Attention	—	—	—	—	—	—	—	—
3. Advertising	—	—	—	—	—	—	—	—
4. New Rate Structure	—	—	—	—	—	—	—	—
5. New Terms & Conditions	—							
6. New Service Procedures	—		**CALLS (+ OR -)**					—
7. New Information Required	—	—	—	—	—	—	—	—
8. New Product Introduction	—	—	—	—	—	—	—	—
9. General Activity Level	—	—	—	—	—	—	—	—
10. Product Performance	—	—	—	—	—	—	—	—
11. Competitors' Actions	—	—	—	—	—	—	—	—
12. Other	—	—	—	—	—	—	—	—
E. Total (add 1 through 12)	—	—	—	—	—	—	—	—
F. Projected Calls (C + E)	—	—	—	—	—	—	—	—

tomer service environment, the number of calls is often primarily a function of the total number of customers or constituents in the organization's universe. It is possible to project calls based on historical data, utilizing the relationships between calling volume and total customers (calls per customer). To the degree that the future repeats the past, this forecast will be accurate.

Part D of the form is where judgment plays a significant role. In this section, you customize the forecast by adding or reducing calls, based on information you develop from your own and others' input. For some of these factors, you may have some hard data that you can use. For others, you'll be making more of an "educated guess."

The factors in Part D are only examples, derived from the following list. You will need to create your own list specific to your environment — for example, if you are a support center for broken-down or stranded vehicles, weather would be a key influence on call load.

You will need a routine mechanism or forum for blending judgment into the forecast. A fairly common approach in call centers is a weekly forecasting meeting. These meetings typically include members of the scheduling department and a representation of supervisors and managers from the call center and other departments. The meeting will typically last only 30 or 45 minutes. It often works like this:

- The person in charge of the meeting prepares an agenda of items to be discussed.
- The scheduling person (or team) prepares the quantitative forecast before the meeting.
- During the meeting, the attendees discuss issues that may influence the forecast, such as those in Part D of the worksheet. Each participant brings a unique perspective to the process.
- As each issue is discussed, the forecast is adjusted up or down, based on what the group believes will happen.

The collaborative approach is most effective when key team members who are accountable for staffing take an active role in forecasting (in large call centers, they can be rotated through this process). The forecast not only improves as a result of their perspective, but they gain an understanding of the factors that contribute to staffing. As a result, they more effectively lead their teams.

Measuring Accuracy — Strive for Five

How accurate should your forecast be? Large agent groups (i.e., 100 or more agents) generally see relatively stable call arrival patterns and should strive for plus or minus 5 percent (or better) of call load down to specific intervals. Small groups (i.e., 15 or fewer agents) often have more volatile patterns and should shoot for plus or minus 10 percent. Those in-between

MEASURING FORECAST ACCURACY

		Call Volume				The accuracy of forecasting must be measured here...
		Forecast	Actual	Difference	Percent*	
8:30	9:00	342	291	51	17.5%	
9:00	9:30	399	343	56	16.3%	
9:30	10:00	461	499	-38	-7.6%	
10:00	10:30	511	582	-71	-12.2%	
10:30	11:00	576	649	-73	-11.2%	
11:00	11:30	605	578	27	4.7%	
11:30	12:00	572	513	59	11.5%	
12:00	12:30	505	412	93	22.6%	
12:30	1:00	456	540	-84	-15.6%	
		4427	4407	20	0.5%	Not here!

*Variance of forecast to actual

should strive for something close to 5 percent. This is not to suggest you can't do better. But if your forecast is much further off the mark, your staffing calculations, schedules and budgets will be unacceptably inaccurate.

It's essential to measure forecast accuracy by interval, rather than as an average over a day or more. One way to assess how you're doing by interval without producing mounds of detail is to create a table that summarizes the percent of intervals that fall within various ranges of accuracy. You determine the thresholds — and you can tighten them down the road as forecasts become more accurate.

FORECAST ACCURACY BY INTERVAL

Accurate Within:	Percent of Intervals
5% or less	11%
5.1% to 10%	11%
10.1% to 15%	33%
15.1% to 20%	33%
Over 20%	11%

You can summarize a week, month, year or more in this way, and still provide meaningful data. This approach isn't perfect — e.g., it doesn't tell you which intervals were most important. But it's a lot better than most cumulative summaries, and will get your team focused on intervals and on moving the numbers in the right direction.

Common Forecasting Problems

Over the years, our team at ICMI has investigated why some call centers have accurate forecasts and others don't. Ten common problems tend to consistently emerge, and they are summarized here (in no specific order). In centers with inaccurate forecasts, usually two or three of these issues are most prevalent. The good news? You can avoid these problems, and the remedies in most cases are fairly obvious.

1. NO SYSTEMATIC PROCESS IN PLACE. There are often two erroneous beliefs that some managers use to justify the absence of a systematic forecasting process. Some say, "Our environment is too unpredictable. We're growing; we're introducing new products... There is no way we can expect to produce an accurate forecast." However, there are many call centers in highly volatile environments that do a respectable job of forecasting.

Others aren't convinced that forecasting is worth the time. Yep, it takes time — but not nearly as much as some imagine. Further, a good forecast will save a lot of time later on.

2. AN ASSUMPTION THAT "THE FORECASTING SOFTWARE KNOWS BEST." If you have forecasting software or a workforce management system, don't blindly relinquish decisions to the program, assuming that it knows best. The software doesn't know what the marketing department is about to do, or that average handling time will be affected by changes you are making to your systems. And if you have busy signals, you will also need to ensure that the system incorporates adjusted offered calls, not just calls received by the ACD system.

Further, it is important to understand the assumptions your forecasting software is making. Some of the techniques it will utilize are user-definable.

For example, you can program the system to give more weight to recent historical data, or you can tell it to ignore data that varies beyond X percent of the norm. It's a great idea to have the supplier provide a flow chart of the methodology the system is using and decision points where your input is necessary.

3. NOT FORECASTING AT THE AGENT GROUP LEVEL. Even a perfect forecast of the aggregate call load will be of limited use if you route calls to specialized groups. If you have a group of French-speaking agents handling services A, B and C, you will need to forecast calls from French-speaking callers who need help with those services.

4. THE FORECAST IS TAKEN LIGHTLY. If the forecast has been wildly inaccurate in the past or if no one understands the assumptions used in the process, it will not be given the prominence it needs in the planning steps to follow.

5. EVENTS THAT SHOULD BE EXCEPTIONS BECOME A PART OF THE FORECAST. Utilities tend to get lots of calls when storms knock out power, the travel industry gets swamped during airline price wars, and many call centers have, on at least one occasion, dealt with calls from an unannounced marketing campaign. (Have your agents ever had to sheepishly ask a caller, "Um, what does the ad say we are offering?")

Those preparing the forecast have to be aware of the root causes of calls in order to make a good judgment on what is likely to continue (and therefore should be built into the forecast) versus the exceptions.

6. GOOD TIES WITH OTHER DEPARTMENTS DON'T EXIST. Most of what happens in a call center is caused by something going on outside the call center. The forecast is doomed if strong ties with other departments don't exist.

7. PLANNING IS DONE AROUND GOALS, NOT REALITY. If staffing is based on a talk time of 210 seconds when actual talk time is more like 300 seconds, the resulting staff calculations and schedules will be based on a pipe dream. Sure, maybe talk time ought to be 210 seconds, and improved training, streamlined procedures and better systems would make that possible. But fudging on reality in the planning process is no way to achieve better results or build confidence in the forecast.

8. NO ONE IS ACCOUNTABLE. As vital as a good forecast is, often there is no one who spearheads the effort. Someone needs to be responsible for bringing the various types of input together, ensuring that it is integrated into the forecast, and investigating which assumptions were off when the forecast is not accurate.

9. AGENTS ARE MIXING FLEXIBLE ACTIVITIES INTO THE AFTER-CALL WORK MODE. If agents are not using work modes consistently, especially after-call work, then accurate forecasting will be elusive.

10. NOT MAKING THE CONNECTION WITH STAFFING. Forecasts mean nothing unless they are tied to staff and trunks required. That is the subject of Chapter 7.

Look Back and Adjust

The call centers that produce accurate forecasts are not necessarily those that have the most stable environments. Rather, they have a group of people (or an individual) who have made accurate forecasting a priority. They have taken responsibility, established good ties with other departments, pulled in the data required, and established a forecasting process they are continually improving. They set accuracy goals and monitor progress. They consider accurate forecasting to be mission-critical.

Forecasting takes practice. You will never learn all there is to know about it — but you'll get better at it. One of the most important steps you can take to improve accuracy is to compare your forecasts to actual results and then ask, "Why?"

Points to Remember

- Forecasting is a blend of art and science, and incorporates both quantitative and judgmental approaches.
- The forecast should accurately predict all three components of call load: talk time, after-call work and volume. Volume alone is meaningless.
- The forecast should reflect adjusted offered calls, or the individuals who try to reach you.
- There are a variety of quantitative forecasting methodologies. Time-series forecasting is popular for call centers.
- You need mechanisms, such as a collaborative weekly meeting, to blend good judgment into your forecasts.
- You should create a forecast for each agent group.
- A good forecast provides a solid foundation for the planning steps that follow.

CHAPTER 7:
Determining Base Staff and Trunks Required

Having the right number of properly skilled people and supporting resources in place at the right times...

ICMI

The key to achieving service level and response time objectives ultimately comes down to having the right people in the right places at the right times, supported by the right system resources. With a reasonably accurate forecast, base staff and trunking calculations are usually straightforward.

However, there are two caveats to getting this part of planning right: 1) You will need to use the right methodology in your calculations; and 2) trunking and related system resources should be calculated with an understanding of staffing requirements because staffing impacts delay, which affects the load that trunks must carry.

In this chapter, we'll dispel some common myths about staffing and trunking. We'll go through the mechanics of correct calculations and how existing software tools can be applied to the task. We'll explore how text-chat, long calls and other types of contacts impact requirements. And we'll review important definitions and measurements related to this aspect of planning.

113

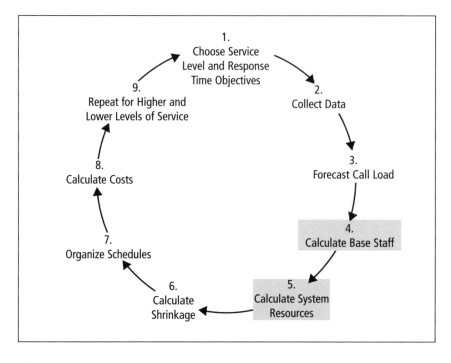

The Relationship between Staff and Trunks

To understand the association between staff and trunks, you'll need to know some key definitions. When interpreting the diagram of the definition, assume a "straight-in" environment, where callers dial a number and are routed directly to the agent group handling the calls. (This example assumes no IVR involvement).

- **DELAY:** Delay is everything from when the trunk is seized to the point at which the caller is connected to an agent.
- **AGENT LOAD:** Agent load includes the two components of handling time — talk time and after-call work.
- **TRUNK LOAD:** Trunk load includes all aspects of the transaction other than after-call work, which does not require a circuit. The "caller's load" is the same as the trunk load, other than the short time it takes for the network to route the call to the call center.

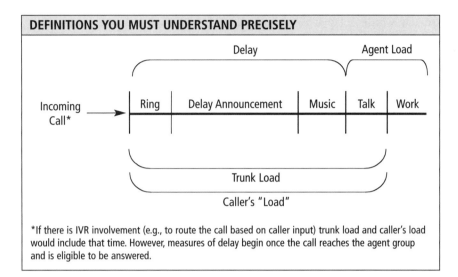

DEFINITIONS YOU MUST UNDERSTAND PRECISELY

*If there is IVR involvement (e.g., to route the call based on caller input) trunk load and caller's load would include that time. However, measures of delay begin once the call reaches the agent group and is eligible to be answered.

Notice that agent load and trunk load both include talk time. However, trunk load carries the delay, which is not a direct part of the agent load. And the agents handle after-call work, which is not carried by the trunks.

This realization leads to two important considerations when calculating staff and trunks:

1. STAFF SHOULD BE CALCULATED IN CONJUNCTION WITH TRUNKS. The more staff handling a given call load, the less delay callers will experience. In other words, staffing impacts delay; therefore, it directly impacts how many trunks are required. There is no way to know base trunking needs without knowing how many staff will be handling the projected call load.

2. THERE IS NO SINGLE STAFF-TO-TRUNK RATIO YOU CAN COUNT ON. You may have heard the rule of thumb that you need 1.5 trunks per agent (e.g., 15 trunks for every 10 agents). If that's the ratio you end up needing, it's purely chance. There is no ratio that can be universally applied. The reasons? For one, after-call work, which occupies agents but doesn't require trunks, is different from one call center to the next. Second, caller tolerances vary widely among organizations, as influenced by the seven factors affecting tolerance (Chapter 3). If you have a high service level, the trunks will carry little delay. If your service level is low, the trunks will have to carry more delay and, consequently, you will need more trunks.

There's a better way to determine resources than to depend on ratios that may not work: calculate staff, then calculate trunks the right way. Whatever the staff-to-trunk ratio turns out to be, that is what will work for you.

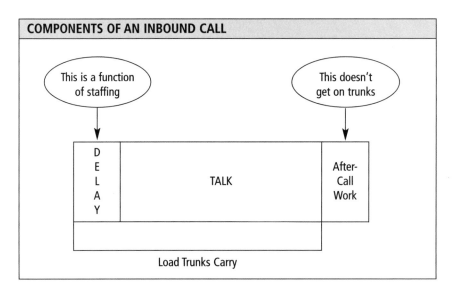

COMPONENTS OF AN INBOUND CALL

This is a function of staffing

This doesn't get on trunks

| D E L A Y | TALK | After-Call Work |

Load Trunks Carry

INTEGRATE BUDGETS

Despite the inextricable relationship between staff and trunks, call centers have traditionally paid for these resources out of different budgets. Telecommunications costs are paid out of one budget, and staffing and other costs often come out of another. Unfortunately, that will cause inaccurate budget projections and could lead to what the late quality guru W. Edwards Deming called "sub-optimizing," where one aspect of the operation is optimized in a vacuum while overall costs and performance suffer. Staff and trunks are a classic example of the need to look at the big picture.

"Wrong" Ways to Calculate Staff

To calculate how many agents you need, why not use this formula? Take the average handling time of a call (average talk time + average after-call work) and multiply it by the number of calls forecasted. Then, divide the result by 1,800 seconds (the total seconds in a half-hour). You may even build in extra time, such as an added 10 percent or 20 percent, assuming agents will actually need a breather now and then.

Or what about this formula? Determine the actual average calls per agent in a group. Then, divide that into the number of calls forecasted. Or use target objectives, as in "our agents ought to be able to handle X calls per half-hour, therefore…"

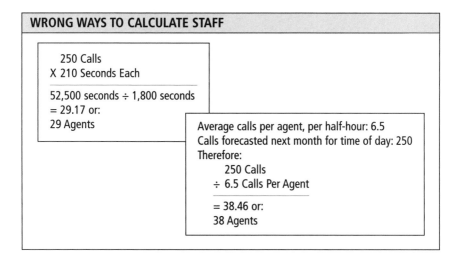

These methods may sound logical, and some call center managers use them. Unfortunately, they are dead wrong. They do not relate the outcome to a target service level. Further, they are based on moving targets. The average group productivity (calls that the group can handle) is not a constant factor. Instead, it is continually fluctuating because it is heavily influenced by vacillating call loads and the service level objective. But the biggest problem is that these approaches ignore a fundamental driving force in call centers that handle inbound contacts (Chapter 3): *Calls bunch up!*

The following figure illustrates a possible queuing situation. (It's not as complicated as it first looks!)

SIMULATION OF QUEUING SITUATION					
Arrival		**One Agent Case**		**Two Agents Case**	
(1) Arrival number	**(2)** Time of arrival	**(3)** Time call is answered	**(4)** Waiting time (min.)	**(5)** Time call is answered	**(6)** Waiting time (min.)
1	0:04.3	0:04.3	0	0:04.3	0
2	0:04.4	0:07.3	2.9	0:04.4	0
3	0:15.7	0:15.7	0	0:15.7	0
4	0:17.3	0:18.7	1.4	0:17.3	0
5	0:21.1	0:21.7	0.6	0:21.1	0
6	0:22.1	0:24.7	2.6	0:22.1	0
7	0:25.4	0:27.7	2.3	0:25.4	0
8	0:26.3	0:30.7	4.4	0:26.3	0
9	0:27.4	0:33.7	6.3	0:28.4	1.0
10	0:27.5	0:36.7	9.2	0:29.3	1.8
	Average Delay:		2.97		.28

In this scenario, 10 calls arrive in a half-hour, and each call is assumed to last three minutes. The second column shows when each of the 10 calls arrives. The third column gives the time each call is answered, and column four is the waiting time (the difference between when a call arrives and when it is answered).

For example, call number two arrives 4.4 minutes into the half-hour, but has to wait 2.9 minutes before being answered because the first call is still in progress. With one agent, the waiting times build throughout the half-hour and beyond, and service is poor. With two agents, it's a different story; service is much better and waiting times are minimal.

If sorting out staffing for random call arrival is this involved with two agents, imagine a scenario with 15 agents. Or 115! The point is, if you want to determine staffing correctly, you need the right tools. You need a method that takes the usual randomness of call arrival into consideration. That means using the Erlang C formula (or a variation of it) or computer simulation.

Staffing the "Right" Way

As introduced in the first chapter, the widely used Erlang C formula was developed in 1917 by A.K. Erlang, a Danish engineer with the Copenhagen Telephone Company. Erlang C can be used to determine resources in just about any situation where people might wait in queue for service — whether it is at a ticket counter, a bank of elevators or toilets in a stadium. Erlang C (and variations of it) is currently built into virtually all of the commercially available workforce management software packages.

Erlang C calculates predicted waiting times (delay) based on three things: the number of servers (i.e., agents); the number of people waiting to be served (i.e., callers); and the average amount of time it takes to serve each person. It can also predict the resources required to keep waiting times within targeted limits, and that's why it is useful for call centers.

As with any mathematical formula, Erlang C has built-in assumptions that don't perfectly reflect real-world circumstances. For one, it assumes

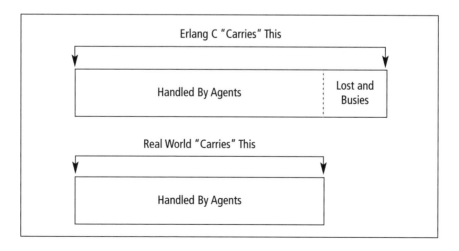

ADVANTAGES OF ERLANG C	DISADVANTAGES OF ERLANG C
• Assumes random call arrival and that calls queue if an agent is not immediately available. • Is accurate at good service levels, where abandoned calls and busy signals are minimal. • Is easy and quick to use, and is available in software programs from a wide variety of sources. • Illustrates call center tradeoffs well (e.g., when service level goes up, occupancy goes down). • Is the basis for staffing calculations in almost all workforce management programs.	• Assumes no abandoned calls or busy signals. • Assumes "steady-state" arrival, or that traffic does not increase or decrease beyond random fluctuation within the time period. • Assumes you have a fixed number of staff handling calls throughout the time period. • Assumes that all agents within a group can handle the calls presented to the group. • Calculations assume no calls in queue from the prior half-hour (unless the user or workforce management system makes this adjustment).

that "lost calls are delayed." In plain English, that means that the formula assumes that calls are queued. No problem with that. The problem is, it assumes that callers have infinite patience — they will wait as long as necessary to reach an agent and nobody will abandon. *Oops!*

Erlang C also assumes that you have infinite trunking and system capacity, or that nobody will get a busy signal. But some call centers have quite a problem with busy signals. *Oops again!*

The result, in a nutshell, is that Erlang C may overestimate the staff you really need. If some of your callers abandon or get busy signals, your agents won't have to handle all of the calls Erlang C is including in its calculations. For a given level of staff, Erlang C predicts that conditions will be worse than they really are. Erlang C also assumes that you have the same level of staff on the phones the entire half-hour. In reality, if service level starts taking a nose-dive, you may be able to add reinforcements on short notice. All

VARIATIONS ON ERLANG C

Many workforce management vendors use traffic engineering formulas that are modifications of traditional queuing formulas. For example, Pipkins developed the "Merlang" formula, a modification of A.K. Erlang's original work, which can adjust for busies, abandoned calls and variations in agent group structure. And Mike Hills, president of HTLT Technologies, produced the Hills B formula, which "is designed to overcome 'deficiencies' associated with the use of Erlang C and other classic queuing models." Says Dr. Hills, "Erlang C is fatalistic and can overestimate required staff by 20 percent. No formula is perfect, but we have built-in assumptions that better model the real environment."

things considered, Erlang C overstates how bad things will be for poor service levels.

So then why is Erlang C so popular? As you might guess, there are defensible reasons to use it. For one, it's a planning tool, and most call centers are *planning* to have good service levels. Erlang C is fairly accurate for good service levels — and when service level is decent, you should theoretically have little in the way of lost calls or busy signals. If you do have a lot of calls disappearing or getting busy signals, it's probably because you don't have enough staff to handle the load. In that case, who's worried about overstaffing? As your staffing more accurately reflects the workload demand, Erlang C will inherently become more accurate.

Further, if you adjust for abandoned calls and busy signals, and retry rates turn out to be higher than you estimate, you could wind up underestimating staff. (And frankly there's a little industry secret... shhh... some call center managers have decided that a little over-calculation as a safety net isn't such a bad thing. They figure that they fail to get full effective use of their already authorized headcount anyway, due to staff turnover and the time it takes to hire and train replacements.)

Finally, from a practical sense, many staffing and scheduling programs do, in fact, use modified versions of Erlang C and enable you to adjust variables as you see fit. Just be sure to have the supplier review with you the assumptions being made — your CFO will probably ask you the same thing.

Erlang C is designed for straightforward environments, like sales calls going here and technical support calls going there. But the realities of today are not so straightforward. You may have complex routing contingencies in place, such as agent groups that overlap, skills-based routing and complex network interflow.

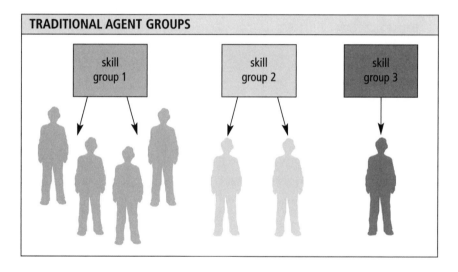

Enter computer simulation. What staffing simulation does for call centers is comparable to what flight simulators do for airplane manufacturers. Boeing, Airbus and other suppliers spend a lot of time simulating their new aircraft designs. They fail a lot — on computer. But by the time the real thing is produced, they know the ins and outs of good design intimately.

Similarly, you can use simulation to resource your call center without making too many real live mistakes. There are a variety of standalone simulation packages available, and some workforce management suppliers are building simulation capabilities into their systems.

But computer simulation has some downsides, too. For one thing, simulation is designed for modeling, design and verification, and is generally

ADVANTAGES OF COMPUTER SIMULATION	DISADVANTAGES OF COMPUTER SIMULATION
• Can be programmed to assume a wide variety of variables, including overlapping agent groups and skills-based routing. • The assumptions can include lost calls and busy signals. • Can often be programmed to use the terminology of your systems. • Results may cover a wide range of variables and include value-added analysis. • Results may be more credible to decision makers who are not familiar with alternative queuing formulas.	• Takes time to set up and use. • Requires a relatively advanced user. • Is a standalone tool that is generally not integrated with forecasting and staffing modules. • Does not tell you what to do (it instead illustrates what will happen based on variables you input). • Is more expensive than standalone Erlang C programs or entry-level staffing and scheduling packages.

not meant to be a forecasting and scheduling tool. As a result, if you want the time-saving benefits of software, you will still need a forecasting and scheduling system.

Second, simulation software takes more time and expertise to set up and use than Erlang C. Like a flight simulator, you have to run it over and over to identify potential results. That is a phenomenon of its added flexibility, and the time spent will be time saved if you have a complex environment that requires a simulator's perspective. But it takes more effort and knowhow to feed variables into the program and interpret the results.

So, what should you use? For fairly straightforward environments with good service levels, Erlang C or variations of it will likely be sufficient. And even if you have a more complex environment, there is something to be said for a combination of Erlang C, intuition and experience. But if you really want to understand requirements in the most complex settings — e.g., where you are using skills-based routing extensively or have a complex network with many call-handling variables in play — no formula will ever beat simulation.

Just remember, whatever methodology you use, no formula or program can perfectly predict outcomes. As much science as may be involved it's inexact and must be augmented with common sense and resource plans that are at least somewhat flexible.

Basic Staffing

One of the advantages of using Erlang C is that it is a great educational tool, and it illustrates queue dynamics and resource tradeoffs well. So, that's what I'll be using here to outline basic staffing requirements and tradeoffs in a call center setting.

For most of us, Erlang C in its raw beauty is unwieldy at best and totally unusable at worst. That's what prompted various sources to publish Erlang C tables before computers came along. But using an Erlang C table isn't that easy either because you have to take factors from the table, multiply them against the "holding time" and so on, to get usable answers. And using an Erlang C table is anything but self-evident if you want to relate staffing to service level. Thank goodness for software, which makes using the formula quick and easy!

(Note, in the examples to follow I am using QueueView, a low-cost soft-

ERLANG C

$$P\,(>0) = \frac{\dfrac{A^N}{N!}\dfrac{N}{N-A}}{\displaystyle\sum_{x=0}^{N-1}\dfrac{A^X}{x!} + \dfrac{A^N}{N!}\dfrac{N}{N-A}}$$

Where   A = total traffic offered in erlangs
              N = number of servers in a full availability group
              P(>0) = probability of delay greater than 0
              P = probability of loss — Poisson formula

ware program provided by ICMI. Other staffing calculators are available from a wide variety of sources.)

Erlang C requires you to input four variables:

- **AVERAGE TALK TIME, IN SECONDS.** Input the projected average for the future half-hour you are analyzing.
- **AVERAGE AFTER-CALL WORK, IN SECONDS.** Input the projected average for the future half-hour you are analyzing.
- **NUMBER OF CALLS.** Input the projected volume for the future half-hour you are analyzing.
- **SERVICE LEVEL OBJECTIVE, IN SECONDS.** If your service level objective is to answer 90 percent of calls in 20 seconds, you will input 20 seconds. If it's 80 percent in 15 seconds, plug in 15 seconds. In other words, the program needs the Y seconds in the definition, "X percent of calls answered in Y seconds."

Input the numbers and — *voilà!* — the output provides a wealth of information and insight into the dynamics of call center queues (see table, "Erlang C for Call Centers — Staffing Module"). Probably the first column you'll look at is labeled "SL," which is service level. That's the X percent to be answered in the Y seconds you input. In the first row, the number 24 means that you'll answer 24 percent of the calls in 20 seconds. The next row is 45 percent, meaning 45 percent answered in 20 seconds.

Let's say your objective is to answer 80 percent of calls in 20 seconds. Keep going down the rows and... hey, where's 80 percent? The answers go from 73 percent to 82 percent, but where's 80 percent? You guessed it — the program is calculating staff required, and people come in "whole numbers," so some rounding is involved. Since 82 percent meets your standard, that's the row you would then concentrate on.

Next, glancing across that row you can see that you need 34 agents (first column), average speed of answer will be 13 seconds (third column), etc. In other words, each column provides insight and information into the service level you choose.

125

ERLANG C FOR CALL CENTERS — STAFFING MODULE								
Average talk time in seconds: 180 Calls per half-hour: 250				Average after-call work in seconds: 30 Service level in seconds: 20				
Agents	P(0)	ASA	DLYDLY	Q1	Q2	SL	OCC	TKLD
30	83%	209	252	29	35	24%	97%	54.0
31	65%	75	115	10	16	45%	94%	35.4
32	51%	38	74	5	10	61%	91%	30.2
33	39%	21	55	3	8	73%	88%	28.0
34	29%	13	43	2	6	82%	86%	26.8
35	22%	8	36	1	5	88%	83%	26.1
36	16%	5	31	1	4	92%	81%	25.7
37	11%	3	27	0	4	95%	79%	25.4
38	8%	2	24	0	3	97%	77%	25.3
39	6%	1	21	0	3	98%	75%	25.2
40	4%	1	19	0	3	99%	73%	25.1
41	3%	1	18	0	3	99%	71%	25.1
42	2%	0	16	0	2	100%	69%	25.0

Source: International Customer Management Institute, Annapolis, Md.

Here's what the column headings stand for:

AGENTS: Number of agents required to be plugged in and available to handle contacts. In this example, 34 agents will achieve a service level of 82 percent answered in 20 seconds.

P(0): Probability of a delay greater than zero seconds. In other words, the probability of not getting an immediate answer. In this example, about 29 percent of calls will be delayed. That means 71 percent of callers won't be delayed, but instead will go right to an agent.

ASA: Average speed of answer. With 34 agents handling calls, ASA will be 13 seconds. ASA is the average delay of all calls, including the ones that aren't delayed at all. In this example, 250 calls are included in the calculation. (See discussion on why ASA is often misinterpreted, Chapter 4.)

DLYDLY: Average delay of delayed calls. This is the average delay only of those calls that are delayed — 43 seconds, in this example. DLYDLY is a better reflection than ASA of what's actually happening to the calls that end up in queue. But keep in mind, it's still an average. Some calls wait five seconds and others may wait several minutes. If calls end up in queue any amount of time, they will be included in the calculation.

Q1: Average number of calls in queue at any time, including times when there is no queue. The label is somewhat of a misnomer, because Q1 incorporates all calls into the calculation, including those that don't end up in queue. However, this column makes a useful contrast to the next, Q2.

Q2: Average number of calls in queue when all agents are busy or when there is a queue. In the example, an average of six calls are in queue, when there is a queue. Again, this is an average, and some of the time there will be more than six calls in queue, some of the time less. But this figure can provide useful guidance for what to look for when monitoring real-time information, and can also be useful for determining overflow parameters. It can also be of help when estimating the "queue slots" required by some telco-based ACD systems.

SL: Service level, the percentage of calls that will be answered in the number of seconds you specify — 82 percent in 20 seconds, here.

OCC: Percent agent occupancy. The percentage of time agents will spend handling calls, including talk time and after-call work. The balance of time, they are available and waiting for calls. In the example, occupancy will be 86 percent. Notice the tradeoff: When service level goes up, occupancy goes down. We will discuss this dynamic in Chapter 9.

TKLD: This column is the hours (erlangs) of trunk traffic, which is the product of (talk time + average speed of answer) x number of calls in an hour. Since Erlang B and other alternatives used for calculating trunks often require input in hours, these numbers can be readily used as is. The actual traffic carried by trunks in a half-hour will, in each row, be half of what is given.

The mechanics of staffing are easy enough. Plug in your numbers and the program gives answers. It's the interpretation that takes a bit of thought and application.

A good question to ask for any service level is, "What happens to the calls that don't get answered in Y seconds?" Programs that calculate delay can be very useful in answering this question. (The following is also part of ICMI's QueueView program.)

ERLANG C FOR CALL CENTERS — DELAY MODULE													
Average talk time in seconds: 180						Average after-call work in seconds: 30							
Calls per half-hour: 250						Service level in seconds: 20							
|◄——— Number of callers waiting longer than x seconds ———►|													
Agents	SL%	5	10	15	20	30	40	50	60	90	120	180	240
30	24	203	199	195	191	184	177	170	163	145	129	101	80
31	45	156	149	143	137	126	115	105	97	74	57	34	20
32	61	118	111	104	97	85	74	65	56	38	25	11	5
33	73	89	81	74	67	56	47	39	32	19	11	4	1
34	82	65	58	52	46	37	29	23	18	9	5	1	0
35	88	47	41	36	31	24	18	14	10	4	2	0	0
36	92	34	29	24	21	15	11	8	6	2	1	0	0
37	95	24	20	16	14	9	6	4	3	1	0	0	0
38	97	16	13	11	9	6	4	2	2	0	0	0	0
39	98	11	9	7	5	3	2	1	1	0	0	0	0
40	99	7	6	4	3	2	1	1	0	0	0	0	0
41	99	5	4	3	2	1	1	0	0	0	0	0	0
42	100	3	2	2	1	1	0	0	0	0	0	0	0

Source: International Customer Management Institute, Annapolis, Md.

As you can see, 34 agents will result in a service level of 82 percent of calls answered in 20 seconds. But here we get additional insight into what happens to individual calls. Sixty-five callers will wait five seconds or longer. In the next five seconds, seven of those callers reach agents, so only 58 callers are waiting 10 seconds or longer. In the next five seconds, six more callers will reach agents, leaving only 52 callers waiting 15 seconds or more. At this service level, one caller is still waiting at three minutes.

Note an important implication of delay: Because of random call arrival, different callers have different experiences even though they called during the same half-hour, and even though the call center may be hitting its target service level. (Some call centers attempt to set two service levels for the same queue, e.g., to handle 80 percent of calls in 20 seconds and the rest within 60 seconds. As you can see here, that is not possible — 80/20 and 100/60 are distinctly different service levels.) What's the worse case that your organization is willing to tolerate? That becomes a key question when exploring these tradeoffs.

If you have never used an Erlang C program, we recommend that you get one and experiment with it. You will learn more about call center dynamics and tradeoffs in an hour or two than it once took someone years of using tables or — heaven forbid — the raw formula to learn.

So far, you have calculated staff required to handle a specified mix of inbound contacts that must be handled when they arrive, for one half-hour of the day. You will also need to calculate base staff for each half-hour of the day and for every unique group of agents — sales, customer service and other types of groups you have. In Step 6 of the planning and management process, we will discuss how to factor in breaks, absenteeism and non-phone activities so that the schedule (Step 7) reflects the total staff you need.

RESPONSE TIME CONTACTS

Recall the two major categories of inbound transactions defined in Chapter 4: Those that must be handled when they arrive and those that can be handled at a later time. Staffing for contacts that must be handled when they arrive — defined by service level — should be calculated using Erlang C or computer simulation.

Calculating staff requirements for a workload that does not have to be handled at the time it arrives is generally based on the centuries-old "units-of-output" approach. Here's the logic: If you get 60 email messages that have an average handling time of four minutes, that's four hours of workload. One agent working non-stop could handle the load in four hours. If you need to complete the transactions within two hours, you will need a minimum of two agents working over a period of two hours. So, as with service level and inbound telephone calls, the email workload and response time objective dictate staff requirements. Accordingly, the basic formula for calculating the minimum staff required is:

BASIC RESPONSE TIME FORMULA

$$\frac{\text{Volume}}{(RT \div AHT)} = \text{Agents}$$

Volume = Number of contacts to be handled
RT = Response time
AHT = Average handling time

Volume is the quantity of transactions you must handle, AHT is the average amount of time it takes agents to handle the transactions (the equivalent of average talk time and average after-call work for inbound telephone calls), and response time is the time you have to respond to customers after receiving their messages. Using the formula, you could handle the 60 messages previously mentioned in two hours with two agents: $60 \div (120 \div 4) = 2$.

There are several things to keep in mind:

• There are many ways you can slice and dice base staff schedules to achieve your objectives. In fact, in the example, you could have 60 agents rush in and handle all 60 transactions just before the promised response time and still meet your objective. What you are really doing is looking for an efficient way to distribute the workload across your schedules within the promised response time.

• The basic response time formula assumes a "static" amount of work to be completed — in other words, that you have a defined amount of work that has already arrived and is waiting to be processed. However, email and other contacts that can be deferred arrive in your center throughout the day in patterns that are often similar to phone traffic. With 24-hour response time objectives, projected workload can simply be built into the following day's staffing requirements. But if you have more aggressive response time objectives, you'll need to look at both on-hand workload and projections by interval to determine staffing requirements.

- When response time objectives are less than an hour, traffic engineers generally recommend using Erlang C or computer simulation to calculate base staff. This would be a queuing and service level scenario, like inbound telephone calls.

- Breaks, absenteeism and other activities that keep agents from the work need to be added to base staff calculations (a step we'll cover in the next chapter).

- An "efficiency factor" acknowledges that agents cannot handle one transaction after another with no "breathing" time in between. For example, if you want to build in an efficiency factor with a ceiling of 90 percent, divide base staff calculations by .9 to determine if additional agents are required.

In short, meeting response time objectives requires:

- Setting response time objectives.
- Forecasting these transactions, within time-frames specific enough to calculate base staff required.
- Calculating base staff needed.
- Factoring in breaks and other activities that will take staff away from the work.
- Factoring these staffing needs into overall schedules.

OUTBOUND CONTACTS

There are three general types of outbound contacts. Each has implications for staffing requirements:

1. OUTBOUND THAT IS A PART OF THE INBOUND WORKLOAD. For example, calls to an emergency roadside service from stranded customers often involve outbound calls to arrange towing or repair services. Whether these outbound contacts happen during calls from customers, or immediately

following the calls as part of after-call work, they should be considered part of inbound handling time. As such, they should be inherently included in base-staff requirements for the inbound call load.

2. **OUTBOUND CONTACTS THAT ARE SCHEDULED.** In many cases, outbound calls to customers or prospects can be scheduled based on factors such as convenience to customers, highest probability of making successful connections, etc. Within these blocks of time, contacts can be placed and handled one after another. Base-staff requirements can be calculated using traditional response time calculations — e.g., a minimum of five agents would be required to handle 20 hours' worth of calls in four hours time. As with other response time calculations, a reasonable efficiency factor should also be included in the assumptions.

3. **OUTBOUND CONTACTS THAT ARE NEITHER A PART OF RANDOMLY ARRIVING INBOUND LOAD NOR SCHEDULED.** In every call center, there are at least some outbound calls to colleagues or customers that are neither part of the inbound load nor specifically scheduled. If significant enough to merit consideration in resource requirements, they can be reflected in Step 6, covered in the next chapter.

Staffing for Non-Traditional Groups

Today's environment is often characterized by complex transactions and sophisticated routing alternatives. You may be utilizing skills-based routing, overlapping agent groups, sophisticated network environments and other configurations that go beyond simple agent groups. Your environment will dictate the staffing methodology that will yield the best results.

SKILLS-BASED ROUTING

Available in ACD routing systems for well over a decade now, skills-based routing is a powerful capability designed to match each caller with the agent who has the skill set best-suited to handle the call on a real-time basis. It has been a boon to the efficiency and quality of services provided by call

SKILLS-BASED ROUTING

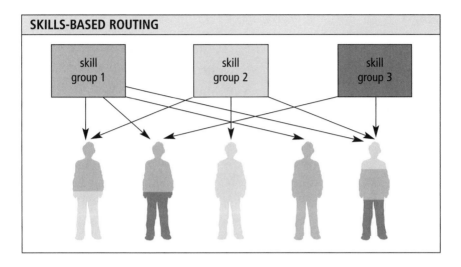

centers that, by nature, have overlapping groups or complex routing contingencies. And variations of skills-based routing are also working their way into multimedia queuing environments. But to be effective, skills-based routing must be managed well. In this environment, Erlang C's assumption of traditional agent groups no longer fits, but computer simulation can help fill the gap.

The basic requirements for skills-based routing include:

- Identify and define the skills required for each call type.
- Identify and define individual agent skills.
- Prioritize agent skills, based on individual competency levels.
- Devise and program an appropriate routing plan into the ACD.

Although specific programming approaches vary by system, you will essentially create two "maps" when you set up your ACD for skills-based routing. One will specify the types of calls to be handled and the other will identify the skills available by agent. As an example, the maps for a technical support center handling calls across Europe might look like this:

MAP 1

English-speaking callers who need assistance with Internet access.

English-speaking callers who need assistance with printers.

English-speaking callers who need assistance with storage devices.

English-speaking callers who need assistance with PCs.

French-speaking callers who need assistance with Internet access.

French-speaking callers who need assistance with printers.

French-speaking callers who need assistance with storage devices.

French-speaking callers who need assistance with PCs.

German-speaking callers who need assistance with Internet access.

German-speaking callers who need assistance with printers.

German-speaking callers who need assistance with storage devices.

German-speaking callers who need assistance with PCs.

And so on. The second map might look like this:

MAP 2

TOM — Speaks English, Dutch and French. Trained on Internet access and printers.

ANGELIQUE — Speaks French and Italian. Trained on printers, PCs and storage devices.

ERIK — Speaks Swedish, French and English. Trained on Internet access and PCs.

MARIA — Speaks Spanish, Italian and French. Trained on printers and storage devices.

Consider a simple case that illustrates the basic steps in staffing for skills-based routing. Assume you have two languages to handle — English and Spanish. And let's say that you have four call types to handle — orders and technical support calls in each language. The agent skills can be illustrated as shown.

AGENT SKILLS									
Caller Types (Based upon IVR menu selections)	Agent Type 1	Agent Type 2	Agent Type 3	Agent Type 4	Agent Type 5	Agent Type 6	Agent Type 7	Agent Type 8	Agent Type 9
Orders — English	X	X						X	X
Orders — Spanish				X		X		X	X
Tech Support — English		X	X		X				X
Tech Support — Spanish			X			X	X		X

Next, let's assume that your plan is to route calls to the least-skilled agent who can handle the call because you want to preserve your more experienced or skilled agents for less common or more complex calls. Consequently, the routing plan would appear as shown.

ROUTING PLAN				
Call-Routing Hierarchy	Order-English	Order-Spanish	Tech Support–English	Tech Support–Spanish
Skill Choice 1	Agent Type 1	Agent Type 4	Agent Type 5	Agent Type 7
Skill Choice 2	Agent Type 2	Agent Type 8	Agent Type 2	Agent Type 6
Skill Choice 3	Agent Type 8	Agent Type 6	Agent Type 3	Agent Type 3
Skill Choice 4	Agent Type 9	Agent Type 9	Agent Type 9	Agent Type 9

You set up the simulator the same way you program the maps into your ACD. You tell it what types of calls you are going to get and the skills of your group. You also plug in the same data required by Erlang C: volume of each transaction you expect, and corresponding talk time and work time estimates. Additionally, you can specify caller tolerance levels by type of call, trunking configurations and other conditions.

We used this data to run three different scenarios, all using the same call load and service level objective:

- Conventional ACD groups (one group for each call type)
- Skills-based routing
- Universal agents (a fully cross-trained group)

As the results in the table indicate, skills-based routing is more efficient than separate, segmented groups. Also note that universal agents, where each agent is fully cross-trained and speaks both languages, is the most efficient arrangement.

RESULTS OF EACH SCENARIO			
Time Period	Separate Groups by Language and Call Type	Skills-Based Routing Scenario	Universal Agents
9:00-9:30	30	27	24
9:30-10:00	43	41	39
10:00-10:30	64	62	59
10:30-11:00	58	56	52
11:00-11:30	44	41	40
11:30-12:00	31	28	27

In general, skills-based routing works best in environments that have small groups where multiple skills are required. It can also help to quickly integrate new agents into call handling, by sending only certain calls to them. It also has the potential to improve efficiency by matching callers with "just the right agent."

Skills-based routing has some disadvantages, though. In application, it seems to be Murphy's Law that the agent with just the right skill is on break at the wrong time. Mapping out skills and programming routing scenarios is one thing; getting people in the right place at the right times can be quite another. Small, specialized groups are tough to manage — and they can eliminate the efficiencies of pooling, common to conventional agent groups.

Further, routing and resource planning become more complex. Be pre-

to a second site, and the balance, 40 percent, to go to a third site.

Erlang C will generally provide good results in this environment. Even if you change call allocation throughout the day based on evolving circumstances, Erlang C will be an effective planning tool. As with ACD groups in a single site, you will forecast the call load you anticipate and run Erlang C calculations for each site.

2. NETWORK INTERFLOW. Networks that are designed to interflow calls are a step up from straight percent allocation. In this type of environment, calls initially presented to one site can be simultaneously queued at other sites, based on thresholds you define. As circumstances allow, calls can then be sent from an original site to a secondary site.

Contingencies will vary based on how you program the environment. The criteria that determine how calls are interflowed can run the gamut, from availability at each site to the types of calls you are handling. For example, you might immediately send high-priority calls to available agents in any site, but queue lower priority calls longer for intended agent groups. Given the variables, simulation can help to model and test the environment under different conditions.

3. VIRTUAL CALL CENTER. In a true, virtual environment — becoming more common as network services advance and costs of running traffic over distances fades — each call is routed to the first available agent (or longest-waiting agent). Other contingencies notwithstanding, this environment represents a traditional agent group regardless of where agents are, and Erlang C will produce accurate calculations.

LONG CALLS

Long calls pose another staffing challenge. Thirty-minute reporting periods provide an adequate level of detail and accuracy for most call centers. However, some centers, particularly those in help desk environments, handle calls that are complex enough that average handling time approaches or exceeds 30 minutes.

When long calls are not distributed as Erlang C assumes, they may violate the assumptions of the formula. Compounding the problem is the fact that some ACDs count calls in the period in which they begin, but report average handling time in the period in which they end. Consequently, reported averages can be skewed.

If your AHT approaches 30 minutes, you may need to adjust your default reporting interval to an hour versus a half-hour. Most Erlang C programs will allow you to define the interval you want to examine. Alternatively, you can program a simulator to model the mix of contacts you are handling. If, on the other hand, long calls are not common, but they do occasionally occur, you will need to adjust your statistics — remove them from assumptions — before using your historical data.

You will also need to consider how you manage long calls. Many technical support environments have established a second tier of staff to handle long and/or complex calls. You will need to manage the service level for both tiers, or it will tend to suffer in both. But when managed well, this approach can ensure that long calls don't tie up the primary group and cause erratic service levels.

PEAKED TRAFFIC

Peaked traffic, as discussed in Chapter 3, is a surge beyond random variation within a half-hour, which poses a unique staffing challenge. For the purposes of this discussion, there are two types of peaked traffic — the type you can plan for, and incidents that are impossible to predict.

The calls that utilities get just after a major power outage will surge far beyond normal random variation. Similarly, if a national news program unexpectedly provides your telephone number to the viewing audience as part of its story, you will get unannounced peaked traffic — and it will be quite an experience!

The problem is, you can't predict these events, and you're probably not willing to staff up for them just in case they happen. So staffing for unexpected peaks falls more in the category of real-time management or disaster recovery planning.

On the other hand, peaked traffic that you are expecting belongs squarely in the realm of fundamental call center planning. Forecasting, staffing and scheduling to meet a specified service level still apply. However, planning must happen at much more detailed periods of time, often in five- or 10-minute increments. For a given service level, peaked traffic requires more staff than random traffic, and agents will have a lower occupancy over a half-hour period.

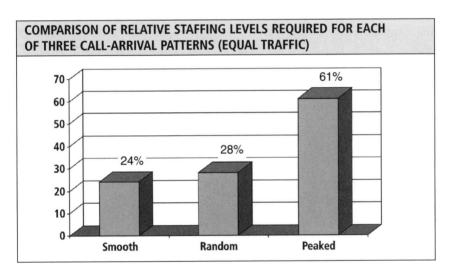

COMPARISON OF RELATIVE STAFFING LEVELS REQUIRED FOR EACH OF THREE CALL-ARRIVAL PATTERNS (EQUAL TRAFFIC)

Most use Erlang C to calculate base staff for predicted peaks. If you expect 200 calls in a five-minute span, that's the equivalent of 1,200 calls in a half-hour. If you use an Erlang C program based on half-hour data, you will assume 1,200 calls for the calculations. Alternatively, some staffing programs allow you to specify the timeframe you choose, and can accommodate short intervals.

But common sense is required. If you have 75 people to handle the 200 calls, and the calls come in at virtually the same time, you know that the first 75 are going to be answered immediately. The next 75 are going to have to wait, and the average wait will be similar to the average handling time of the first 75 calls. The last 50 calls will have to wait something like two times the average handling time of the calls.

The situation can be similar to a bus dropping people off in front of a sports arena. Those reaching the gates first get quick service. For others, service levels can be dramatically different, depending on where they end up in the line. Consequently, how peaked the traffic is (how concentrated it is within a small period of time) will dramatically impact service level.

TEXT-CHAT

Text-chat is a service level-oriented contact, and the essential planning steps apply. You can determine the most conservative (highest) estimate of agents you'll need by assuming that each agent can interact with only one customer at a time, then using Erlang C or simulation to calculate staff requirements based on the usual input — number of contacts, average session transaction time (the equivalent of AHT), and your service level objective. However, this can overestimate actual requirements in many cases; between workflow-routing options and technology possibilities, there really is no "one-size-fits-all" approach. You will need to make some key decisions to deliver acceptable levels of service efficiently in your environment.

Let's review some important terms. The following are definitions that we use and recommend. (Note: Depending on the application the roles may be reversed — e.g., the agent may make an initial request to a customer browsing the organization's Web site.)

SESSION: The whole of the text-chat interaction, from hello to goodbye.

EXCHANGE: A part of a session that begins with an inquiry from the customer and concludes with a response from the agent.

SESSION RESPONSE TIME: The time it takes the organization to respond to the initial request for a session from the customer.

EXCHANGE RESPONSE TIME: The time that elapses between the customer sending a question or comment and the delivery of the agent's response.

CUSTOMER RESPONSE TIME: The time is takes the customer to read an agent's reply and send a response.

EXCHANGE HANDLE TIME: The time it takes for the agent to prepare and deliver a response during an exchange.

SESSION HANDLE TIME: The cumulative total of the exchange handle times for the session.

SESSION TRANSACTION TIME: The time elapsed from the beginning of the initial exchange to the close-out.

CLOSE-OUT: The moment in time when the session is considered to be complete.

While some organizations use text-chat extensively, it makes up a relatively small portion of the contact workload in many others. If you're just starting out, you'll need to answer a fundamental question at some point: When do you move from "educated guessing" to staffing approaches that are more scientific? After all, if you only need one or two agents handling text-chat, advanced mathematical approaches won't yield any more accuracy than common sense.

We believe that a sensible threshold is five — when you need five or more agents handling text-chat at any one time, a more disciplined approach will begin to pay off.

Another important decision is around the number of simultaneous sessions you allow agents to handle. Some systems can be configured to enable 16 simultaneous sessions per agent — which, of course, is impractical from a human standpoint in most cases. The number of maximum concurrent sessions you allow will impact response times, customer satisfaction, employee morale and even reporting. Our advice to those just starting out: Go with one until you get a better read on what's possible and get the kinks worked out of the system.

To determine how far beyond one concurrent session you can move, some basic math comes in handy. Let's assume that you set the maximum number of concurrent sessions at five. It's simple and valuable to develop

THE REPORTING CHALLENGE

Although multiple concurrent chat sessions can improve productivity, they can also make reporting more difficult. Consider again the example of five concurrent sessions, where all five customers initiate an exchange at the same time. The last customer served will have to wait 6.25 minutes for a response — but most of that time was spent on other exchanges with other customers. The reporting challenge is accounting for these variables.

For example, when a customer initiates an exchange, the reporting system must note how many concurrent exchanges are already in queue for that agent in order to determine the exchange handle time. The customer who is fourth in line will wait a total of five minutes for a response. Divide that wait time by the number of exchanges in queue, and you'll come up with the exchange handle time of 1.25 minutes (5 ÷ 4) — but you can see that reporting must acccount for many variables.

In short, these are issues you'll need to review with your supplier. How does the system make these calculations and what do the reports produced really mean?

worst-case estimates. The formula: Multiply the maximum number of concurrent sessions you expect by the average exchange handle time. The result will give you an idea of what could happen (worst case) to customer wait times. For example, if five customers initiate an exchange at the same time, and the average exchange handle time is 1.25 minutes, the last customer in line will have to wait 6.25 minutes for a response (5 x 1.25). This scenario won't happen often — but if and when it does, the delay would be well beyond the expectations of most customers. So, five concurrent sessions would be too high for an organization focused on delivering high levels of service.

Another decision you must make is when an agent will receive a session. If a customer's initial request is immediately delivered to an agent, you can send an automated, personalized greeting from that agent to the customer. If you decide to wait on routing, you will need to deliver either a blank text-chat box or one with a generic greeting. Here's the staffing tradeoff: If you provide the more personalized approach, you will need to live with the chance that you may be tying up an agent too early — some customers will request a chat session but then never initiate the exchange, and the agent will be left waiting for a question that never comes. Given this possibility, you will probably want to allow relatively more concurrent sessions per agent than in a scenario where an agent is selected only after an exchange is initiated.

You will also need to define when a session ends. Often, the point of close-out is clear — but sometimes it's not. For example, customers may get what they need and ignore further attempts at communication; they may step away from their computers; or they might head off to competitors' Web sites. (Text-chat is often perceived to be less personal than phone calls, and customers may apply different rules of courtesy.) While your agent waits for a response, the session is considered active. So you'll need to

SERVICE LEVEL IN THE WORLD OF TEXT-CHAT

Call center professionals often liken the time it takes to receive a reply to an email or text-chat to what service level means to phone contacts. But there is an important difference: Speed-of-answer statistics associated with phone calls are based on *when the call reaches the agent.* But speed-of-response for email and text-chat is based on *when the customer receives a reply,* which can only happen after the agent actually handles the inquiry.

Is this distinction important? In the world of email — where response time is typically measured in hours or days — not usually. But text-chat is different. Response time is measured in seconds or minutes, and the time required for the agent to craft the reply must be taken into account. We've seen cases where well-intentioned executives set a response time target for exchanges of one minute or less when it takes longer than that to create the right reply! That's a recipe for disaster (or, at the least, for missed targets). It is up to the management team to establish workable objectives supported by the right level of resources.

decide on procedures to try to re-engage the customer, and when the agent can, in effect, "give up" and close the session. Staffing implication: The longer the threshold until close-out, the more time the agent will spend waiting for an exchange that may never occur; accordingly, a long threshold would suggest you can allow a relatively higher number of concurrent sessions per agent.

In short, staffing for text-chat revolves more around questions of workflow and technology application than on mathematical calculations. As volumes rise, we expect to see common practices emerge. Even then, you'll need to make decisions in each of these areas that are right for your organization and customers.

Calculating Trunks

You will need enough trunks to carry the delay that callers experience (the time from the moment calls arrive at the telephone system until agents say "hello") and the conversation time (talk time), for the period you are analyzing. The general method for calculating trunks is as follows:

1. Forecast the call load (work load) to be handled for the busiest half-hour in the foreseeable future.

2. Compute the number of agents required to handle the forecasted call load at your service level objective.

3. Determine the trunk load, according to the call load you will be handling and the service level you can realistically achieve. The trunk load represents how much time in hours callers are in queue or connected to agents over an hour.

4. Determine the number of trunks required to handle the calculated trunk load, using an appropriate formula.

Erlang B (or variations of it) is widely used and is often available in published tables, workforce management programs or in staffing calculators (including QueueView, the program that I am using for examples). There

FORMULA	ASSUMPTIONS
Erlang B	Assumes that if callers get busy signals, they go away forever, never to retry. Since some callers retry, Erlang B can underestimate trunks required.
Poisson	Assumes that if callers get busy signals, they keep trying until they successfully get through. Since some callers won't keep retrying, Poisson can overestimate trunks required.
Retrial Tables	Used less frequently by traffic engineers, but correctly assumes that some callers retry and others will go away

are also other alternatives you can choose from and each has built-in assumptions. And bandwidth calculators are emerging as VoIP applications become more common. With any of the usual formulas used for calculating trunks, you will need to specify the probability of busy signals you can live with, because if you specify none, you'll need as many trunks as there are calls. But if you can tolerate even a small probability of busy signals (e.g., 1 percent) then the number of trunks required becomes much more realistic. In the staffing sample on page 126, 38 trunks are required to handle 26.8 hours of traffic with a 1 percent probability of busy signals.

If you have more than one trunk group, you will allocate the trunk load among your trunk groups, before calculation. For example, if 25 percent of the traffic will arrive on a trunk group that handles local calls and the other 75 percent on a group that carries toll-free traffic, you will need trunks to handle 6.7 hours of traffic in the first group (.25 x 26.8 hours)

ERLANG B FORMULA

$$P = \frac{\dfrac{A^N}{N!}}{\displaystyle\sum_{x=0}^{N} \dfrac{A^x}{x!}}$$

Where   A = total traffic in erlangs
N = number of trunks
P = grade of service

and 20.1 hours in the second (.75 x 26.8 hours).

You may have an IVR that callers go through before they reach an agent (to enter their account number, route themselves, etc.). If so, the time callers spend in the IVR will have to be factored into the calculations. And if trunks are shared among different agent groups, that would also be a consideration. Regardless, the basic concept holds true: Staffing impacts trunking requirements. Delay is key — the fewer people you have for a given call load, the more trunks you'll need.

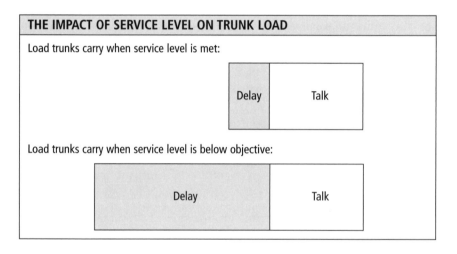

THE IMPACT OF SERVICE LEVEL ON TRUNK LOAD

Load trunks carry when service level is met:

Delay | Talk

Load trunks carry when service level is below objective:

Delay | Talk

My purpose here is to illustrate the relationship between staff and trunks, and introduce the basics of calculating the trunks you need. As with Erlang C, Erlang B will be inaccurate when assumptions built into the formula do not line up with reality. There are many possible trunking scenarios that go beyond the scope of this chapter, and we highly recommend that you get the help of a competent telecommunications professional to help you engineer your system — but ensure that they understand the relationship between trunks and staff. And make sure that staffing and trunking are coordinated activities, both in calculations and in your budgets.

Points to Remember

- Staffing and trunking are inextricably related. The load carried by trunks and the telecommunications network will be impacted by the service level the call center is achieving.

- The Erlang C formula is commonly used for calculating base staff and is easy-to-use and widely available. Computer simulation is more difficult to use than Erlang C, but can more accurately model complex environments.

- No staffing methodology is perfect, and it is important to understand the assumptions each makes and to blend in a good dose of common sense.

- Base staff calculations tell you how many agents you need to handle the workload at the service level and response time targets you've set. But many things can keep agents away from the work, and Steps 6 and 7 — covered in the next chapter — incorporate these activities so that schedules are realistic and reflect total staffing needs.

CHAPTER 8:
Successful Scheduling

Where are they?

ANONYMOUS CALL CENTER MANAGER

A ccurate scheduling is more challenging than ever. A number of trends have contributed to this complexity. For instance, today's call centers support a broader range of products and services than they did in the past. Technology has enabled many simple transactions to be automated, leaving agents with increasingly varied and demanding calls that often necessitate more offline research, follow-up and training. And the majority of customers are using a variety of contact channels to interact with organizations.

The irony is that the very forces that are making scheduling increasingly difficult in many centers have created an environment in which accurate scheduling is paramount. It's an

CONSEQUENCES OF BEING OVERSTAFFED

- Unnecessarily high staffing costs
- Underutilization of staff
- Boredom of staff
- Loss of credibility in budgeting

CONSEQUENCES OF BEING UNDERSTAFFED

- Unhappy callers
- Abandoned calls
- Longer calls
- More errors and rework
- Higher telephone network usage and costs
- Staff stress and burnout

unenviable tradeoff: Get your schedules right or brace for chaos.

Fortunately, the core objective of scheduling — get the right people and supporting resources in the right places at the right times — hasn't changed. Nor have the principles driving the process: correctly identifying and categorizing the different types of activities; making accurate base staff calculations; anticipating shrinkage requirements; using scheduling alternatives that provide necessary flexibility; and ensuring that things go as planned (e.g., through effective schedule adherence).

From one perspective, a schedule is a high-level forecast. It incorporates all of the planning steps discussed in previous chapters and predicts who needs to be where, doing what and when. It is also a "game plan" — one designed specifically for agents to follow.

> **Thank you for calling. Currently our agents are either:**
> - On a break
> - At lunch
> - Making calls
> - In a meeting
> - Helping a colleague
> - In the restroom
> - Working on a project
> - Rebooting their computer
> - Researching something
> - Sick
> - On vacation
> - In a coaching session
> - Catching up with internal email
> - Getting supplies
> - Showing visitors around the call center
> - Stuck in after-call work
> - In training
> - Assisting other customers
>
> **Thank you for your patience, and please continue to hold...**

The Scheduling Challenge

Before we head into the next two planning steps, let's take stock of where you are in the planning process. You chose service level and response time objectives (Step 1), acquired the necessary planning data (Step 2), and forecasted the workload associated with the various types of work you must handle (Step 3). You then calculated base staff and trunks required (Steps 4 and 5).

At this point, if you graph out half-hour staffing requirements for any day of the week, you will see that you need different levels of agents every half-hour. And, you'll need different levels of staff for each day of the week and different seasons of the year. Scheduling for an average half-hour of the day, average day of the week or average month of the year will mean being either overstaffed or understaffed much of the time. Consequently, schedules need to reflect the workload as it changes throughout the day, week and year.

Effective scheduling depends on both longer-term budgets and short-term execution. You'll need a big enough bucket of resources to work with — in other words, do you have the staff you need on payroll (or through contracts) to put schedules together that match the workload? We'll cover longer-term staff planning and budgeting in Chapter 10. Short-term execu-

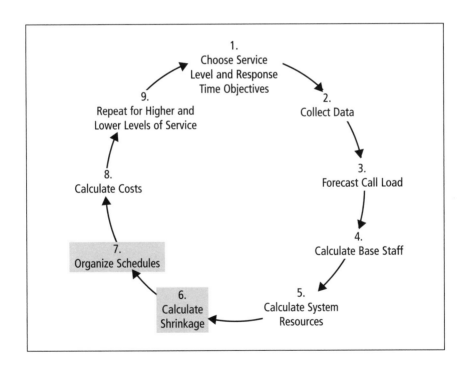

tion is at the other end of the spectrum — you can accurately forecast the workload, know how many people you need and schedule accordingly, yet still miss your service level and response time objectives by a long shot because your agents aren't in the right places at the right times. We'll look at schedule adherence in Chapter 14.

Accounting for Shrinkage

Have you ever looked at a supervisor monitor or conducted a headcount on the floor and wondered, "Where is everybody?" I have a hunch that every call center manager has asked that question at one time or another! Part of the answer is schedule adherence. But another part is realistically anticipating the things that can occupy agents' time.

Rostered staff factor (RSF), alternatively called an "overlay," is a numerical factor that leads to the minimum staff needed on schedule over and above base staff required to achieve your service level and response time objectives. It is calculated after base staffing is determined and before schedules are organized.

Calculating RSF is a form of forecasting. The major assumption is that the proportion of staff off the phones will be similar to what is happening now. In other words, if one person is on break in a group of 10, 10 people

ROSTERED STAFF FACTOR (SHRINKAGE) CALCULATIONS

	Base Staff Required					On	Rostered Staff
	Phone	Email	Absent	Break	Training	Schedule	Factor
08:00-08:30	18	4	2	0	0	24	1.09
08:30-09:00	20	4	2	0	4	30	1.25
09:00-09:30	20	4	2	0	4	30	1.25
09:30-10:00	25	5	2	3	4	39	1.3
10:00-10:30	25	5	2	3	4	39	1.3
10:30-11:00	31	5	2	3	4	45	1.25

$$\text{Rostered Staff Factor} = \frac{\text{On Schedule}}{\text{Base Staff Required}}$$

will be on break in a group of 100. An illustration of how to calculate RSF is shown in the table.

The mechanics include five steps:

1. ENTER THE BASE STAFF REQUIRED BY HALF-HOUR. What base staff includes will depend on the structure of your groups. For example, if you have separate agent groups for transactions that must be handled when they arrive (i.e., phone calls) and transactions that can be handled at a later time (i.e., email), the base staff entered represents one of those groups. You will need RSF calculations for each group. On the other hand, if you set up groups that handle both types of transactions, base staff is first calculated for both types of work separately and then added together. You would then calculate RSF for the combined group.

2. IDENTIFY THE THINGS THAT ROUTINELY KEEP AGENTS FROM THE WORKLOAD. The next three columns reflect the numbers of staff absent, on break and in training, as they now occur. These categories are just examples, and you can include research, outbound calls (those that are not part of talk time or after-call work, nor otherwise included in base staff calculations) and other activities. You may also want to further subdivide the categories. For example, absenteeism can be divided into planned absenteeism, such as vacations, and unplanned absenteeism, such as sick leave.

3. ADD BASE STAFF TO THE NUMBER OF AGENTS WHO WILL BE AWAY FROM THE WORKLOAD, FOR EACH HALF-HOUR. The "on-schedule" column is the sum of the entries in previous columns, by half-hour.

4. CALCULATE RSF. The last column is derived by dividing the staff required on schedule by base staff required for each half-hour. The proportions are the mechanism you will use to project future schedule requirements.

5. USE THE FACTORS WHEN ORGANIZING FUTURE SCHEDULES. The result of these calculations is a set of factors reflecting expected requirements by half-hour. You multiply them against the base staff you will need when assembling future schedules. For example, if you are putting togeth-

er a schedule for four weeks from now, and you need 32 base staff between 8:30 and 9:00, you will need to schedule 40 agents (32 x 1.25) for that half-hour — plus any staff required to be working on projects, in meetings or anything else not included in the calculation.

WHAT TO INCLUDE

While breaks and absenteeism should almost always be included in RSF calculations, other activities require some analysis and judgment. For example, should training be included? If training schedules frequently change and/or require differing proportions of staff, keep training out of calculations and, instead, factor it into schedules on a case-by-case basis. But if training happens in predictable proportion to the base staff required, include it. Note: After-call work is already included in base staff calculations (as part of average handling time) so it should not be included in RSF factor calculations.

In many call centers, RSF factor falls between 1.1 and 1.4 throughout the day, meaning that a minimum of 10 percent to 40 percent additional staff are required on schedule over those handling the workload. But don't trust rules of thumb; you will need to produce your own calculations. If activities not related to the workload are significant, RSF can be as high as 2.0, meaning that you'll need to schedule two people for each agent required. This is fairly common in some technical support environments that require extensive offline research.

We recommend that you initially produce a table of factors for each day of the week and for each agent group you will be scheduling. Then, adjust the calculations as circumstances dictate (i.e., for vacation season or major changes in training schedules).

IMPROVING ACCURACY

Larger call centers will pick up some accuracy by going through this planning step in 15-minute increments. In smaller centers, half-hour peri-

SHRINKAGE VERSUS ROSTERED STAFF FACTOR

For years, many have used the terms rostered staff factor (RSF) and shrinkage interchangeably to refer to the reality of needing more staff on schedule than the base staff required to handle customer contacts. There's nothing wrong with that, as long as it's understood that, in that context, the terms refer to the overall concept of needing more staff on schedule than base staff required to handle the workload.

Others use the terms more specifically — nothing wrong with that either, as long as the context is understood. When differentiated — and it's subtle in concept — shrinkage refers to *how much loss* (shrinkage) there is between scheduled staff and base staff, while rostered staff factor looks at *how much needs to be added* to base staff required to reach schedule requirements.

What's not subtle is how the calculations for each are used when they are diffentiated in this way. Consider an example where base staff is 40, 10 agents will be involved in other activities, so the schedule requirement is 50 agents.

The RSF is 50/40, or 1.25
Application: 40 x 1.25 = 50 agents
(or)
The shrinkage (loss) = 10/50, or 20%
Application: 40 / (1 - 20%) = 50 agents

Uh, oh… you can see what's coming here. Some mistakenly apply shrinkage in place of what should be RSF, and end up with too few scheduled agents. And others mistakenly apply RSF in place of what should be shrinkage, and end up with too many scheduled agents.

Investment analysts often have to remind clients of a similar principle in the world of finance. If a $5,000 investment drops by 20 percent, the new balance is $4,000; $4,000 would need to grow by 25 percent (4,000 x 1.25) to again reach $5,000. Many call center managers have found themselves in a similar education process: "Yes, scheduled staff shrinks by 20 percent, which is why we need 25 percent additional staff above base-staff requirements for that increment!"

(continued next page)

In that sense, RSF has some advantages — it's easier to explain. Correctly applying either method at the interval level will lead you to the same answers — however, you have to take shrinkage a step further to calculate staff required, while RSF provides requirements more directly. The RSF methodology also tends to fit nicely into the logical progression of planning, e.g., calculate staff and supporting resources (Steps 4 and 5), determine and apply RSF (Step 6), organize schedules (Step 7). Shrinkage tends to jump from schedules (Step 7) to determining loss or shrinkage (Step 6), to applying the formula to base staff (Step 5) to get back to schedule requirements (Step 7). It's a small point that doesn't matter if either approach is used correctly — but I do prefer the RSF approach when explaining these principles to others.

Shrinkage has some advantages, as well. It's the term that, more often than not, has been adapted by workforce management suppliers (consequently, I run into people who have been in the industry for years and have never heard of RSF). And it's used more broadly in other environments — e.g., in retailing environments, inventory shrinkage can be caused by loss, damage or theft. (That can be a mixed blessing — if you do an Internet search on "shrinkage" you will find pages of definitions and sites having nothing to do with call centers.)

Finally, the time horizon you are considering may impact the approach you use. As described here, RSF and shrinkage are for scheduling (near and medium term) purposes. When we look at a longer planning horizon — e.g., to determine full-time equivalent requirements (Chapter 10), we'll use a shrinkage-like approach in the methodology. But caution is in order: Any mismatch of time — e.g., taking a calculation for shrinkage or RSF determined over a broader timeframe, and applying it to smaller increments — simply doesn't work.

There are different ways to get from point A to point B, and organizations, systems and individuals tend to use the same or similar terms differently. When used correctly and in the right context, both shrinkage and RSF lead to the *same answer*. It's essential to recognize the assumptions you are making and use the right calculations in the right context.

ods are sufficient, but you should use numbers that are conservative. For example, if you have two people on break the first 15 minutes of the half-hour, and four on break in the second half of the period, use four in the calculations.

If you calculated staff for hour increments due to long calls (as discussed in Chapter 6), you can also generally calculate RSF by hour, since scheduled breaks and lunch tend to get moved around by long calls. If you find that hours are not picking up the activity accurately, drop to half-hour increments.

If you are handling peaked traffic, you can usually use half-hour or 15-minute increments for RSF even though you calculated base staff for even shorter periods. Naturally, you will plan any activities that are flexible around the inbound peaks.

A PREREQUISITE TO EFFECTIVE BUDGETS AND SCHEDULES

Frankly, the phenomenon of rostered staff factor *really bugs* some financial people — and understandably so. "You mean to tell me we need to hire 42 people so we can have 30 on the phones handling calls?" (In your defense, *they* go on breaks, take vacations and handle a variety of tasks too, but I wouldn't recommend that argument!) There is simply no substitute for showing them what's going on and why the extra staff is required. As a result, RSF calculations are necessary to communicate budget requirements effectively.

An added advantage of making this effort is that it will force you to examine these activities — should they be happening when and to the degree that they are? Some changes may provide better coverage or make scheduling easier or more acceptable to agents. Like any aspect of planning, examine how accurate your predictions are compared to actual results, and adjust accordingly.

After you have calculated RSF, you know your staffing requirements accurately down to specific times of day. The next challenge is to identify scheduling alternatives and parameters so that you can organize schedules that closely match staffing requirements.

CAN YOU SKIP STEP 6?

Why bother with RSF — Step 6 in the planning process — if you know how many staff you will need simply by adding the columns together? Better yet, why bother with any of it, if your scheduling package inherently accounts for these sorts of things? Can you calculate base-staff requirements, then jump right into scheduling — skipping step 6 altogether?

With a scheduling package, you can, in a sense, do just that. After calculating base-staff requirements, you will begin building schedules — and yes, they will account for and include breaks, holidays, training and other factors. But Step 6 is still important, for several reasons:

- Simply understanding the principle is key to understanding the spread between base-staff and schedule requirements — and you'll need to explain this principle to others in various planning and budgeting settings.
- There will be times when you'll want to model the schedule requirements for different workload scenarios, without laboring though the minutia of adding up individual shrinkage components; there's nothing that beats the speed and accuracy of having an accurate set of factors.
- Because it is a ratio, RSF can be easily tracked and graphed, enabling you to see relative trends and identify improvement opportunities. That is much more difficult when looking at a full-blown schedule.

Scheduling Alternatives

Considering that staffing needs fluctuate significantly throughout the day, month and year, what alternatives exist for having an adequate number of people in place without being overstaffed much of the time? After all, there aren't too many people who like to work half-hour shifts.

Fortunately, quite a few alternatives exist. Here we've listed some of the

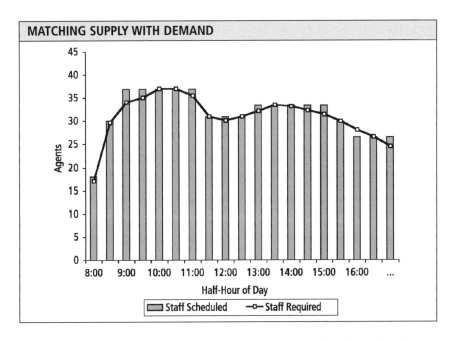

MATCHING SUPPLY WITH DEMAND

strategies that call centers are using. Of course, not all will be feasible for you. This aspect of planning involves putting the cards on the table — identifying the scheduling approaches that could work in your specific environment.

USE HIRING TO YOUR ADVANTAGE. Important criteria when hiring new agents should be the hours and days they can (or can't) work.

UTILIZE CONVENTIONAL SHIFTS. Many call centers have a core group of agents who work traditional five-day-a-week shifts during normal hours (e.g., 9 a.m. to 5 p.m.). That's just fine, assuming there are additional scheduling options to address variability in workload within and beyond these hours.

ADJUST BREAKS, LUNCH, MEETING AND TRAINING SCHEDULES. Even slight changes to when these activities are scheduled can mean that a few more people are handling contacts at just the right times. And that can make a big difference (review the staffing calculations in Chapter 7 and notice the impact that just one person will make on service level when it is

161

low). This alternative is available to virtually every call center.

STAGGER SHIFTS. For example, one shift begins at 7 a.m., the next at 7:30 a.m., the next at 8 a.m., etc., until the call center is fully staffed for the busy mid-morning traffic. This is a common and effective approach. Be sure to tweak these shifts as necessary to account for changes in calling patterns.

OFFER CONCENTRATED SHIFTS. Given the choice, some agents will opt to work fewer days with more hours per day, while others would rather work fewer hours in a day, even if that means a six- or seven-day workweek. In one example, global investment firm AMVESCAP's Retirement Resource Center has benefited from offering 10x4 workweek shifts, with some of the most experienced, longest-tenured agents bidding for them. Roughly 10 percent of the center's agents work from 10 a.m. to 9 p.m., four days a week. Each of these agents' extra day off rotates weekly so that, once a month, each person gets a Friday off — for a three-day weekend. (Nobody is ever off on Monday, the center's busiest day.) In addition to meeting the center's peak coverage requirements, the 10x4 work schedule has boosted the number of skilled agents on staff for the night shift.

USE AN ENVELOPE STRATEGY. With more types of work to handle in today's environment, many call centers are using an "envelope" strategy (see figure). This approach recognizes that some types of work have to be handled at specific times of the day, and other types of work allow more flexibility. The idea is to move in and out of the various types of work as circumstances dictate. Collateral work provides flexibility, if it is planned and managed well.

OFFER OVERTIME. No additional training is required, and many agents will volunteer for the extra work. However, overtime can be expensive as an ongoing strategy and, once again, there is the question of whether or not agents can perform at high levels throughout extended shifts.

GIVE AGENTS THE OPTION TO GO HOME WITHOUT PAY. Often referred to as LWOP (leave without pay, pronounced "el-wop"), this is a popular

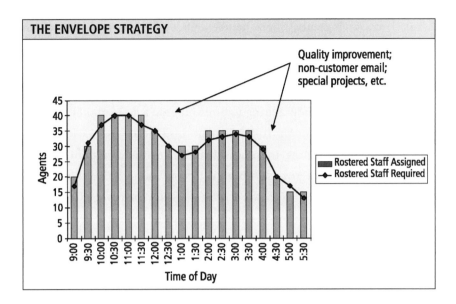

THE ENVELOPE STRATEGY

approach on slower days, and there are usually enough agents willing to take you up on it.

SCHEDULE PART-TIMERS. Some call centers are prevented from using part-time help by union agreements or by practicalities (e.g., complex call center services requiring extensive training). But when available and practical, this is a popular and common approach.

ESTABLISH REINFORCEMENTS. When contact-handling duties are combined with other tasks, such as correspondence, outbound calling or data entry, the agents assigned to these collateral duties can act as reinforcements when the contact load gets heavy. Often called the "reinforcement method," this approach is a bit like being able to bring in part-timers on an as-needed basis (keep an eye on the workload being put aside so that you aren't creating downstream problems). Initially, you many need to tackle training, scheduling, cultural — and perhaps even pay and union issues.

CREATE A SWAT TEAM. This approach takes the reinforcement method to the larger organization. Vanguard, the large financial services company, helped to pioneer this approach and it was not out of question to see the company's founder and former chairman, John C. Bogel (who now runs a financial research center), help handle calls. A similar arrangement has paid dividends for People's Bank's call center in Bridgeport, Conn. For years, the center has been using former skilled agents — many of whom work in the company's marketing or accounting departments — to manage seasonal call spikes without having to hire and train a large number of temporary staff or to outsource. To implement this kind of approach successfully, you'll need to address training, scheduling, pay and cultural issues.

ARRANGE FOR SOME AGENTS TO BE ON CALL. Although this alternative is impractical for many, it can work in situations where events cannot be precisely predicted (i.e., catalog companies during the initial days of a new promotion). Typically, for this approach to be effective, agents must either live near the call center or be equipped for telework.

OFFER SPLIT SHIFTS. Granted, split shifts — where agents work a partial shift, take part of the day off, then return later to finish their shifts — are not common. They are typically used in cases where college students need to work around class schedules. But don't count this alternative out in other settings. A group of agents in one of MetLife's call centers once volunteered to work in the mornings and then come back for the less popular evening shift. They were happy to have the free midday time to play golf — not a bad arrangement!

SEND CALLS TO AN OUTSOURCING AGENCY. Today, outsourcers of all types and capabilities are available. The best agencies can handle complex types of contacts and the full range of customer contact channels. In fact, some outsourcers today specialize in providing support for specific contact channels.

COLLABORATE WITH SIMILAR ORGANIZATIONS. Some progressive call centers have formed successful "staffing alliances" with other centers that have different seasonality patterns. The two centers "loan" agents to one another to help each company effectively handle its peak contact periods, and to eliminate the costs that would be incurred if each had to hire and train temporary staff each year. While not yet a common practice, we are seeing more of these types of arrangements all the time.

STAFF-SHARING PARTNERSHIP HELPS EASE SCHEDULING DILEMNA

If you can't beat your seasonal staffing crunch, join a contact center that faces similar challenges. That's what Day-Timers' Customer Contact Center and Accor Reservations Center did. Both centers were growing tired of hiring extra staff to handle peak-season call volumes, then laying them off (or relying on natural attrition) when things slowed down. When the two non-competing centers realized that their respective peak seasons were "counter-cyclical" — meaning that volumes got kicking for one organization around the same time that volume started dropping off at the other — they had an idea: Form a staff-sharing alliance that enables each center to cost-effectively manage its seasonal peaks and valleys.

Here's how the innovative staffing alliance works: Just prior to Accor's peak season, a group of Day-Timers' agents are trained to take reservations calls for the hotel giant. Then, when Accor's call volume begins to dissipate, the "shared" Day-Timers agents go back to handling calls for Day-Timers. Soon thereafter, when Day-Tmers' peak season is about to hit, a group of Accor agents are trained to handle calls for the calendar, planning and organization supplies company.

To simplify compensation issues, the two centers simply "swap" hours. Each center tabulates the number of hours its agents work for the other company, including call-handling and training. For example, if during a given season, Day-Timers' agents spend 13,000 hours taking calls or attending training for Accor, then Accor agents are scheduled for 13,000 hours during Day-Timers' peak season. If either company requires more hours, they are billed at the average agent rate, plus a 10 percent administrative fee.

To ensure call quality during high-volume seasons, each company conducts quality monitoring of the other's agents, as well as their own. The reports are shared so that each center can compare those results with their own reports.

Source: *Call Center Management Review*

SET UP A TELEWORK/HOME-AGENT PROGRAM. This is not a scheduling alternative, per se, but it can create an environment in which unpopular shifts will be more palatable and where agents can handle contacts on short notice. Numerous organizations have successfully implemented work-at-home agent programs, benefiting not only from enhanced scheduling flexibility but also increased productivity and agent retention. Some companies have embraced "extreme telework" where the large majority — in some cases 100 percent — of staff are home agents. For example, JetBlue Airline's only in-house agents are those completing the center's five-week new-hire training program. And some outsourcing agencies — WillowCSN, Alpine Access, Working Solutions and others — are staffed primarily with home agents.

SACRIFICE SERVICE LEVEL FOR A PLANNED PERIOD OF TIME. It may be unrealistic for some customer service or technical support centers to meet service level (and response time) objectives during the initial weeks of a new product introduction, or during the busiest season. As a result, some conscientiously "sacrifice" service level for several weeks or more and rely on customers to understand. This must be carefully planned, and to be acceptable to customers, it must fall within the realm of their expectations.

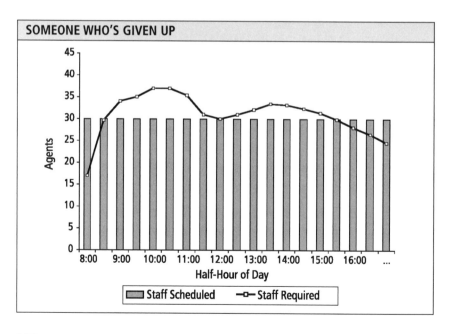

Sometimes we hear defeatist attitudes related to staffing and scheduling: "Hey, they're going to give us what they are going to give us" (see "Someone Who's Given Up"). But there are many scheduling alternatives available, even in relatively restrictive environments. Further, would senior management be persuaded by budgetary requests based on solid planning? The answer is often an unequivocal, "yes."

Putting the Pieces Together

Scheduling is inherently an iterative process — effective scheduling will always involve a certain amount of trial and error. As you identify scheduling alternatives, there are a number of important considerations:

AGENT PREFERENCES. If you involve agents in identifying scheduling possibilities up front, they will often generate ideas you didn't consider and will better accept and adhere to the schedules that are produced. Education on the implications of service level, quality and the impact of each person help enormously (see discussion of the impact of one person, in the next chapter).

AGENT GROUP STRUCTURE. How specialized are your skill requirements? Some call centers can't say with precision where contacts go because their skills- or contingency-based routing environments are so complex. Keep your routing contingencies simple enough to manage. Then invest the time necessary to forecast, staff and schedule for the specialized mix of contacts the call center is handling.

SCHEDULE HORIZON. How far in advance will you determine schedules (the schedule horizon)? If you schedule further out, say for two or three months from now, your schedules will be less efficient. They will be locked in place, even if call load deviates from the forecast. But a big plus is that they will be more agreeable to your staff, who prefer to know their work schedules well in advance. On the other hand, if you use a shorter timeframe, the scheduling process will be less popular with agents, but schedules will likely be more accurate. This issue is a balancing act.

UNION, LEGAL AND CONTRACT REQUIREMENTS. You will need to carefully consider union, legal and contractual requirements to ensure that you are scheduling within acceptable parameters. Restrictions on part-time staff, hours worked and overtime pay will impact the alternatives you can use. If you are in a union environment, an open, collaborative environment with union representatives — as well as educating them on the principles covered in Chapters 7 through 9 — can help immensely.

Scheduling software can be a big help in shuffling the pieces and generating schedules according to the parameters you establish. Conversely, it can turn out schedules that people will look at and say, "Are you kidding? There's no way we can adhere to that." So you'll need to define the rules and manage the process for best results.

As in other aspects of planning, you'll need to make sure that the software is considering all of the alternatives and parameters unique to your environment. You will also need to be realistic about agent preferences and encourage their involvement. In short, this, like other planning steps, should be a collaborative effort; it involves a great deal more than mechanics.

How Did It Go?

Want to really know how well scheduling is going? Make a line graph of your service level as it was during a recent week (you can also do this for response time). The following line charts represent agent groups in three different call centers (note, the hours and days of operation are different for each). Each chart covers a specific week, and each line represents a different day.

Because these graphs display actual results by half-hour, versus results for a single day or averages for a week or month, they can expose recurring problem areas. The first graph illustrates a fairly consistent service level that is centered around the call center's target of answering 85 percent of calls in 30 seconds (minus a few short-lived problem areas). A consistent, on-target service level such as this is what you are striving for. If the graph doesn't look consistent, keep in mind that because service level is a high-level report, these graphs won't show stable, repeating patterns usually inherent with handling time or volume graphs.

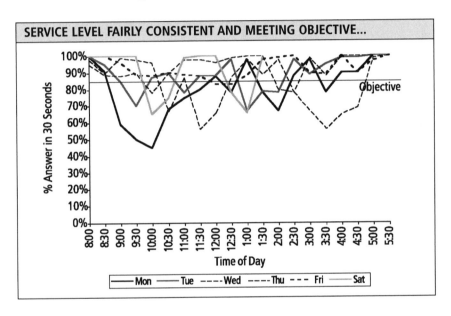

The next graph illustrates a service level that isn't so hot. You can see that service level is relatively consistent from day to day, but well below the call center's objective of answering 75 percent of calls in 20 seconds. It dips mid-morning, mid-afternoon and some around lunch time — probably the result of breaks and lunch.

The afternoons are consistently more… well, inconsistent. My hunch is, call-related or non-phone work is building up through the first part of the day and being squeezed into the afternoons, often at the expense of service level. Monday (probably the busiest day of the week) takes a beating. Service level also drops Thursday afternoon, possibly the result of meet-

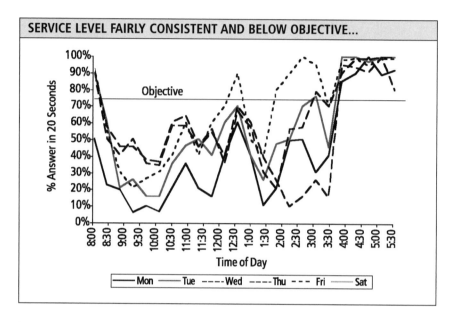

ings, training or some other activity that occupies part of the staff. Based on these observations, you should investigate the following:

• Can breaks and lunch be adjusted to provide better coverage during the mornings and afternoons? For example, can you move lunch to a later time for some agents? Granted, you have to be reasonable — few would want to take a break at 9 a.m. or eat lunch at 3 p.m. But even slight adjustments can yield significant results.

• Is phone-related and non-phone work being forecasted and managed as well as possible? Do supervisors and agents know when to move from handling incoming calls into other types of work? Do they have real-time information on service level? Can some of the work be shifted into the evening when service level is high?

• Are there any scheduling strategies available that would provide better coverage on Monday? Are there any activities on Monday (non-phone work, meetings, training, etc.) that can be moved to another day? Is there any way to provide better coverage Thursday afternoon (maybe not; this may be the best time for the event that is affecting service level)?

• Do the resources exist to achieve the service level target, especially on Monday? Consistent results such as these can indicate that, when all is said and done, the group is doing about as well as it can. In that case, only additional staff or a reduction of call load is going to improve results.

The next figure reveals an erratic service level that is usually below management's objective of 80 percent answer in 20 seconds. This may be an indication that the resources to meet the objective are adequate, but that they aren't in the right places at the right times.

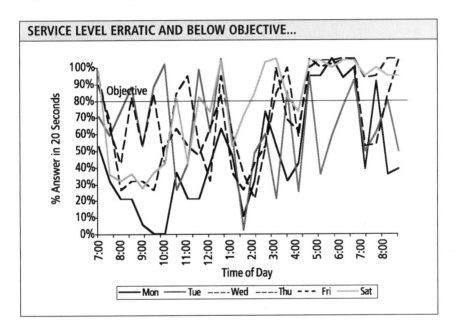

There are probably inconsistencies in how agents are handling the workload. Further, agents may not understand or have information on service level. Some of the issues to investigate include:

• Is non-phone work being forecasted and managed as well as possible? Can some of the non-phone work be moved into the evening when service level is generally better?

• Do supervisors and agents have real-time information on service level

171

so they know when to sign-off or go into other work modes versus when to "plug in" and help handle the queue?

- Do agents use the after-call work mode consistently? Do they know what constitutes after-call work, or are they mixing other activities into this mode?

- Are there scheduling strategies available to provide better coverage on Mondays?

- Is staffing adequate to achieve service level, assuming breaks, training and non-phone work are being scheduled as appropriately as possible?

Staffing and scheduling is an art that takes time, practice and collaboration to master. As the environment becomes more complex, this step becomes more important. The results you are getting are telling, and you'll learn a lot by making the effort to compare what actually happens to what was scheduled to happen.

Scheduling is a creative process that requires support from call center

FIVE WAYS TO GET BETTER SCHEDULING RESULTS

The very forces that are making scheduling difficult — more complex products and services, additional contact channels, faster pace of change, and the need for diverse agent skills — are creating an environment in which accurate scheduling is absolutely essential. Fortunately, scheduling is a process that can be learned and continuously improved — you get better at it with practice! We've found that organizations getting the best scheduling results commonly take steps beyond the mechanics of calculating required staff and putting schedules together. Here are five of their secrets.

1. Clarify Your Organization's Values. This involves a dialog and set of decisions with the organization's senior level management around key questions; e.g., what is the call center's mission? How committed are you to providing good service even when the forecasts may be uncertain? What are your priorities — which activities get done first? What alternatives exist to maintain consistent service levels — from scheduling options to backup from other departments or outside help? Be ready for these discussions; they are opportunities to clarify direction and make a case for the resources and support that the call center requires.

2. Model Different Scenarios. Modeling, or periodically creating test schedules with different sets of variables, can be a big eye-opener for possibilities and solutions. What's the impact of changing call-routing alternatives? Agent group structure? Schedule horizon? Training and meeting schedules? Shifts? While modeling takes time — you're basically having a person or team produce example schedules under different parameters — you'll get this investment back in multiples, in the form of better decisions that come from an understanding of tradeoffs and points of leverage. (Scheduling software can be a big help in this effort, particularly in larger or more complex centers.)

3. Ensure that All Activities Are Included. Too often, call centers have extra work outside of the schedule that is unaccounted for but that exacts a heavy price in psychological weight and creates fires when it's ignored for too long (e.g., unfinished projects or case work that results in additional contacts or repetitive work). Take an inventory of activities — and make it is as comprehensive and specific as possible.

4. Resolve the "Power Struggles." If power struggle sounds a bit dramatic, you ought to see some of the challenges those in forecasting and scheduling roles have encountered: Requests from other areas preempting schedules, unplanned marketing campaigns, unannounced schedule exceptions among agent teams, and unclear lines of authority between supervisors and workforce planners. These challenges are not insurmountable — unless they go unaddressed.

5. Ensure that the Process Is Simple, Flexible and Inclusive. Effective scheduling will always involve a certain amount of trial and error. It's important to keep your routing contingencies simple enough to manage, and get people involved in helping to identify scheduling possibilities and solutions. Education on the implications of service level, quality and the impact of each person is essential (see next chapter).

leadership, depends on ongoing communication, and is implemented only through effective collaboration throughout the call center. It takes an ongoing commitment — but as a prerequisite to a stable and well-run call center, it's worth the effort many times over.

Points to Remember

- Scheduling is both a forecast and a game plan. It requires accurate planning and good schedule adherence.
- An important prerequisite to effective scheduling is to get your arms around all of the activities that occupy agents' time, and build schedules that are realistic.
- Many scheduling alternatives exist, even in relatively restrictive environments. You should regularly reassess which alternatives are feasible in your call center, and how you can use them.
- Creating service level graphs by half-hour will reveal how well schedules are matching agents to the workload and will expose recurring problem areas.

Part Three:
Understanding Call Center Dynamics

CHAPTER 9:
How Contact Centers Behave

CHAPTER 10:
Communicating with Senior Management

CHAPTER 11:
Real-Time Management

There are important fundamental principles that govern how customer contact centers behave. Understanding them is key to everything from communicating with senior management and making a case for the budget you need, to managing the center in "real-time."

CHAPTER 9:
How Contact Centers Behave

Every why hath a wherefore.

SHAKESPEARE, THE COMEDY OF ERRORS

As surely as the laws of physics define the parameters for air travel, fundamental principles govern call centers. When these principles are misunderstood or ignored, the results are often poor or volatile service levels and response times, inappropriate staffing, excessive costs and unhappy customers.

Six "immutable laws" are at work in any call center that handles at least some inbound customer contacts. (Reason: Many of these laws are driven

---

SIX IMMUTABLE LAWS IN CALL CENTERS

1. For a given call load, when service level goes up, occupancy goes down.
2. Keep improving service level and you will reach a point of diminishing returns.
3. For a given service level, larger agent groups are more efficient than smaller groups.
4. All other things being equal, pooled groups are more efficient than specialized groups.
5. For a given call load, add staff and average speed of answer will go down.
6. For a given call load, add staff and trunk load will go down.

177

by random call arrival — see Chapter 3.) They are immutable in the sense that they are unchangeable, always have been with us, and always will be with us. Understanding these dynamics is key to cultivating an effective planning process, setting fair standards, preparing accurate budgets, and communicating call center activities to upper management and others.

When Service Level Goes Up, Occupancy Goes Down

As discussed in Chapter 4, service level is expressed as "X percent of calls answered in Y seconds." Occupancy is the percent of time during a half-hour that those agents who are on the phones (or available to handle other types of contacts) are actually handling contacts (e.g., in talk time and after-call work). The inverse of occupancy is the time that agents spend waiting for calls, plugged in and available.

As the table illustrates, a service level of 80 percent of calls answered in 20 seconds (82/20, to be precise) equates to an occupancy of 86 percent (given that call load). If service level drops to 24 percent answered in 20 seconds, occupancy goes up to 97 percent.

Avg. Talk Time: 180 sec; Avg. Work Time: 30 sec; Calls: 250				
Agents	SL% in 20 Sec.	ASA	Occupancy	Trunk Load (in hours)
30	24%	208.7	97%	54.0
31	45%	74.7	94%	35.4
32	61%	37.6	91%	30.2
33	73%	21.3	88%	28.0
34	82%	12.7	86%	26.8
35	88%	7.8	83%	26.1
36	92%	4.9	81%	25.7
37	95%	3.1	79%	25.4
38	97%	1.9	77%	25.3
39	98%	1.2	75%	25.2
40	99%	0.7	73%	25.1
41	99%	0.5	71%	25.1
42	100%	0.3	69%	25.0

The relationship between occupancy and service level is often misunderstood. The incorrect logic goes something like, "If agents really dig in, service level will go up and so will their occupancy." In reality, if occupancy is high, it is because agents are taking one call after another and another, with little or no wait between calls. Calls are stacked up in queue and service level is low. In the worst scenario, occupancy is 100 percent because service level is so low that all callers spend at least some time in queue.

When service level gets better, occupancy goes down. Therefore, average calls taken per agent will also go down. That suggests that setting standards on number of contacts handled is inherently unfair, because agents can't directly control occupancy. Further, that would conflict with an important objective: ensure that enough agents are available to handle calls so service level objectives are achieved. (We will discuss individual performance standards in Chapter 14.)

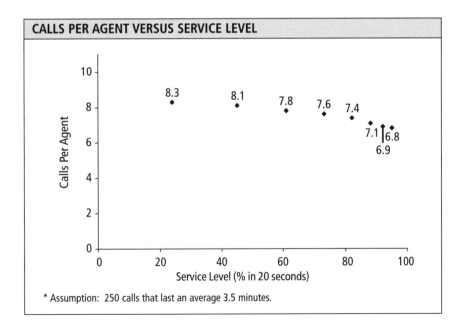

Occupancy is driven by random call arrival and is heavily influenced by service level and group size (see the third immutable law). Some managers can't stomach this reality — heaven forbid any "unproductive" time. However, the time that agents spend waiting for calls is sliced into 12 seconds here, two seconds there, and so on — a factor of how contacts are arriving.

In many centers, agents handle various non-phone or response time-oriented work that is less time-critical when the inbound call load slows down. In fact, blended environments (where agents move in and out of these types of work as circumstances dictate) make a lot of sense because no one has a perfect forecast all of the time, and schedules don't always perfectly match staff to the call load (see Chapter 8). But don't be misled. When other work is getting done, there are either: a) more agents on the phones than the baseline staff necessary to handle the call load at service level, at that time; or b) the service level objective is sacrificed. In other words, don't try to force occupancy higher than what base-staffing calculations predict it should be.

WHAT'S TOO HIGH?

As any agent knows, periods of high occupancy are stressful. Studies suggest that agents begin to burn out above around 90 percent occupancy if the condition lasts for an extended time, e.g., several half-hours in a row (some have the threshold as low as 88 percent, others as high as 92 percent). Most call center managers agree, but unfortunately, a high occupancy tends to feed on itself. Taking breaks is a natural reaction to high occupancy, and this tends to compound the problem.

As an example, consider this scenario. Jen, Ben and Mary are three of 32 agents plugged in and taking calls. Staffing calculations predict that the average occupancy for the half-hour for 32 agents will be 91 percent and service level will be just above 60 percent answer in 20 seconds.

Jen: *Whewww... it's call after call this morning. I need a breather! I don't have a scheduled break for a while so, let's see... I think I'll head to the water cooler for a couple of minutes.*

OOPS. Now there are only 31 agents on the phone. If traffic keeps arriving at about the same clip, service level will drop and occupancy will go... up.

Ben begins to ponder... *Things sure are busy today, just one call after another. And this caller sure is friendly. Wish everyone was this pleasant. I wonder what the weather is like where she is...*

So Ben takes a little bit longer on the call, service level drops another notch, and occupancy goes up more. Mary really begins to feel the load...

Mary: *This call doesn't really require wrap-up, but...*

This is the proverbial "vicious cycle." If things are chronically backed up, service level will consistently be low and occupancy will be high. The real fix, of course, goes to the fundamentals of managing a call center — a good forecast, accurate staffing calculations and schedules that match people to the workload.

OCCUPANCY VERSUS ADHERENCE TO SCHEDULE

Notice an important distinction that this law reveals. When adherence to schedule improves (goes up), occupancy goes down. Why? Because when agents are available to handle more calls, service level will go up. And when service level goes up, occupancy goes down.

When adherence to schedule improves (goes up), occupancy goes down.

The terms adherence to schedule and occupancy are often incorrectly used interchangeably. They not only mean different things, they move in opposite directions. Further, adherence to schedule is within the control of individuals, whereas the laws of nature outside of an individual's control determine occupancy.

The Law of Diminishing Returns

Economists identified the law of diminishing returns many years ago as it applies to manufacturing environments, but it also significantly impacts call centers. It can be defined this way: When successive individual agents are assigned to a given call load, marginal improvements in service level that can be attributed to each additional agent will eventually decline.

The figure, "Law of Diminishing Returns," is based on the data from the first table (based on Erlang C). It shows that 30 agents at the given call load will provide a service level of just over 23 percent in 20 seconds. Keep in mind, these numbers will not be exact — at that low of a service level, many of the calls may get cleared via busies and abandons, so Erlang C may exaggerate how bad things will be. But the exact results notwithstanding, service level will be poor.

With 31 agents, things improve dramatically. Service level jumps to 45 percent, a quantum improvement. Adding one more person yields another big improvement. In fact, adding only four or five people takes service

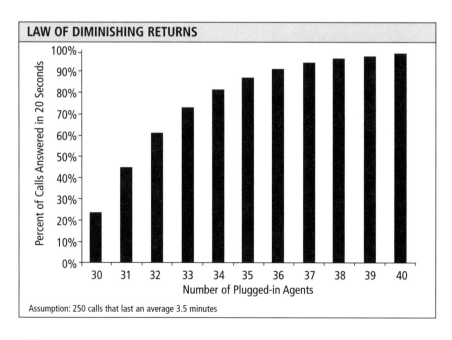

LAW OF DIMINISHING RETURNS

Percent of Calls Answered in 20 Seconds

Number of Plugged-in Agents

Assumption: 250 calls that last an average 3.5 minutes

level from the depths of poor service to something respectable. That, of course, means a commensurate drop in average speed of answer (ASA) and trunk load.

The same principle is true for larger groups, as the next table shows. Each person has a significant positive impact on the queue when service level is low, even in groups with hundreds of agents.

Avg. Talk Time: 180 sec; Avg. Work Time: 30 sec; Calls: 1,000 in 1/2 hr.				
Agents	SL% in 20 Sec.	ASA	Occupancy	Trunk Load (in hours)
117	7%	607	100%	437.0
118	24%	135	99%	175.0
119	39%	69	98%	138.0
120	51%	42	97%	123.5
121	61%	29	96%	115.9
122	69%	21	96%	111.4
123	75%	15	95%	108.4
124	80%	11	94%	106.3
125	85%	9	93%	104.8
126	88%	7	93%	103.7
127	91%	5	92%	102.9
128	93%	4	91%	102.2
129	94%	3	90%	101.7
130	96%	3	90%	101.4
131	97%	2	89%	101.1
132	97%	2	88%	100.8
133	98%	1	88%	100.7

Call center managers who struggle with a low service level will like this law because it often doesn't take a lot of resources to improve things dramatically. On the other hand, those who want to be the "best of the best" in terms of service level find that it takes a real commitment in the staffing budget. The relationship between varying levels of resources and service level ought to be demonstrated in the budgeting process.

Viewed from a different angle, if you have the right number of people handling contacts to begin with, but just a few of them unplug or go unavailable at an inopportune moment, things begin to back up. Think of what a stalled car blocking just one lane can quickly do to a busy expressway. This phenomenon has been referred to as "falling in the swamp."

SWAMP-AVOIDANCE STRATEGIES

Here are some steps you can take to avoid this pitfall:

• Educate every agent on these principles and relay — directly, consistently and often — how important they are to the call center's success. Each person matters! And what they do impacts customers, the organization and their peers. Everyone needs to be aware of just how much they contribute, even if they are tempted to feel like just one of many. (There are resources that can get you started — for example, ICMI has ready-to-go educational programs that cover what agents, managers and others need to know about call centers and call center dynamics.)

Educate every agent on these principles and relay — directly, consistently and often — how important they are to the call center's success. Each person matters!

• Provide real-time queue information to agents. Readerboards from a variety of manufacturers provide current data on the queue, and most have color-coded information for easy interpretation or to make the point (red means "help!"). And information delivered to desktop and phone displays can provide detailed insight into the queue and how variables are evolving. We will discuss real-time information in more detail in Chapter 11.

• Fix the basics, if necessary. If queues are predictably and consistently backed up, occupancy will be high and you will have to be sensitive to the need for more breaks, even though they add to the problem. The real fix is in improving the planning process and making an effective case for the necessary resources.

Ultimately, there is a fine line between a service level that's good for everybody (callers and agents alike) and one that snowballs out of control, zapping the productivity and fun out of the environment.

SMALL IMPROVEMENTS, BIG RESULTS

From another perspective, the law of diminishing returns reveals why improvements to call processes can yield such dramatic results. Some examples we have witnessed include:

• A consumer resource center for a major manufacturing company improved call tracking in its database system, clarified codes and agent training on call tracking, and assigned a small team to prepare reports for the quality assurance, marketing and consumer relations departments. While sales went up, call volume dropped by 7 percent, the result of pre-empting calls at the source. Service level improved by 30 percent during busy half-hours.

• An insurance company, which upgraded its computer systems to provide quicker response time, cut nine seconds off average handle time. Service level went up from 60 percent answer in 20 seconds to about 80 percent answer in 20 seconds during busy half-hours.

• A financial company, which added additional services to its existing IVR application, reduced traffic to its customer service group by around 5 percent. Service level improved by over 15 percent during busy half-hours. (Note: New IVR and Web services won't always reduce the number of calls requiring live answer. We'll discuss this more in Chapter 16.)

Larger Groups Are More Efficient

Average group productivity (contacts that a group handles) is not a constant factor. Instead, it's constantly fluctuating because the number of calls to handle and the service level objective determine it. Therefore, if you hold the service level constant, and provide the correct number of staff on the phones to achieve it, you'll find that average productivity is relatively lower at lower call volumes and relatively higher at higher call volumes. Since the number of calls is changing throughout the day, so is average group productivity. (When we use the term "group," we are not referring to supervisory groups or teams, we are referring to call-answering groups or queues, which could contain many supervisory groups.)

Why? Mathematically, larger groups of agents are more efficient than smaller groups, at the same service level. Therefore, larger groups assigned to heavy mid-morning traffic will be more efficient than smaller groups handling the lighter evening load. So, calculating staff the wrong way — assuming fixed productivity at different call volumes — will be highly inaccurate (see chart).

Calls in Half-hour	Service Level	Agents Required	Occupancy	Avg. Calls Per Agent
50	80/20	9	65%	5.6
100	80/20	15	78%	6.7
500	80/20	65	90%	7.7
1,000	80/20	124	94%	8.1
Assumption: Calls last an average 3.5 minutes.				

This is yet another reason why setting standards on the number of contacts that agents handle is an inherently unfair way to measure productivity. Attempting to compare groups or sites in a networked environment may also be misleading (the exception would be a network that finds the longest waiting agent, regardless of location — a true virtual group).

Despite mathematical efficiencies, there is a point where groups become large enough that occupancy becomes too high for agents to handle. Some managers believe that the number of agents in a single group should be limited to 125 to 150 people. However, there are plenty of call centers that have much larger groups (i.e., the U.S. Social Security Administration, Centrelink Australia, Indian Railways, United Airlines and others can have hundreds or even thousands of agents in a single agent group).

A better approach than establishing a strict limit to group size is to watch occupancy and take appropriate measures when it edges above 90 percent. For example, in the scenario on page 183, scheduling 129 plugged-in agents is recommended, even though the required service level may be exceeded. Callers sure won't mind, and your staff will have a fighting chance at being able to function proficiently throughout their shift.

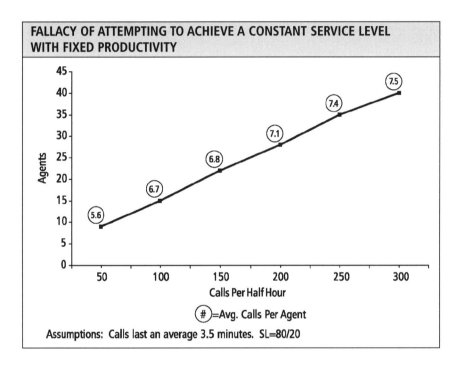

FALLACY OF ATTEMPTING TO ACHIEVE A CONSTANT SERVICE LEVEL WITH FIXED PRODUCTIVITY

Assumptions: Calls last an average 3.5 minutes. SL=80/20

The Powerful Pooling Principle

The powerful pooling principle is a mathematical fact, based on the laws of probability, and is well-rooted in telecommunications engineering practice. It states: Any movement in the direction of consolidation of resources will result in improved traffic-carrying efficiency. Conversely, any movement away from consolidation of resources will result in reduced traffic-carrying efficiency. Put more simply, if you take several small, specialized agent groups, effectively cross-train them and put them into a single group, you'll have a more efficient environment.

Note in the table on page 186, which compares service level to group size, 15 agents are required to provide a service level of 80/20. But only 124 agents are necessary to handle a load 10 times as large, not 150 agents (10 x 15 agents).

The pooling principle should be a consideration from the highest levels of strategic planning (How many call centers should you have? How should existing call centers be networked?) to the moment-to-moment decisions about overflowing calls among groups.

In one sense, pooling resources is at the heart of what ACDs and networks do. In fact, when ACDs first came into the market in the early 1970s, the big challenge was to get users to abandon the "clientele" approach.

THE POWERFUL POOLING PRINCIPLE

- Handle *more calls*, at the same service level, with the same number of agents
- Handle the same number of calls, at the same service level, with *fewer agents*
- Handle the same number of calls, at a *better service level*, with the same number of agents

A clear trend today, though, is the recognition that different types of callers often have different needs and expectations, and that different agents with a mix of aptitudes and skills are required. New capabilities in the intelligent network and in intelligent ACDs give call centers the means to pool resources, as well as segment and prioritize their customer base. Skills-based routing is a notable example (see Chapter 7).

But have we gone full circle? In 30 years, have we moved from specialization to consolidation and then back again to specialization? Can we have specialization without foregoing the benefits of the powerful pooling principle?

It depends. Consider two perspectives. Skills-based routing can yield efficiencies over specialized, individual groups. However, when not managed well, the number of contingencies can multiply beyond the center's ability to understand and handle them. The interplay can become stupefying. And the whole notion of call answering groups and traditional call center organization can begin to erode.

One thing is for sure: As real and pervasive as the pooling principle is, it is not an all-or-nothing proposition. There is a continuum between pooling and specialization.

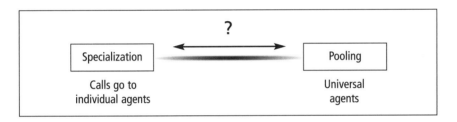

Your objective should be to get as close to the pooled end of the spectrum as circumstances allow without going too far— if you try to consolidate too much you may increase AHT to the point that efficiency gains are lost. This requires a certain degree of experimentation. More specifically, it means taking steps such as hiring multilingual agents, expanding responsibilities for existing agents, and improving information systems so that all agents are equipped to handle a variety of contacts.

Add Staff, and ASA Goes Down

Anyone who has ever waited in line knows that if there were a few more tollbooths or a few more people behind the counter, the line wouldn't be so long! And when someone behind the counter goes on break (invariably, just as you enter the queue!), the wait will increase.

The same principle is at work in call centers. When more agents are plugged in and handling contacts, assuming they are proficient and equipped to do so, the queue will be shorter. Fewer agents mean a longer queue. This principle leads to the next immutable law...

Add Staff, and Trunk Load Goes Down

When more agents are assigned to a given call load, trunk load (the load on the telecommunications network) goes down. The converse is also true: When fewer agents are available to handle a given call load, trunk load goes up because delay increases (see discussion on trunks in Chapter 7).

Each customer connected to your system requires a trunk, whether they are talking to an agent or waiting in queue. If you have toll-free service (or any other service which charges a usage fee), you are paying for this time. Telecommunications costs are inextricably wrapped in staffing issues. If service level is continually low, the costs of network services will be high.

See the following table for another scenario that illustrates the inherent tradeoffs between staffing levels and service level, average speed of answer, occupancy and trunk load. Recall from Chapter 7 that trunk load represents how much time in hours callers are queued up for and/or talking to agents in this group over the equivalent of an hour. Staff is calculated for a half-hour's traffic, but the trunk load is converted to an hour's traffic sim-

Avg. Talk Time: 180 sec; Avg. Work Time: 30 sec; Calls: 350 in half-hour				
Agents	SL% in 20 Sec.	ASA (in sec.)	Occupancy	Trunk Load (Erlangs)
42	29%	144	97%	62.9
43	47%	63	95%	47.3
44	61%	35	93%	41.8
45	72%	21	91%	39.1
46	80%	13	89%	37.6
47	86%	9	87%	36.7
48	90%	6	85%	36.1
49	93%	4	83%	35.8
50	95%	3	82%	35.5
51	97%	2	80%	35.3
52	98%	1	79%	35.2

ply because telecom managers almost universally use hour increments for engineering and management purposes.

UNDERSTANDING TRUNK LOAD

Let's run through one of the trunk-load calculations manually just to see where they come from. Using the scenario in the table, assume that you will have 46 agents handling calls and, therefore, will be able to achieve a service level of 80/20. Here's how the calculations produced an estimated 37.6 hours on the trunks:

• First, you can see that calls will be queued for agents an average of 13 seconds (ASA) and will be connected to agents an average of 180 seconds (average talk time), for a total of 193 seconds. The 180 seconds represents the forecast for what average talk time will likely be; the 13 seconds ASA comes from the Erlang C calculation.

• Since the table provides call volume for a half-hour, multiply 350 calls by two to assume 700 calls in an hour.

• Since the assumed 700 calls spend an average 193 seconds queuing for and connected to agents, the trunk load in seconds is 135,100 seconds (700 calls x 193 seconds).

• Finally, since trunk load is customarily presented in erlangs — hours of traffic over the course of an hour — divide 135,100 by 3,600 (the number of seconds in an hour) and you come up with 37.6 hours, just as the Erlang C table provides. To use the correct telecom lingo, you'll have the equivalent of "37.6 erlangs of traffic" on the trunks for this agent group during this time period. (Note: This example does not add the time calls may spend in the IVR before arriving at the agent group.)

The big variable is average speed of answer (average delay) before calls get connected — it goes up (gets worse) with fewer agents, and goes down (gets better) with more agents. Glance through the table, and you'll see that, if 50 agents are handling calls, ASA will be a projected 3 seconds. If 42 agents are handling calls, ASA will be a projected 144 seconds. In short, the number of staff you have in place determines the average delay, which is a key variable in trunk load — and therefore in what you pay for toll-free services.

THE IMPACT OF STAFF ON TOLL-FREE COSTS

You can see from the following figure that telecommunications costs are inextricably wrapped up in staffing issues. Saving a nickel on staffing levels can result in spending a dime on the network. Of course, there may also be other considerations — busies and abandons (likely at low service levels), and answer-delay (whereby the ACD doesn't immediately return "answer-supervision" to the long-distance carrier) may lower toll-free costs. And as the telecommunications world transitions to VoIP, contracts are becoming less time- and distance-sensitive. Nonetheless, the tradeoff between staff and network costs is direct and reasonably predictable.

As you decide on service levels and how to allocate budgets, you should incorporate network costs. All other things being equal, if your service level is low, adding an agent will often bring total costs down because network

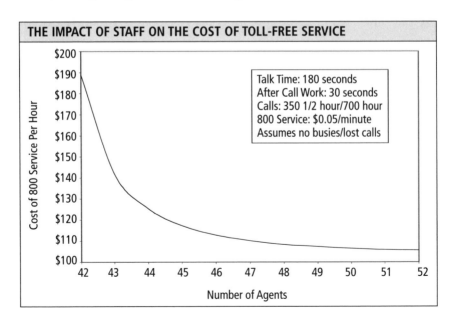

THE IMPACT OF STAFF ON THE COST OF TOLL-FREE SERVICE

Talk Time: 180 seconds
After Call Work: 30 seconds
Calls: 350 1/2 hour/700 hour
800 Service: $0.05/minute
Assumes no busies/lost calls

costs drop dramatically. Many managers who see these numbers naturally want to calculate the point where staffing and network costs are optimized. Just remember, that's not necessarily the place to set your service level objective, as service level should also consider caller needs and expectations. Assuming your network costs are low, you'll likely need to provide better service levels than this tradeoff in isolation would indicate.

The staff versus toll-free costs tradeoff used to be much more dramatic. In North America, for example, toll-free costs are currently just pennies a minute, depending on the negotiated contract, volume discounts, etc. In the days when toll-free service was 15 cents, 25 cents and higher, improving service level meant huge drops in network costs, often producing savings that far surpassed the cost of adding staff. With low network costs, the tradeoff is much less significant.

Even so, the process of assessing the impact on network costs will underscore the importance of considering both agent and network costs together. The fact is, no matter how low your toll-free costs, improving service level will save at least some money on network services; these savings should be factored into predictions of overall costs.

THE COST OF DELAY

The direct expense of putting callers in queue is called the "cost of delay." It is expressed in terms of how much you pay for toll-free service each day (or month, or hour, or half-hour) just for callers to wait in queue until they reach an agent. You may want to plot the cost of delay each day.

Making a graph of your cost of delay is simple. First, take the total delay for the day, as reported by your ACD, and convert that into minutes or hours. Next, multiply the minutes or hours of delay by the average per-minute or per-hour cost of your toll-free service. Then add that figure to a day-by-day graph that illustrates these costs (see the graph "Cost of Delay"). The whole process takes only a few minutes.

The cost of delay graph will be a constant reminder that poor service is not cheap. And it will catch the interest of senior managers, who will look at the graph and say things like, "You mean that's what we're paying just for callers to wait? Why, we could use that money for…"

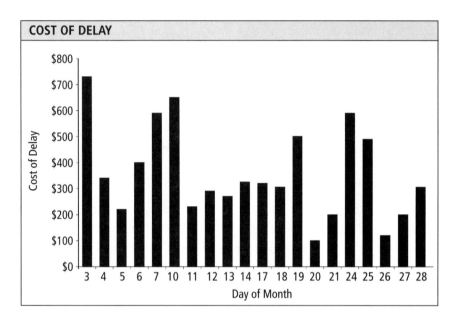

Points to Remember

- There are immutable laws at work in any call center that handles at least some inbound contacts.
- A common theme runs through these laws: Do a good job of matching staff with the workload or bad things will happen.
- The impetus doesn't fall solely on those who do the planning and scheduling. Designing and managing a call center requires a big-picture perspective and the collaborative effort of all involved.
- A good understanding of the immutable laws is a prerequisite to developing an accurate planning process, setting fair objectives and standards,

developing a good strategy and just about every other aspect of effective management

- It's important that agents, senior level managers and others who work in or support the call center are aware of these principles.

CHAPTER 10:
Communicating with Senior Management

Talk low, talk slow and don't say too much.
JOHN WAYNE

Call center managers have the responsibility of succinctly, but adequately, conveying call center budgetary requirements, activities and contributions to senior management. And that can be quite a balancing act! There's a lot going on in call centers, and simplified budgetary requests and summary reports often gloss over important details. Complex budgets and reports filled with pages of numbers may give more information, but senior managers may not have the time — nor the expertise — to read and understand them.

Consequently, conveying requirements and information in a thorough, but straight-forward format is critical to success. For many call center managers, determining what to include and how to present the material can be one of the most difficult tasks they face. But when done correctly, these reports will give senior management an accurate understanding of what is going on in the center, what resources are needed and what objectives are realistic.

In this chapter, we will review the essential processes of budgeting and reporting. And we'll hopefully help you find the right balance in producing and communicating critical information.

What Senior Level Managers Should Understand About Call Centers

Call centers have become recognized as an important factor in competitiveness, are significantly impacting the allocation of organizational resources, and are playing a vital role in emerging information- and communications-oriented economies. As a result, selling senior management on the call center concept is becoming much easier.

But at a more detailed level, a prerequisite to getting good support from senior management — and from managers in other key areas, such as marketing, information systems, telecommunications and human resources — is that they have at least a basic working knowledge of how call centers tick. The following is a summary of a dozen things that they need to know.

1. **CALLS BUNCH UP.** As discussed in Chapter 3, calls arrive randomly (or as peaked traffic). Senior management needs to know that planning for a workload that arrives randomly is different than planning for workload in other parts of the organization. Customers decide when and how they will contact the organization, and the resulting work will not arrive in a nice, even flow. Agents can't complete work in advance and set finished work aside. Consequently, staffing and productivity issues must be considered in this context.

2. **THERE'S A DIRECT LINK BETWEEN RESOURCES AND RESULTS.** You may need 36 people on the phones to achieve a service level of 90 percent answer in 20 seconds, given your call load. But if you have 25 and are told to hit 90/20, that's not going to work. That's an example of mutually exclusive objectives. It behooves the call center management team to constantly reinforce the fact that a certain level of resources is required to achieve a specified result (see Chapter 7 and the FTE budgeting section in this chapter).

3. **"STAFFING ON THE CHEAP" IS EXPENSIVE.** If you provide toll-free service for callers, you are paying for the time they spend waiting in queue

(see Chapter 9). However, there are less measurable but very real costs you will also incur that senior management needs to be aware of: high occupancy, if chronic, leads to burnout and turnover. Further, average handling time will increase as more callers comment about the long wait and as agents need more "breather" breaks because there is no time in between calls.

4. THERE'S GENERALLY NO INDUSTRY STANDARD FOR ACCESSIBILITY. No single service level or response time objective makes sense for every call center (with the only exceptions being regulated industries that have mandated service levels). Different organizations place different values on customer service, and each will have different staffing costs, network costs, and numbers and types of callers. Instead of looking for industry standards, determine a service level objective that makes sense for your organization, according to your callers' needs, your goals and your cost structure. (See Chapter 4.)

5. WHEN SERVICE LEVEL IMPROVES, PRODUCTIVITY DECLINES. As discussed in Chapter 9, when service level goes up, occupancy goes down. Senior management should understand that the better the service level you provide, the more time your agents will spend waiting for calls to arrive.

6. YOU WILL NEED TO SCHEDULE MORE STAFF THAN BASE STAFF REQUIRED. If you hear senior management complaining, "You mean we need to hire 30 people so that we can have 25 people on the phones handling calls?" then you need to explain why. They need to recognize that schedules should realistically reflect the many things that can keep agents from taking calls (Chapter 8).

7. STAFFING AND TELECOMMUNICATIONS REQUIREMENTS SHOULD BE DETERMINED TOGETHER. Staffing and trunking issues are inextricably associated, as discussed in Chapter 7 and Chapter 9. Budgets should consider both staffing and telecommunications costs and their impact on one another.

8. BUY THE BEST SYSTEMS YOU CAN AFFORD. Senior managers should be aware that technologies make up a relatively small portion of expenditures — generally less than 15 percent or even 10 percent of the call center's budget over time (with the exception of large databases, CRM or other system overhauls, which may justifiably fall outside this rule of thumb). And yet, when selected and applied wisely, they can have enormous impact on results. It often makes sense to buy the system that has more capacity, better reports and more advanced features. Few have regretted buying too much, but many regret being encumbered day after day by a system that doesn't quite meet their needs.

9. IT AND TELECOM PEOPLE SHOULD SUPPORT CALL CENTERS, NOT MANAGE THEM. Competent IT and telecom professionals are worth their weight in gold. But when they wield too much control, it usually stems from the notion that call centers are "technology operations" — an assumption that will bog down the IT department and hamper the call center.

10. SUMMARY REPORTS DON'T GIVE THE REAL PICTURE. Interpret summary reports of call center activity with caution — they can be very misleading. For example, daily reports of service level may look good, but the report conceals the fact that you got walloped in the morning and had agents sitting idle much of the afternoon. Even half-hour reports can be misleading. They illustrate average staffing for specific periods, but reality unfolds moment by moment, day by day.

11. CALL CENTERS — AND CONTACTS THEMSELVES — ARE BECOMING MORE COMPLEX. Traditional service-only centers — that have historically existed as islands unto themselves and that have often been viewed as a necessary cost — have evolved into more dynamic and holistic operations that contribute to and require the support of departments across the organization. These centers need the executive support and budget for the cross-functional tools, processes, training and human resources necessary to compete in today's complex and ever-changing environment.

12. CALL CENTERS HAVE BECOME INCREASINGLY IMPORTANT TO THE ORGANIZATION'S SUCCESS. Call centers have become increasingly vital to the organization's ability to understand and serve diverse customers, capture marketplace intelligence and work across departments to improve products and services. (This is a theme that runs throughout the book, but is covered more extensively in Chapters 1, 2, 13 and 17.) To fulfill this potential, call centers need commitment and involvement from the top to ensure that they get the support and resources they need.

I am convinced that the only way to really understand the unique call center environment is to spend some time in it. Senior level executives who have made the effort to understand — at least at a basic level — call center issues and processes invariably come away with better insight into evolving customer requirements and interdependencies across the larger organiza-

---

SIDE-BY-SIDE WITH SENIOR MANAGEMENT AT BT AMERICAS

Senior managers at many companies find out what's happening in their call centers through memos, reports and meetings. At BT Americas, execs also get the lowdown directly — through one of its centers' headsets. Each year, over the course of two weeks, dozens of senior managers for the communications solutions provider travel to the company's Regional Center of Excellence in Atlanta to spend an entire day listening in on customer calls with an agent and, importantly, identify at least one critical customer issue that they must later help to resolve.

"It demonstrates BT's senior management commitment both to our customers and to our call center representatives," says Thom Ray, vice president of service operations for BT Americas. "It provides senior managers across BT — regardless of what specific organization they are in — the opportunity to spend an entire shift with a customer-facing person, and to listen, learn and proactively support the individual [agent with whom they are seated]." Since launching this initiative in the Atlanta center, BT Americas has implemented numerous improvements, ranging from better workflows to enhanced customer information on agents' desktops and more dynamic call-routing processes.

Source: *Call Center Management Review*

---

tion. In many cases, these executives then encourage and sometimes even mandate ongoing involvement from their executive teams.

Principles of Effective Budgeting

An important part of ensuring that call centers fulfill their potential is to see that they get the resources they need. That, of course, requires an effective budget — and a clear understanding of what the return on those investments should be.

A budget is simply a summary of proposed or agreed-upon expenditures for a given period of time, for specified purposes. Sounds tame enough — but the process of putting a budget together is often seen by call center managers as tedious, time-consuming and, some say, distracting from "more important management responsibilities." We cannot forget, however, the outcome of this much-maligned process: the funding the call center has with which to accomplish its purpose.

Here are the essential principles we've uncovered in analyzing and working with call centers that consistently get the right amount of funding, at the right times, for the right things:

VIEW THE BUDGET AS MUCH MORE THAN A DOCUMENT. Those who picture rows and columns of line items and figures when they think of "budget" are missing the larger opportunity. The budget is a process. More specifically, it's a set of internal negotiations that lead to decisions on how money will be spent. I've seen managers spend many hours — make that many days — putting the details together, only to have their priorities swept away or diluted in a matter of minutes in the CFO's office. I've also seen powerful (and positive) budgetary agreements happen over lunch, literally on the back of a napkin. Remember, it's the effectiveness of your case, not the detail of your analysis, which matters most.

When you see the budget as a process of negotiations and decisions — not just a document — you spend more of your time and talent on opening channels of communication, educating decision makers and highlighting key priorities and tradeoffs. In short, you focus on ensuring that the process creates the right results.

ANSWER THE BIG QUESTION — WHY? Why are we spending this money? Why does the call center exist? Why are we spending more (or less) than last year? These answers must form the backdrop of the budgetary process. They are sometimes addressed in the communication that takes place during the process, and also may be summarized in budgetary documents. Regardless, those who are involved in preparing and approving the budget need a common understanding of the value the call center contributes to the organization.

REMEMBER TO FOCUS ON RESULTS. Handling 4.2 million calls, achieving 92 percent first-call resolution or hitting service level targets are NOT results decision makers are looking for — they are only means to an end. Higher levels of customer retention, improved sales and revenues, streamlined costs, contributions to more effective products, services and processes — these are examples of results that truly impact the organization.

Handling 4.2 million calls, achieving 92 percent first-call resolution or hitting service level targets are NOT results decision makers are looking for — they are only means to an end. Higher levels of customer retention, improved sales and revenues, streamlined costs, contributions to more effective products, services and processes — these are examples of results that truly impact the organization.

BASE THE BUDGET ON A CLEAR STRATEGY. A prerequisite to a successful budgeting process is agreement on the call center's direction and priorities. A customer access strategy is the framework that defines how customers will interact with the organization. By defining who your customers are, when and how they desire to reach you, the means by which you will identify, route, handle and track those contacts, and how you will leverage the information that comes from them, the customer access strategy is the *de facto* blueprint for the budget (see Chapter 2). Without this foundation, budgetary decisions are likely to head off in many unrelated directions and may be at odds with your organization's larger objectives.

ENSURE THAT BUDGETING IS AN EXTENSION OF RESOURCE PLANNING. In well-run call centers, forecasting, staffing, scheduling and cost-analysis are ongoing responsibilities. These activities should take much of the work out of the budget process, because the budget should ultimately be based on the same workload predictions.

There's an important principle at work here. Objectives should drive the budget, not the other way around. If your budget is based on precedent (last year's numbers), arbitrary decisions, or anything other than the objectives identified in your customer access strategy and workload predictions, then you are at a disadvantage from the get-go. It's time to rethink the assumptions that drive the process (see figures).

THE RIGHT WAY: KEY OBJECTIVES DRIVE THE BUDGET			
• Choose service level and response time objectives • Forecast call load (contacts)	• Calculate base staff • Calculate trunks	• Calculate schedule shrinkage • Organize schedules	• Calculate costs; compare to alternative service levels • Finalize budgets

———————————————————————————————➤

THE WRONG WAY: THE BUDGET DRIVES KEY OBJECTIVES			
• Determine budget	• Estimate feasible schedules and probable schedule shrinkage	• Determine staff and trunk load capacities	• Estimate feasible service levels based on available resources

———————————————————————————————➤

IDENTIFY KEY TRADEOFFS. For example, what happens if the forecast is high? Low? What happens if you provide better levels of service? Lower levels of service? How much would you save/spend if...? Once the budget for expected workload is established, along with recommended resources, it is fairly straightforward to rerun scenarios for both different workload assumptions and alternative service levels. These illustrations will contribute to good budgeting decisions and will improve understanding of call center dynamics.

LOOK FOR OPPORTUNITIES TO MAXIMIZE CROSS-FUNCTIONAL RESOURCES. Often, an organization's overall results can be improved by investing more in one area, to the benefit of others. Rather than focus on expenditures in a departmental vacuum, effective budgetary-thinking maximizes cross-functional resources.

For example, marketing managers are often willing to provide the call center with budget to capture and analyze information on consumer trends and expectations, because they can save substantial money on target marketing. Legal departments are increasingly helping the call center make the case for investments that will improve tracking and consistency in customer contacts. And product development budgets may be directed, in part, to the call center for improved analysis on customer suggestions and input. These possibilities become evident to the degree that relationships exist and collaboration is in place among functional areas.

HIGHLIGHT INVESTMENT OPPORTUNITIES. As with many organizations in general, most call centers are consistently searching for ways to do more with less. But there's also a place for making some high-leverage investments in sensible areas, including:

- Planning and process improvements
- Selective technology investments
- Management-level education
- Cross-sell and upsell programs
- Focused agent and supervisor coaching initiatives

• Research and development

The key is selection — to focus on those areas that are most likely to yield an acceptable return on investment.

PRESENT THE BUDGET FORMALLY. This recommendation may seem odd, given the emphasis on the budgetary negotiations and decisions. But a formal presentation can be an important part of the process. For example, it can be the catalyst for getting all decision makers together at one time. (How many times did you answer the same questions for different people last year?) All in attendance will hear the questions and comments of the others, saving time and raising the general level of understanding more quickly — and you will be duly motivated to "have your ducks in a row."

KEEP THE PRESENTATION SHORT AND UNCLUTTERED. Use graphs and illustrations where possible. Provide backup material as necessary, such as actual system reports (but only as backup and not as a part of the main presentation). And sprinkle the conversation with real examples; e.g., "Sarah Johnson, a small-business owner in Seattle and a four-year customer, was one of the 4,200,000 contacts we handled last year. She called us because she was concerned that..." Examples bring realities to life. And service tradeoffs become much more relevant when Sarah Johnson and 4,199,999 other customer contacts are at stake.

ANTICIPATE AND PREPARE FOR THE "USUAL QUESTIONS." They will come up throughout the process. Examples:

• What did we spend on the call center in total last year?
• What's our cost per contact? Is it going down or up?
• What's our contact per customer ratio? Sales per customer?
• What are you doing to reduce unnecessary contacts?
• Can we use the resources we have now to handle the expected workload?

You know these and other questions will be asked. Prepare for them.

Some may be relevant, some may be less important — but having a competent grasp of the facts will provide you with credibility throughout the process.

ENSURE THE BUDGETING PROCESS IS HONEST AND RESPONSIBLE. You should be realistic and candid about the recent past and whether or not the call center has been meeting its objectives. The budget must put that in context with customer and agent satisfaction, and with the objectives and funding being proposed. It must support the mission of the organization and dovetail with the roles and requirements of other areas. And it must be honest about opportunities and challenges.

Yes, effective budgeting requires some number-crunching and analysis. But above all, it requires a clear direction, good communication and a solid understanding of the call center's needs and strategic contributions. This is a process that will bring the totality of your leadership, communication skills and professional expertise to bear. Don't treat it as a once-a-year event. It should be part of a continuous effort. Revisit it often and, as with other aspects of planning, make adjustments as necessary.

GROWTH OR CONTRACTION — PLAN ACCORDINGLY

Growth in workloads remains one of the biggest challenges facing many customer contact centers. As long as your call center is growing, senior level management will understandably need to know why the call center represents a growing percentage of the organization's expenses, and where

FRANK & ERNEST by ® Bob Thaves

Reprinted with permission.

the money is going.

An important principle in managing growth is to do an analysis of the likely impact of growth in advance. The objective is to avoid surprises so you aren't going into the budget process "behind the power curve."

Accurate growth projections often take the form of a document that illustrates projected costs and time-frames, such as 10 percent growth in call load, 20 percent growth, 30 percent growth, and so on (up to at least two times the current size). Your analysis should consider each major call center component and answer important questions like, when will you need a new ACD cabinet? More IVR ports? More trunking capacity? More space? Additional supervisors or analysts? What is the ideal lead time for each increment of growth? How long does it take to recruit, hire and train agents?

Contraction is also a planning challenge. Even as many grapple with growth, long-established call centers in some vertical sectors have contracted or closed. For example, many airlines have successfully encouraged a growing portion of customers to use self-service systems for inquiries, bookings and check-in. In these cases, plans and budgets must anticipate how call centers can be scaled down as workload drops — react too slowly, and expensive and unnecessary resources drive up costs. But cut too quickly, and service will be poor.

Because the document is a projection, it won't precisely predict required resources. It's not a budget, per se. But it will illustrate required lead-times and key decision points necessary to align resources with workload. As industry consultant Laurie Solomon puts it, "This analysis gives you the information you need to minimize costly surprises and thrown-together solutions."

Getting Staffing Budgets Right

In many organizations, staffing makes up between 65 to 75 percent of the call center's budget. This one slice of the budgetary pie trumps tech-

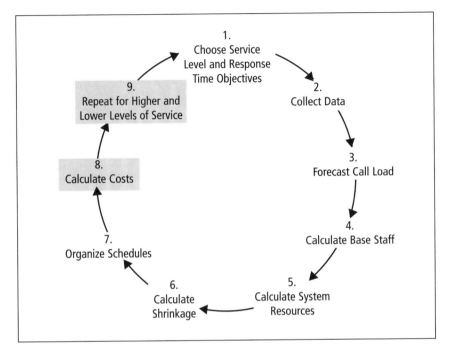

nology costs, facilities and telecommunications costs combined — and getting it right is a make-or-break factor in the call center's efficiency and effectiveness.

Let's take a look at the basics of longer-term staff planning. As discussed in Chapter 8, effective scheduling depends on both longer-term budgets and short-term execution. You'll need a big enough bucket of resources to work with — in other words, the right number of staff on payroll (or through contracts) to put schedules together that match workload requirements. You'll also need to manage schedule adherence, a subject we'll pick up in Chapter 14.

A long-term staff plan (sometimes called budgetary staffing plan) generally represents staffing requirements at a monthly level for the next 12 months. The goal is to accurately predict the paid hours required to handle the workload at your target service level and response time objectives. The best long-term plans are set up so that they are easily adjusted and clearly demonstrate the "whys" behind budget requirements to all involved, especially those who will approve the required funds.

Projections should be based on both an accurate workload forecast and the required staff for the workload, accounting for "availability factors" that keep agents from handling the work. Staff availability can be grouped into three categories:

PRESENCE. Is the agent working today (i.e., is he or she in the building)?

UTILIZATION. Is the agent scheduled to handle customer contacts?

RANDOM. Is the agent actually handling a contact (i.e., in talk time or after-call work)?

Let's go through a staffing example that accounts for each of these categories and leads to the number of full-time equivalents (FTEs) required to handle the workload. Here, we'll look at just one month, but you'll normally be projecting out for 12 months or more. Note that throughout the example, rounding variations can produce slightly different totals and results. (This example was prepared by Jay Minnucci and Dan Rickwalder of ICMI, and is based on a staffing model available from ICMI's Consulting Division.)

BEGIN WITH WORKLOAD

The workload forecast is the primary driver of staffing needs. Workload includes the projected volume of contacts multiplied by average handling time; the result is then converted into staff hours required. Let's say your July projections for telephone contacts (we'll factor email contacts into the model later) are as follows:

JULY WORKLOAD — CALLS		
Item	Projection	Rationale
Call volume	89,857	Based on forecasts
AHT (sec.)	210	Based on forecasts. Typical since last system upgrade.
Workload (hours)	5,242	Calculation: (volume x AHT) ÷ 3,600 (sec. in an hour)

So, you will have a projected 5,242 hours of workload to handle in July. (If you're remembering from Chapter 6 that average handling time often varies increment by increment — you're right. This estimate is a broad brushstroke used for longer-term staffing calculations, and is based on the number you're most likely to see on average over the month. It's OK to use it this way for longer-term budgeting purposes — just don't try to base half-hour by half-hour staffing calculations and schedule requirements on an average!)

IDENTIFY AVAILABILITY FACTORS

Next, you'll calculate agent availability factors, beginning with presence. The typical variables that will keep agents from working include vacations, absenteeism, leave of absence, disability, jury duty and holidays. They might be as follows for the month of July:

AVAILABILITY: PRESENCE				
	Projection			
Item	**In units at left**	**As % of paid time**	**Rationale**	**Percent of paid time calculation**
Holidays (days per agent for the month)	1.00	4.35%	As per holiday calendar	1 ÷ 23 (number of paid days in the month)
Disability (days per agent for the month)	1.20	5.22%	Based on past history for this month	1.20 ÷ 23
Vacation (days per agent for the month)	1.60	6.96%	Based on past history and vacation policy	1.60 ÷ 23
Total absence	3.80	16.52%	Sum of presence factors. Presence will be 83.48% (100% - 16.52%)	3.80 ÷ 23

According to the calculations, you'll lose an estimated 16.52 percent of paid hours to these factors. Agents will be at work 83.48 percent of paid hours (100% - 16.52%), or 33.39 hours out of the 40-hour work week.

Next, you will project utilization, which includes all of the things that keep your agents from handling contacts even though they are at work — e.g., breaks, meetings, training and various projects. These variables might be as follows:

AVAILABILITY: UTILIZATION				
	Projection			
Item	**In units at left**	**As % of paid time**	**Rationale**	**Percent of paid time calculation**
Breaks (minutes per day)	30.00	5.22%	Per work rules	(30 minutes ÷ 480 paid minutes per day) x presence factor of 83.48%
Meetings (hours per month)	3.00	1.36%	Three one-hour meetings per month	3 ÷ 184 (number of paid hours in the month) x presence factor of 83.48%
Training (hours per month)	2.50	1.36%	Required for new application training	2.5 ÷ 184
Coaching (hours per month)	2.00	1.09%	Two one-hour coaching sessions per month	2 ÷ 184
Committee (hours per month)	2.00	0.91%	As requested by VP of Customer Service	(2 ÷ 184) x presence factor of 83.48%
Total non-phone utilization (hours per week)	3.97	9.93%	Out of a 40-hour week, an agent will be utilized for non-phone tasks an average 3.97 hours (40 x .0993)	The sum of all utilization categories

Note that lunch is missing from the list — since it is not paid time it is not included in this model. Also, the factor used for breaks is adjusted for presence (you shouldn't count breaks for agents not at work).

Consequently, if agents are not at work 16.52 percent of the time (meaning they are at work 83.48 percent of the time), then the factor would be 30 minutes (time on breaks) divided by 480 minutes (minutes in day), multiplied by 83.48 percent; the result is 5.22 percent and not the usual 6.25 percent many managers associate with breaks. Conversely, training and coaching percents are not adjusted by the presence factor because these activities will be rescheduled when missed due to absence.

So, you're down another 9.93 percent off of total payroll hours to account for variables that keep agents off the phones. Added together, presence and utilization factors total 26.45 percent. Put another way, your projections show that agents will be scheduled to handle contacts 73.55 percent of the time (100% - 26.45%).

But you're not there yet. There's a third category of factors, which can be termed random, that also need to be included. Don't let the term trip you up — schedule adherence isn't random from a mathematical sense like random call arrival — e.g., we can positively impact schedule adher-

AVAILABILITY: RANDOM FACTORS				
	Projection			
Item	In units at left	As % of paid time	Rationale	Percent of paid time calculation
Adjustment for adherence (90% of scheduled time on phones)	10%	7.36%	As per objectives and past history	10% x scheduled rate of 73.55%
Adjustment for occupancy (85% of time in talk and after call work)	15%	9.93%	85% occupancy is from Erlang C calculations based on volume, handle time and service level objectives	15% x manned percent of 66.20%
Total random	6.91	17.29%	Out of a 40-hour week, agents will lose an average 6.91 hours to random factors	The sum of all random categories

ence (see Chapter 14). But while you can accurately predict the total amount of time that will go to these factors, they are random because you cannot predict minute-to-minute impact. This inability to control the timing of these events is what separates them from activities like breaks, meetings and training.

In the example, you will subtract adherence time from your scheduled rate of 73.55 percent because, again, you do not want to double-count time for agents not on the phones (or handling other types of contacts). Following this logic, you'll also need to remove adherence time from scheduled time when calculating occupancy so that you do not include hours lost to schedule adherence in the occupancy rate.

The expected occupancy rate is determined by running enough Erlang C calculations (based on expected volume, average handling time and service level scenarios) that you feel comfortable you've identified a "typical" occupancy rate. (Yes, if you're remembering from Chapters 7 and 9 that occupancy varies increment by increment, you're right. As with average handling time, this estimate is a broad brushstroke used for longer-term staffing calculations, and is based on the number you're most likely to see over the month.)

AVAILABILITY SUMMARY		
Item	As % of Paid Time	Meaning
Presence factors	16.52%	6.61 hours per FTE per week (40 x .1652)
Utilization factors	9.93%	3.97 hours per FTE per week (40 x .0993)
Random factors	17.29%	6.92 hours per FTE per week (40 x .1729)
Total non-availability	43.74%	17.50 hours per FTE per week (40 x .4374)
Design factor	56.26%	22.50 hours per FTE per week spent handling contacts: (100% - 43.74%) x 40
Rostered staff factor	1.78	Need 1.78 FTEs for every 40 hours of workload per week (100 ÷ 56.26)

You have now identified all of the factors keeping your agents from handling the workload, and can convert that into a rostered staff factor, as shown in the chart on the previous page.

All of the factors keeping your agents from handling the workload total 43.74 percent. Consequently, agents are projected to spend 56.26 percent of their time (100% - 43.74%) actually handling contacts. This is converted into a longer-term rostered staff factor of 1.78, which is the ratio of staff needed on schedule divided by staff needed to handle the workload (100 ÷ 56.26).

CONVERT TO FULL-TIME EQUIVALENTS (FTES)

Using full-time equivalents (FTEs) instead of headcount will allow you to accurately account for part-timers; so the final step in determining required staff is to convert these figures into FTEs. If a full workweek is 40 hours, one full-time employee working 40 hours is one FTE. Two part-time employees, working 20 hours each, would equal one FTE — as would four employees who work 10 hours each.

To convert the workload to FTEs, multiply the workload hours by the RSF and divide by the number of hours per month worked by a full-time employee. For example:

TELEPHONE FTEs REQUIRED	
Item	Amount
Telephone workload hours	5,242
Telephone staff ratio	1.78
Telephone staff hours required (5,242 x 1.78)	9,331
Staff hours per FTE for the month	184
Telephone FTEs Required (9,331 ÷ 184)	50.71

Going through a similar process for non-realtime work might produce the following:

EMAIL FTEs REQUIRED	
Item	Amount
Email workload Hours	1,365
Email staff ratio	1.51
Email staff hours required (1,365 x 1.51)	2,061
Staff hours per FTE for the month	184
Email FTEs required (2,061 ÷ 184)	11.20

Adding phone and email FTE requirements yields a total of 61.91 FTEs:

TOTAL FTEs REQUIRED	
Item	Amount
Telephone FTEs required	50.71
Email FTEs required	11.20
Total FTEs required	61.91

The end result of this section of the model is the number of agents required on payroll to handle your planned workload and achieve your service level and response time objectives. Since this number often does not match the current staffing in the center, we recommend going one step further with the model and incorporating a staff-planning component that illustrates gaps between the required and the current headcount.

The staff-planning section includes current staff, turnover and new-hire information. It also factors in part-time employees and shows how close your current staff comes to your required staff. Hiring plans are often produced many months in advance (perhaps by someone outside the call center) around general business trends. This section allows you to assess and adjust hiring plans as needed so that they match workload needs as precisely as possible. For example, before going through this final step, your hiring activity might produce the following comparison of required FTE versus planned FTE:

HIRING PLAN (BEFORE)						
	July	Aug	Sept	Oct	Nov	Dec
FTEs required	61.91	55.00	62.50	64.10	65.05	61.00
Planned staff						
Starting FTEs	52.00	58.92	56.56	57.87	59.13	62.36
Attrition %	4%	4%	3%	3%	3%	3%
Net FTEs	49.92	56.56	54.87	56.13	57.36	60.49
New-hire FTEs	9	0	3	3	5	4
Planned FTEs	58.92	56.56	57.87	59.13	62.36	64.49
FTE +/-	-2.99	1.56	-4.63	-4.97	-2.69	3.49

In the example, there are two months (September and October) where you will be understaffed by three or more FTEs, and one (December) where you are overstaffed by more than three. Since your goal is to keep your actual staff numbers as close as possible to required numbers, you can adjust staffing plans (represented by the new-hire FTEs in the next table) to reduce the over/under. The results might be as follows:

HIRING PLAN (AFTER)						
	July	Aug	Sept	Oct	Nov	Dec
FTEs required	61.91	55.00	62.50	64.10	65.05	61.00
Planned staff						
Starting FTEs	52.00	58.92	56.56	60.87	65.08	63.13
Attrition %	4%	4%	3%	3%	3%	3%
Net FTEs	49.92	56.56	54.87	59.04	63.13	61.24
New-hire FTEs	9	0	6	6	0	0
Planned FTEs	58.92	56.56	60.87	65.08	63.13	61.24
FTE +/-	-2.99	1.56	-1.63	0.98	-1.92	0.24

The new plan keeps every month to within three FTEs of requirements. It also reduces total hiring during the six months shown. All in all, it is a better fit to requirements.

Once the plan is created, you are set to go to bat for your staffing needs. You have created a model that is fully adjustable at the workload, staffing factor and staff planning levels. It illustrates staffing needs, while allowing all parties to quickly see the results of changes in any variable.

We've found that talking through the process line by line helps those who are involved in budgeting and approvals understand and participate in the assumptions you're making, and feel much more comfortable about how you reach requirements. There may be spirited discussion along the way about specific issues. But with line-by-line agreement (and changes that may be merited), one plus one plus three should add up to five — not four or six.

Reporting Call Center Activity

Reporting call center activity to senior level management and others in the organization can seem a daunting task. The wide variety of activities in a typical call center, the reality of senior management not having the time nor inclination to pour over detailed reports, and the fact that summary reports often gloss over important information, all contribute to the challenge. Consequently, many diligently prepared reports either go unread or, worse, are misunderstood.

Clearly, good communication doesn't happen just because detailed information is available. Any call center manager buried in system reports yet struggling to convey basic realities can testify to that fact. The process you establish to communicate call center activities is as important as the information itself. The following steps can help you identify and prepare meaningful reports and ensure that they are understood.

1. **DETERMINE YOUR OBJECTIVES.** What are the objectives for the reports? In other words, what should other managers know about the call

center or the information it has acquired, and why? To find the answers, assemble a team for a working discussion. A cross-section of managers from across the organization, call center managers, supervisors and agents should be involved. General areas of concern usually include:

- Customer satisfaction and quality measurements
- Contributions to other business units
- Access alternatives (workload trends, e.g., self-service, telephone, email, text-chat, etc.)
- Costs and revenues
- Queue reports (e.g., service level, abandonment)
- Resource utilization and requirements (e.g., staffing and scheduling needs)

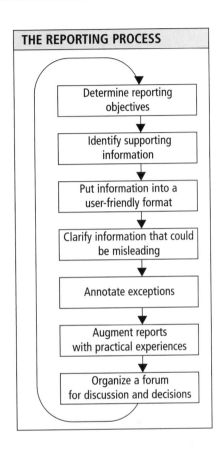

THE REPORTING PROCESS

Determine reporting objectives

Identify supporting information

Put information into a user-friendly format

Clarify information that could be misleading

Annotate exceptions

Augment reports with practical experiences

Organize a forum for discussion and decisions

From these major categories, important measurements will emerge. It's often useful to preface this exercise with a question like, "If we could wave a magic wand, what would we really want to know about our call center?" At this stage, don't be concerned about whether or not you have the reports to support the objectives you identify. Your objectives — not the reports you happen to have — should drive this process.

2. IDENTIFY SUPPORTING INFORMATION. List the possible reporting alternatives under each of the objectives you identified in the first step. Include information from systems, databases, surveys, other departments and external information.

The challenge now becomes one of selection. Stephanie Winston, author of the popular book, *The Organized Executive*, advises that a report should not simply collect facts, but serve as a judgment tool for management. To pare down the lists, Winston suggests asking a variety of questions: Is the report really necessary? What questions does it answer? Which reports would you dispense with if you had to pay for them? Could several reports be combined? Will you act on the information to affect change?

3. PUT THE INFORMATION IN A USER-FRIENDLY FORMAT. Once you have a list of desired reports, the next step is to compile them into a simple, understandable format. This often means creating graphs of the information. For example, simple line charts can illustrate trends that would otherwise appear as hard-to-decipher numbers. Reports that rely on graphs may take more pages, but a 10-page report consisting primarily of graphs is often quicker to read and easier to comprehend than two pages of detailed numbers in rows and columns. Look for data that should be combined to provide a more complete story.

4. CLARIFY INFORMATION THAT COULD BE MISLEADING. As any seasoned call center manager has learned, you can make call center reports say whatever you want them to say. For example, you can prop up service level by generating controlled busy signals, overflowing calls to other groups, or

---

YOU'RE LOOKIN' (TOO?) GOOD...

Reporting the call center in the best possible light can undermine success. There are a lot of ways to produce reports so that the center looks as productive as possible to senior management. However, if you mask serious resource deficiencies or process problems, the call center is less likely to get the resources and support it needs, which, in turn, will undermine the center's ability to perform. There's also the related issue of psychology — when upper-level managers see some room for improvement, they tend to feel more assured that they are getting the whole story.

taking messages for later callbacks. Or you can provide overall reports that combine data and conceal problematic intervals. Clearly, simply providing a high-level report on service level or quality can be misleading — the reader needs more information.

5. ANNOTATE EXCEPTIONS. There will be points that are clearly out of the norm. Don't leave your audience guessing. Explain deviations — both what happened and why. Why did wait times go through the roof in early February? A simple footnote can provide the answer: "Power outage in Northeast — call load 40 percent higher than normal."

6. AUGMENT REPORTS WITH PRACTICAL EXPERIENCES. Giving recipients a report to read on what happens on Monday mornings versus bringing them into the call center to observe what happens is the difference between night and day. You need to do both. Teaching key call center dynamics to managers outside the call center is necessary to create a clear understanding of how cross-functional decisions and actions link with the call center's overall effectiveness. And call center executives need a solid understanding of the concerns, challenges and objectives in other areas of the organization. This mutual understanding forms a strong and essential foundation for effective reporting and communication. (See "Side-by-Side with Senior Management at BT Americas," on page 201.)

7. ORGANIZE AN ONGOING FORUM FOR DISCUSSING AND ACTING ON THE INFORMATION. Presenting data in a clear, concise and actionable format is a start. But reports must be followed with a forum for discussing and acting on the information. This becomes the primary opportunity to turn information into sound business decisions.

We'll pick up with a discussion of important measurements in Chapter 12, and how to use them to improve performance within the call center and organization in Chapter 13. The key point here: Effective call center reporting is an ongoing communication process, not an end result.

Points to Remember

- Senior management needs a basic knowledge of call center principles.
- Anticipating the impact of growth (or contraction) of the call center's workload is critical, and should be a part of the communication and budgeting process.
- Call center managers must develop a budgeting process that builds credibility and clearly demonstrates tradeoffs and decision points.
- An effective staffing budget is fully adjustable, clearly demonstrates the "whys" behind budget requirements, and enables all parties to quickly see the results of changes in any variable.
- Reporting is communication. It happens best as part of a systematic process that ensures that the right information is being delivered to the right people at the right times.

CHAPTER 11:
Real-Time Management

The pessimist complains about the wind; the optimist expects it to change;
the realist adjusts the sails.
WILLIAM ARTHUR WARD

The planning is done, the schedules are in place — and the customer contacts are pouring in. Now what? Even with good forecasts and accurate schedules, the random arrival of calls, emails and Web contacts means that call centers inherently operate in a "demand-chasing" mode. Each moment, there are either more contacts to be handled than resources available, or more resources than contacts. Because supply and demand are rarely equal, demand must be chased with the supply of answering capabilities.

Further, there are those times when planning goes haywire. The forecast may be a bit on the low side. Customers may behave differently than expected. Marketing or some other part of the organization may do something that generates a flurry of contacts without telling you in advance. Unscheduled activities or unplanned absenteeism can cause unexpected staffing problems. In short, even the most accurate call center planning must be augmented by effective "real-time" management: monitoring events as they happen and making adjustments as necessary.

Real-time management should complement call center planning. When the planning is done, it's the moment-by-moment decisions and actions

223

that will enable you to maintain an appropriate service level and response time. Effective real-time management includes establishing a good foundation, monitoring real-time developments and implementing a workable escalation plan.

A Good Foundation

An important prerequisite to effective real-time management is to establish a good foundation before the customer contacts come flooding in. This involves clearing up potential misconceptions among staff, putting the right tools in place, and establishing workable objectives and a good planning process. In other words, it means ensuring that you aren't creating many of the crises to which you are reacting.

SERVICE LEVEL AND QUALITY

One important principle is to make sure that everybody understands the complementary relationship between service level/response time and quality. Supervisors and agents sometimes see little connection between what they do here and now, and what those in planning roles do. They may feel that the pressure of the moment forces them to make tough tradeoffs between seemingly competing objectives.

Although service level/response time and quality seem to be at odds in the short-term, poor quality will negatively impact service level and response time in the long-term, by contributing to repeat and escalated calls, email and Web contacts, as well as other forms of waste and rework. So the emphasis should be on handling each customer contact correctly, regardless of how backed up the queue is.

But supervisors and agents may believe they are getting mixed signals from management: "Hey, you train us to do a quality job, but then you put a lot of emphasis on achieving an efficient service level and response time objective. You put queue displays all over the place and get unhappy when service level and response time drops. What do you really want?"

The answer is: "Both!" Look at the contacts in queue, make sure that people are plugged in and in the right mode, and do what's possible to arrange flexible activities around the workload. But handle each contact right the first time no matter what's happening with service level and response time.

CURRENT DISPLAY...

THE IMPACT OF EACH PERSON

Everybody in your call center needs to be aware of how much impact they each have on the queue. Review the law of diminishing returns in Chapter 9. The message from that discussion, as it relates to real-time management, is clear: When the queue is backed up, each person makes a big difference!

This issue sheds light on the importance of training agents on how a queue behaves (e.g., how fast it can spin out of control) and providing them with real-time information so they can adjust priorities as necessary. Real-time information can be delivered via:

- Graphically displayed queue information on each agent's computer monitor
- Supervisor monitors
- Wall- or ceiling-mounted readerboards
- Displays on telephones programmed to give queue statistics
- Don't have the latest technology? I've known of a few small call centers that post regularly updated results on easels or white boards (not ideal, but it's better than nothing!).

Queue information must be complemented with appropriate training so that agents know what to look for and how to react.

You also need to establish clear expectations on adherence to schedule. Many call centers diligently track adherence factor, which is a measure of how much time agents spend plugged in and available to handle contacts. Often, it's viewed only as an issue of *how much*. Equally important, though, is *when* agents are plugged in and available to handle customer contacts. A key responsibility of supervisors and team leaders is to ensure that people are plugged in when they are most needed. (See Chapter 14.)

AUTO-AVAILABLE AND AUTO WRAP-UP

Most ACD systems can be programmed for either "auto-available" or "auto wrap-up." With auto-available, agents are automatically put into the available mode after they complete a contact. With auto wrap-up, they are automatically put into the after-call work mode.

There is no way you can anticipate in advance how much time after-call work will take for an individual call.

It usually makes sense to program your system to put agents into the mode they will most often need to be in. This can save precious seconds and minimize the need for agents to manually put themselves in and out of modes.

Some managers program their ACD to put agents into the after-call work mode for a predetermined amount of time. This is usually a bad idea. There is no way you can anticipate in advance how much time after-call work will take for an individual contact. If your objective is to give people breaks due to a heavy workload, you are adding more time to each contact, further backing up the queue.

It's a much better idea to give agents control over the mode. (There is one exception to this rule: Some ACDs require a small window of time after a call is disconnected; i.e., a few seconds, to enable agents to put themselves into the after-call work mode.)

Another alternative you have when programming your ACD is to use a feature generally referred to as "call-forcing." Call-forcing is a terrible, autocratic-sounding term, but it is actually a valuable capability. With this feature, calls are automatically connected to agents who are available and ready (thus, obviating the need for them to manually answer calls). Agents are notified that a call has arrived by a gentle beep-tone (zip tone).

Studies indicate that call-forcing can cut four to six seconds off each call. And agents usually like the feature once they get used to it. It chops what would be an extra step out of the process, and they remain in control — if they aren't ready for the next call, they can stay out of the available mode.

CONSISTENCY

Ensure that agents maintain a consistent approach to handling contacts, regardless of queue conditions. Each agent has an impact on the components of workload, and therefore, on the data that will be used in forecasting and planning for future workloads. When the phone queue is building, it can be tempting to postpone some of the after-call work. As discussed in Chapter 6, this skews reports, causes planning problems and may lead to increased errors.

The solution is to define ahead of time which types of work should follow contacts and which types of work can be completed later. Then train agents and supervisors accordingly.

ACCURATE RESOURCE PLANNING

Real-time management can never make up for inadequate planning. The nine-step planning process covered in preceding chapters should be as accurate as possible. This includes:

- Establishing service level and response time objectives that everybody understands

- Accurately forecasting the workload associated with all types of contacts
- Calculating staffing requirements
- Planning for and managing non-phone activities
- Building schedules that match staff with the workload as closely as possible

---

PERPETUATING THE PROBLEM

Real-time management, though essential, has a serious downside. Real-time tactics that enhance supply or curb demand can also undermine the organization's ability to create accurate resource plans. These tactics — e.g., adjusting call-handling processes, overflowing calls to secondary groups, postponing breaks and training, or reassigning agents to unplanned work — can create skewed activity reports. They can defer essential work or training. And they can complicate future workload and schedule predictions. In short, real-time management can perpetuate the imbalances that created the need for reactionary measures. That doesn't mean that real-time tactics shouldn't be used, but you should employ them judiciously and be alert to their implications on planning and management.

Monitoring Real-Time Developments

The second major principle in real-time management is to monitor developments and identify trends as early as possible. The trick is to react appropriately to evolving conditions. Random call arrival means that, at times, it will look like you are falling behind even though you are staffed appropriately. But if you are experiencing a genuine trend, you need to move quickly. Time is of the essence.

INTERPRETING REPORTS

Service level is "rolling" history. The ACD has to look at what happened to the last X calls (e.g., 20), or what occurred in the last X minutes (e.g., five minutes) to make the calculation. Consequently, even though service level is a primary focus in call center planning, it is not a sensitive real-time report.

(Note: With many ACDs, you can define these thresholds. You may need to experiment some. Set them high enough so that the reports aren't jumpy, but low enough so that they provide information that is as current as possible. "From the beginning of the half-hour" or "150 calls" is too much history, and the reports will have little real-time value. But the last 60 seconds or five calls is too little history, and reporting will be volatile. Also note that "screen refresh" does not correlate to the timeframe used for calculations. Your monitors may display updated information every few seconds, but that has nothing to do with how much data your ACD uses for the calculations that require rolling history.)

Service level will tell you what has already happened, given recent unique call volume, random arrival, average handling time and staff availability patterns. But it's important to realize that what is being reported is not necessarily an indication of what is about to happen.

On the other hand, the number of calls presently in queue *is* a real-time report, as is longest current wait and current agent status. Understanding the distinction between reports that are genuinely real-time versus those that must incorporate some history explains apparent contradictions.

For example, service level may indicate 65 percent answer in 20 seconds, even though there are no calls in queue at the moment. Keep watching the monitor, though, and service level will begin to climb. Alternatively, service level may look high at the moment, even though an enormous amount of calls recently entered the queue. Give it a few minutes and, unless circumstances change, it will be at the bottom of the barrel.

There will be at least several minutes delay before service level reflects the magnitude of a trend. As a result, for service level to have meaning, it must be interpreted in light of the recent past, calls in queue and current longest wait. If you focus only on service level, you could misread the situation.

MONITORING REAL-TIME REPORTS

1. Number of calls in queue
2. Longest current wait (oldest call)
3. Service level/average speed of answer
4. Agent status
5. Escalation plan...

Since the number of calls in queue foretells where service level is about to go (unless conditions change), it should be a primary focus, along with longest current wait. As circumstances dictate, you would then assess the state agents are in — signed off, auxiliary, handling calls, etc. — and make appropriate adjustments.

In summary, focus on real-time reports in this order:

1. NUMBER OF CALLS IN QUEUE. This is the real-time report most sensitive to changes and trends. Look at this first.

2. LONGEST CURRENT WAIT (OLDEST CALL). This is a real-time report, but it behaves like a historical report (e.g., many calls can come into the queue, but longest current wait will take some time to reflect the problem). This report gives context to number of calls in queue. For example, if there are far more calls in queue than normal, but longest current wait is modest, you are at the beginning of a downward trend. Now is the time to react.

3. SERVICE LEVEL, AVERAGE SPEED OF ANSWER, AVERAGE TIME TO ABANDONMENT AND OTHER MEASURES OF THE QUEUE AND CALLER BEHAVIOR. These reports provide additional context to number of calls in queue and longest current wait. For example, if service level is low, but there are few or no calls in queue, then you have hurdled the problem and service level will begin to climb. Don't sweat it.

4. AGENT STATUS. This real-time report indicates how many agents are available and what modes they are in. Some call center mangers suggest that agent status should be at the top of the list. Their argument is that if agents are where they need to be, there wouldn't be much of a queue in the first place. There is some logic in that argument. However, I generally place agent status after other reports because it can be difficult to interpret unless you know something about the queue. So what if few agents are taking calls, if few calls are coming in? In that case, you would want agents to be working on other tasks.

In the end, the debate on the order of reports doesn't matter much because you should monitor and interpret them together. With the right training on what real-time information means and the activity it is reporting, experienced agents and supervisors can scan and decipher these reports quickly.

APPLE'S FAST-RESPONSE CULTURE

Apple Computer's call centers face a unique challenge as a result of their company's long-standing commitment to surprise product announcements. Apple's CEO, Steve Jobs, garners worldwide attention when he speaks at major events, such as the MacWorld conference, because the innovative company is intent on maintaining secrecy. No one knows in advance what new products will be introduced — and that includes call center employees. Yet, as Jobs relays an important announcement, the news hits the wires and devoted Apple customers begin calling.

How does the call center team cope? They rely on their finely tuned instant update process. The top-secret information is prepared by a small, but trusted team — not even the Global Training Director gets to see it. Every agent stands by, waiting for the update to be electronically delivered as the information is being made public. The contacts begin arriving and agents — armed with information they received minutes before — handle them smoothly and confidently.

It's a tremendous challenge for the call center, but the team takes pride in rising to it. And it's a great example of anticipating and planning everything possible in advance — so that when the moment arrives, the call center is ready to respond.

Source: ICMI Call Center Insight Tour

DISPLAY THRESHOLDS

Some ACD and wall display systems allow you to establish various priority thresholds. For example, you can color-code information yellow when the queue begins to back up, and red when it's in bad shape. Alternatively, some ACDs, particularly older models, do not have queue displays on phones, but do provide blinking lights. The lights can be programmed to blink more rapidly as the queue builds.

The problem is, the thresholds are often set arbitrarily. Further, agents often do not understand what is expected from them at different levels. If that's the case, real-time information will raise everybody's stress level. And your agents might feel like it's their fault that they can't clear up the queue. Proper programming and training are necessary.

Generally, the first threshold should be set for one call in queue. Agents should proceed normally, and no tactical adjustments are required. The second threshold should indicate that there are more calls in queue than the average expected for the desired service level (see "Q2" in Chapter 7). Routine adjustments should be made (e.g., postpone flexible work) to get the calls answered. The next threshold should indicate that there are more calls in queue than the agents can handle. In this case, more involved real-time tactics (e.g., calling in reinforcements) are required.

You can program some systems to adjust thresholds as calling loads change (10 calls in queue may be no problem during a fully staffed shift, but would be a nightmare for two people handling calls at 3 a.m.). If your system doesn't have that capability, you'll have to either manually adjust threshold settings (impractical in most cases) or program them for typical half-hours and realize that they provide only rough guidance.

COORDINATION

Ever had this happen? Someone looks at the real-time reports and everything is fine, so he or she decides to unplug and begin work on a project or take a break. Unfortunately, others have the same idea at the same time, resulting in queues that spin out of control. Interpreting real-time information when there is no queue is almost as tricky as identifying trends when there is a queue!

Consequently, most large or networked call centers have a designated "traffic control" center that coordinates activities. The traffic controller's authority can range from making informed suggestions on priorities to flatly dictating what can and can't happen at any given time.

Whatever the size of your call center, you will need someone with the whole field in view to monitor conditions. This person (or team) may also produce and interpret intraday forecasts (see Chapter 6) and make adjustments to system or network thresholds.

©King Features Syndicate. Reprinted with permission.

A Workable Escalation Plan

Regardless of what channels you are supporting, to achieve your service level and response time objectives in real time you will need to make appropriate tactical adjustments as conditions change. An important principle in effective real-time management is to outline a workable escalation plan that is in place before a crisis. Most call centers use a tiered approach.

LEVEL 1

The first level of action involves routine, commonsense adjustments that enable you to get the contacts handled. Agent status becomes the focus,

"In Case of Unexpected Call Spike, Break Glass"

©ICMI

Contingency Plan

and many use a variation of the time-honored phrase: "Everybody take a call!" This is generally directed toward people on the floor who are not currently handling contacts. It can also be for agents stuck in wrap-up mode.

At this level, agents make routine adjustments to work priorities. Flexible tasks are postponed. If you have secondary groups handling email, correspondence, outbound calls or data entry, they can be temporarily assigned to the inbound call traffic. You might also overflow calls to agents in other groups (who are trained to handle the calls).

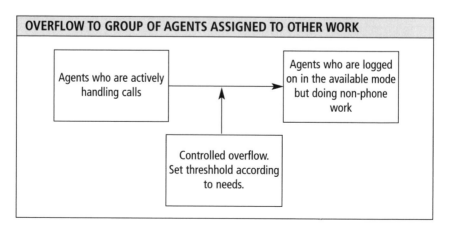

OVERFLOW TO GROUP OF AGENTS ASSIGNED TO OTHER WORK

Agents who are actively handling calls

Agents who are logged on in the available mode but doing non-phone work

Controlled overflow. Set threshhold according to needs.

REAL-TIME TACTICS

- "Everybody take a call"
- Assist people who are stuck in talk time or wrap-up
- Postpone flexible work
- Record appropriate system announcements
- Bring in secondary groups
- Adjust overflow or network parameters
- Reassign agents to groups that need help
- Adjust the placement of delay announcements
- Use supervisors wisely
- Bring in agents who are on call
- Send contacts to outsourcers
- Mobilize the swat team
- Adjust call-routing priorities
- Take messages for callback
- Generate controlled busy signals

Make sure that your agents understand that speeding up their rate of speech will not help. Callers can usually sense they are rushed, and will often dig in their heels to slow things down. However, agents shouldn't go beyond what is necessary to completely satisfy the caller's stated objectives and handle the call with quality.

Hurry? I have no time to hurry. — **Igor Stravinsky**

LEVEL 2 AND BEYOND

If the workload still outpaces the staff required to handle it, the call center can move on to more involved real-time alternatives. For example, it may be feasible to reassign agents from one group to another.

Another possible Level 2 activity is to change system announcements so that they offload what would otherwise be routine calls. Utilities use messages such as, "We are aware of the power outage in the Bay Ridge area, caused by nearby construction. We hope to have power restored by 11 a.m. We apologize for the inconvenience. If you need further assistance, please stay on the line, one of our representatives will be with you momentarily..."

(More routinely, calls can be directed elsewhere: "Thank you for calling ABC airline. If you would like to use our automated flight arrival and departure system, please say or press..." Some call centers also give callers the ability to check the status of an order, listen to specific product information, or hear answers to commonly asked questions while they wait and without losing their place in the queue.)

Sometimes, you can foster empathy with system announcements: "Due to the snowstorm blanketing the East Coast, we are operating with fewer of our associates than normal. However, your call is very important to us. We apologize for the delay and will be with you just as soon as possible. Thank you for your patience." This tactic will backfire if it's overused or stretches the truth.

You might also be able to improve circumstances by changing call-routing thresholds between groups or sites. Most of today's routing systems are based on a form of "if-then" programming logic to automate this process. But there are cases that may require some adjustments. And if you have a network that sends fixed percentages of calls to various sites, you may need

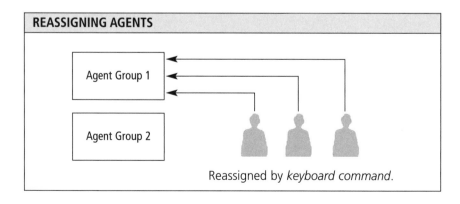

REASSIGNING AGENTS

Agent Group 1

Agent Group 2

Reassigned by *keyboard command.*

to adjust these thresholds.

It may make sense for supervisors and managers to help handle customer contacts. However, this approach must be well thought-out, because if they are unavailable when agents need help, the situation could further deteriorate. Some union agreements restrict supervisors and managers from handling contacts, but if allowed, this can be an effective tactic.

Some call centers take voicemail messages for later callback. However, this approach doesn't work well for most. (Consider the new challenges created: How do you ensure that the callbacks are timely? What do you do when you reach Junior, who informs you that Mom or Dad is unavailable to talk? What is your policy when you reach the caller's voicemail? Or secretary?) This strategy can work in call centers that handle complex calls and have defined customers who are easy to reach. But you may have to experiment with it to find out whether it's workable in your environment. You may also want to consider an alternative — a virtual queue technology, which enables callers to simply hang up and receive a return call without losing their places in queue (see Chapter 3).

Other Level 2 tactics include calling in a swat team, bringing in agents who are on reserve, routing some contacts to established outsourcers, adjusting the placement of delay announcements and generating controlled busy signals.

In sum, establishing an effective escalation plan involves:

- Identifying feasible real-time tactics (ahead of time)
- Determining the conditions in which each should be implemented (ahead of time)
- Monitoring conditions (real time)
- Deciding on adjustments necessary (real time)
- Coordinating and communicating changes to all involved (real time)
- Implementing the tactics (real time)
- Assessing how well the escalation plan worked (after the fact)

An important but sometimes neglected aspect of real-time management is to analyze what happened, once the crisis has passed. How well did your escalation plan work? Were the right tactics deployed? This analysis will help you to fine-tune your escalation plan and improve the planning process. It is especially important if you are responding to more than two or three significant crises per week.

DELAY ANNOUNCEMENTS

Most call centers provide delay announcements to callers who wait in queue. The first announcement recognizes callers, explains the delay and promises that the calls will be answered.

> *Due to our inability to staff appropriately, your call will be delayed... and so will many others.*

The typical behavior of callers who abandon can provide insight into the use of delay announcements. Callers who hang up when they hear the first delay announcement are called "fast

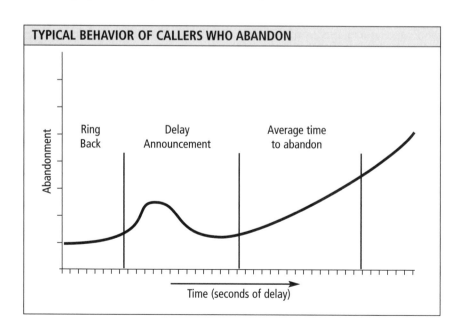

TYPICAL BEHAVIOR OF CALLERS WHO ABANDON

Abandonment

Ring Back | Delay Announcement | Average time to abandon

Time (seconds of delay)

clear-downs." They may have dialed the wrong number or they may just be the type to hang up when it's confirmed that they are in a queue.

Sometimes, repositioning the first delay announcement will lower abandonment. For example, if the delay announcement is normally set to come on after 10 seconds of ringing, moving the threshold to 15 or 20 seconds will give your agents more time to get to callers before they become fast clear-downs. Further, because callers don't mentally register that they are in a queue until they hear the announcement, they may wait longer.

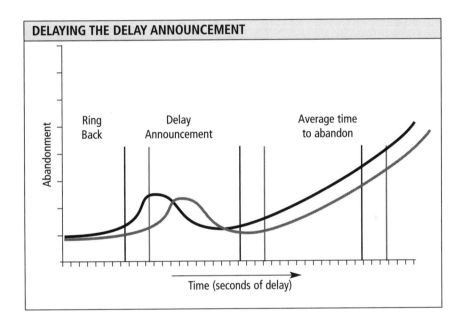

DELAYING THE DELAY ANNOUNCEMENT

Will this work for you? You'll have to try it to find out. Keep in mind, this technique will actually increase average speed of answer and reduce service level. But you have a higher value in mind: To get to as many callers as possible before they give up and hang up.

You may also be able to reduce abandonment by adjusting the position of the second delay announcement. For example, if average time to abandonment is 55 seconds and the second delay announcement is set for 60

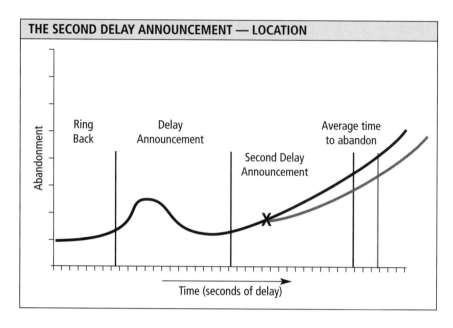

THE SECOND DELAY ANNOUNCEMENT — LOCATION

seconds, you might hang on to more callers by programming it to play earlier. The purpose of the second delay announcement is to give callers who are about to abandon renewed hope that you will get to them: "We haven't forgotten you. One of our agents will be with you momentarily. Thank you for waiting."

The first and second delay announcements are valuable, but repeating delay announcements tend to make things worse. Callers have to mentally tune in every time the announcement is played, which, over time, can make them cynical: "Yes, I know this call is important to you and that you'll be with me momentarily. You've told me eight times so far." And from a practical standpoint, they probably have you on speakerphone while they catch up with other matters — in that case, repeating announcements are repeating interruptions.

ABANDONS OR BUSY SIGNALS?

What if things are really rough? What if you get more calls than expected and have exhausted all other alternatives? Should you continue to let

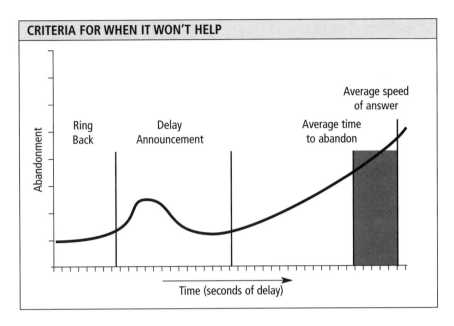

CRITERIA FOR WHEN IT WON'T HELP

Abandonment

Ring Back

Delay Announcement

Average speed of answer

Average time to abandon

Time (seconds of delay)

callers into the queue? The unsavory choice may be to give callers busy signals or let them enter a long queue, only to abandon anyway. (See figure, "Criteria for When It Won't Help.")

Some call centers could never consider using busy signals. Emergency services are a notable example. But for others, generating a busy signal may occasionally be an acceptable alternative. Callers who get busy signals are more likely to make immediate and repeated attempts to reach you than those who abandon.

Two reports, average speed of answer and average time to abandonment, provide useful direction. If ASA is four minutes and ATA is two minutes, then you might begin to block some calls from getting into the queue to force ASA down. The idea is to end up with ASA and ATA in close proximity.

Several technical alternatives exist that allow you to block calls from entering the queue. With older systems, call center managers had to be creative. For example, they could overflow calls to "dummy" answer groups that were busied out. They could also play an "all circuits are busy" message

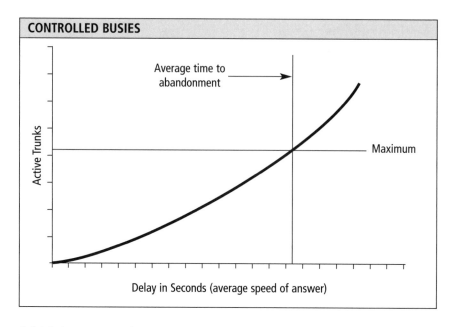

CONTROLLED BUSIES

Average time to abandonment →

Maximum

Active Trunks

Delay in Seconds (average speed of answer)

(which is not a good approach because you or your callers will have to pay for the calls, if toll charges apply). Today, many systems are capable of "controlled" busy signals, whereby the system blocks calls according to the thresholds you program (e.g., seconds in queue or number of calls waiting).

Matching ASA and ATA is by no means a sure-fire approach. Keep in mind, if percent abandonment is low (i.e., 2 or 3 percent), then ATA is irrelevant. When percent abandonment goes up, ATA typically goes up (and becomes more meaningful) because it includes a broader sample of callers in the calculations.

Further, ASA and ATA measure two different populations; ASA includes callers who wait until they reach agents, while ATA considers only those who abandon. Both reports tend to be moving targets, and can fluctuate widely within a few minutes. And callers who get blocked a number of times before reaching the queue tend to be more tenacious and will usually wait longer for an agent.

All of this is to say that this approach must be used judiciously. Busy signals are compelling because they make reports look better and take the pressure off your agents. But some managers depend on them as a crutch for inadequate staffing. That's poor customer service, and it defeats the mission of the call center. This tactic should only be used in extreme or short-lived situations.

Planning and Practice

The call centers that do the best job of real-time management have some important things in common. They plan the escalation procedure ahead of time and define the thresholds that will determine when each tactic should be implemented. They continually review and refine their escalation plan. When the dust settles, they take the time to go back and analyze what happened, what worked and where there were problems. And they continually improve their planning process, so they are not leaving those on the floor with "mission impossible."

Real-time management takes planning, coordination and practice. It's also gratifying. One of the rewards of working in a call center is to step up to a challenge, then be able to look back at the results... and smile.

Points to Remember

- Establish a good foundation ahead of time so that you are not creating many of the crises to which you are responding.
- Provide real-time information to agents and supervisors, and train them on how to interpret the information.
- Plan the escalation procedure ahead of time and define the thresholds that will determine when alternatives are deployed.
- Establish a person or a team to coordinate real-time tactics.
- Review and refine your escalation plan on an ongoing basis.
- Continually improve your planning process. Real-time management will never be an effective substitute for accurate resource planning.

Part Four:
Elevating Quality and Performance

CHAPTER 12:
Establishing the Right Measures and Objectives

CHAPTER 13:
Improving Call Center and Organizationwide Performance

CHAPTER 14:
Boosting Individual Performance

CHAPTER 15:
Building a More Effective Organization

The subjects of quality and productivity have been reassessed with every passing management movement. But high-performance call centers have made a dramatic shift in recent years from contact-processing "factories" to environments marked by high agent skill levels, an incessant focus on customer expectations, and organizationwide contributions to better products and services.

CHAPTER 12:
Establishing the Right Measures and Objectives

The test of any policy in management… is not whether the answer is right or wrong, but whether it works.

PETER F. DRUCKER

Establishing the right measures and objectives is one of the most important responsibilities in leading and managing a call center successfully. When decisions are based on solid information — and when process-improvement efforts are coupled with sensible objectives and accountabilities for individuals and teams — the call center can create substantial value for customers and for the organization.

But there's a significant challenge from the start: Call centers produce mounds of data — the reports that land on your desk could cover a parking lot. Out of all the reports and data that are available, which are best for assessing and guiding your operation's performance? Are you looking at the right things? Are others? Do you agree on what's important and how to interpret results?

In this chapter, we'll look at some important definitions, then identify some of the most common call center measurements. We'll then discuss the performance indicators that matter most and look at how every person has a role in meeting high-level measures and objectives.

Key Definitions

There are quite a few definitions related to measures — e.g., measurement, objective, standard, KPI, target and goal, to name a few. When specifically applied, there are important distinctions in meaning — and whether a measure becomes part of, say, a performance objective or KPI depends on context, use and what you'd like to accomplish. The most important definitions include:

MEASUREMENT: A quantifiable unit, referring to time (e.g., contact handle time), an input (e.g., a telephone call, email message), an output, (e.g., a sale, completed contact) or a ratio expressed with a numerator and denominator (e.g., absenteeism, first-call resolution).

PERFORMANCE OBJECTIVE: Usually stated as a quantifiable goal that must be accomplished within a given set of constraints, a specified period of time or by a given date (e.g., reduce turnover by 20 percent within one year).

STANDARD: A quantifiable minimum level of performance; performance below or outside the standard is not acceptable.

KEY PERFORMANCE INDICATOR: A high-level measure of effectiveness. Some define KPI as the single most important measure in a department or unit, but many call centers have multiple KPIs.

GOAL: The point of arrival — e.g., if a performance objective is to cut turnover in half, and it is currently 40 percent, then 20 percent turnover is the goal.

PERFORMANCE TARGET: An interim improvement point at a specific point in time — a "checkpoint" to reassess progress and correct the action or work plans necessary to reach the final goal.

In this chapter, I refer to measures and objectives somewhat generally. But as you apply them, the context will dictate precise terms and meaning. Ensuring that your team is "speaking a common language" is an important part of using measures appropriately.

Example Call Center Measures

Call center performance measures can be broadly divided into a handful of categories, including:

- Quality
- Accessibility
- Efficiency
- Cost Performance
- Strategic Impact

Let's take a look at common measures within each category. Stick with me here — though this chapter doesn't represent an exhaustive list, there are quite a few we'll run through. Getting a good bird's eye view of the many alternatives from which to choose is a good start to selecting measures and objectives that make sense for your organization.

Also, before we go through the list, it's worth noting that many measures can logically fit into more than one category. Consider agent turnover — is it a measure of efficiency (newer agents tend to be less efficient), cost performance (it can be costly to replace agents), or strategic impact (experience matters)? Or how about contacts by channel, which includes the use of self-service systems — is that a matter of accessibility, efficiency, cost performance or something else (the best answer is "all of the above"). In short, how you categorize measures is not as important as getting them on the table so that you can make sensible choices about which to use and how.

QUALITY

Common measures related to quality include:

CALL (CONTACT) QUALITY: Assigns a value to the quality of individual contacts. Criteria generally include such things as interpreting customer requirements correctly, entering data accurately, providing the correct information, accurate call coding, capturing needed and useful information, etc. (see Chapter 13). Call quality is appropriate in all environments as both a high-level indicator of trends and progress, and as a specific objective for agents and supervisors, contact by contact. Data typically comes from samples via monitoring or recording contacts. Quality is discussed further in Chapters 13 and 14.

FIRST-CALL (FIRST-CONTACT) RESOLUTION: Studies indicate that organizations incur many additional expenses (some hidden and difficult to track) when callers' issues are not fully resolved on the first contact. First-call resolution also greatly impacts customer satisfaction. There is significant value in analyzing relative increases and decreases in first-call resolution in response to changes in call center processes, systems and customer requirements. Consequently, first-call resolution is appropriate in all environments as a high-level objective. Components that lead to first-call resolution should also be built into specific quality objectives for agents — however, because not all aspects are within their control, these components must be selected carefully. First-call resolution may be tracked through quality monitoring samples, a database (e.g., customer information system), call coding, customer surveys (asking customers whether the issues were resolved) or a combination.

ERRORS AND REWORK: As with first-call resolution, there is significant value in analyzing increases and decreases in errors and rework in response to changes in processes, systems and other factors. Measures of errors and rework are appropriate in all environments, and specific components of errors and rework are often built into quality objectives for agents (variables must be selected carefully because not all errors are within their control). Data may come from quality monitoring or recording, a database, call coding or other sources. See Chapter 13.

ACCESSIBILITY

Common measures related to accessibility include:

CONTACTS BY CHANNEL: These are simply measures of the number of contacts by channel; e.g., Web self-service, IVR self-service, telephone, Web chat, etc. It's also a good idea to track the AHTs associated with these contacts so that you have a complete picture of workload by channel. This is essential data for forecasting, and is also useful as a high level indication of relative trends and cost efficiency. Contacts may be tracked by the workforce managment system (WFMS), ACD and other routing systems, email servers, fax servers, Web servers and possibly other sources.

SERVICE LEVEL AND RESPONSE TIME: Establishing service level and response time objectives is a prerequisite to the planning necessary to ensure that the organization is accessible through whatever channel customers use. Real-time reports are also necessary for tactical adjustments. Service level is available directly from ACD (routing system) or WFMS reports. Response time reports may come from additional routing systems, such as email response management systems (ERMS), Web servers, WFMS reports or other sources. See Chapters 4, 7 and 8.

AVERAGE SPEED OF ANSWER (ASA): ASA is often misinterpreted as a "typical" experience, but the average is skewed by many callers who get answered before ASA and some who wait far longer than ASA. ASA comes from the same set of data as service level, and it is not necessary to have both; however, if service level data is not available, ASA can be a substitute. Also, ASA does have important operational applications; e.g., it is a component of trunk load. Data on ASA is available directly from ACD or WFMS reports. See Chapter 4.

ABANDONED AND BLOCKED CALLS: Abandoned and blocked calls are generally caused by insufficient staffing or trunking resources, and should be supporting information to service level and response time reports, not primary objectives. Abandoned calls are available directly from ACD or WFMS reports. Reports on busy signals may come from the ACD (if using ACD-controlled busies), the local telephone company or the interexchange (long-distance) company (IXC). See Chapter 6.

LONGEST DELAY: Also called oldest call, this figure gives you the worst case — the longest amount of time a caller had to wait before reaching an agent or abandoning. It is appropriate in all environments as supporting information to service level and response time objectives, and is available from your ACD, other routing systems, or WFMS.

EFFICIENCY

Common measures related to efficiency include:

FORECAST ACCURACY: Forecasting the workload accurately is a high-leverage activity that is fundamental to managing a call center effectively. Forecasted call load versus actual is appropriate in all environments as a high-level objective, generally reported monthly down to the interval level; it is also used for ongoing tactical adjustments. Forecasted call load is available from the system used for forecasting; e.g., WFMS, forecasting software or spreadsheets. Actual call load may be tracked by the WFMS, ACD, ERMS, fax servers, Web servers or some combination of systems. See Chapter 6.

SCHEDULED STAFF VERSUS ACTUAL: This measure provides a comparison of the number of agents scheduled to the number actually in the center. It is appropriate in all environments as a high-level objective for the center and for teams. As with forecasts, reports should show each interval. The purpose of the objective is to understand and improve staff adherence and schedules. Scheduled staff is available from the system used for scheduling; e.g., WFMS or spreadsheets. Actual staff available is reported primarily by the ACD, or WFMS, with some components available from other systems. See Chapters 8 and 14.

ADHERENCE TO SCHEDULE: A measure of how much time and when during agents' shifts that they are taking or available to take calls. Adherence to schedule is appropriate in all environments as a high-level objective, and is also a common and recommended objective for individuals and teams. The measure is independent of whether the call center actually has the staff necessary to achieve a targeted service level and/or response time; it is simply a comparison of how closely agents adhere to schedules. Data generally comes from ACD or WFMS reports. See Chapter 14.

AVERAGE HANDLING TIME (AHT): AHT is appropriate in all environments for forecasting, planning and process improvement activities; it is generally not recommended as a strict agent standard. In many centers, AHT has been increasing overall as more contacts go to self-serve systems and agent-assisted contacts become more complex; cross-sell and upsell initiatives can also add time to calls. Relative reductions in AHT through better processes, technologies and training can create significant efficiencies. AHT is available from ACD and WFMS reports, and potentially from other routing systems and servers. See Chapters 6 and 13.

OCCUPANCY, CONTACTS HANDLED, NORMALIZED CONTACTS HANDLED: The service level that you are achieving at any given time will dictate the resulting occupancy rate and, therefore, the number of contacts handled. Although occupancy is not within the control of an individual or group of agents, it can be "neutralized" by dividing calls handled by percent occupancy to produce a measure of "normalized contacts handled" — which is more fair and meaningful than calls handled (see Chapter 14). Occupancy and calls handled are available from ACD and WFMS reports, and potentially from other routing systems and servers. See Chapters 7, 9 and 14.

TRANSFERRED OR ESCALATED CALLS: Too many transferred or escalated calls can indicate that calls are not being routed to the right places, or that agents are not sufficiently trained, equipped or empowered to handle calls. These measures are appropriate in all environments, and data is available from applicable routing systems.

COST PERFORMANCE

Common measures related to cost performance include:

COST PER CALL (COST PER CONTACT): Cost per call is appropriate in all environments as a high-level objective (generally reported monthly or quarterly). However, it must be interpreted carefully; e.g., a climbing cost per call can be a good sign (process improvements may result in fewer calls, spreading fixed costs over fewer calls and driving up cost per call). Volume of contacts requires ACD reports, and potentially other systems that track contacts. Cost data comes from several sources; e.g., payroll for staffing costs; budgets for equipment, building depreciation, etc.; and telecommunications reports for toll and line-usage costs.

AVERAGE (CONTACT) CALL VALUE: Average call value is appropriate for revenue-generating environments, such as reservation centers and catalog companies where calls have a measurable value. It is generally reported quarterly or monthly, and sometimes more frequently. Average call value is difficult to apply (and generally not recommended) in call centers where the value of calls is difficult to measure; i.e., customer service centers and help desks. Revenue information comes from any report that indicates revenue generated by the call center; e.g., sales reports, total orders, CRM system reports, etc. Volume of contacts requires reports from the ACD, WFMS or other routing systems that may be involved.

REVENUE: As with average call value, measures of revenue are appropriate for revenue-generating environments and can be reported quarterly, monthly, daily or for specific time periods. Results are often correlated with other variables, such as call center costs, market conditions and revenues through other channels of contact (e.g., retail or direct sales force) to gauge the call center's impact on the organization's profits. Revenue information comes from any report that indicates revenue generated by the call center; e.g., sales reports, total orders, CRM system reports, etc.

BUDGETED TO ACTUAL EXPENDITURES: Often called variance reports, these measures illustrate the differences between projected and actual expenditures for various budget categories. They are appropriate in all environments as high-level objectives, assuming they are considered within the context of changing workload variables and call center responsibilities. They are generally produced both quarterly and annually, and are available monthly in some environments. Budget versus actual information can be formulated from corporate accounting systems or tracked by spreadsheets.

OBJECTIVES FOR OUTBOUND: Outbound measures often include number or percentage of attempted calls, connected calls, contacts, abandoned calls, contacts per hour, contact rate, cost per contact, cost per minute and others. These objectives are appropriate and necessary in environments that include outbound contacts. (And depending on how they are used, they can logically fit into any of the five major categories of measures.)

STRATEGIC IMPACT

Common measures related to strategic impact include:

CUSTOMER SATISFACTION AND LOYALTY: Customer satisfaction is appropriate in all environments and has greatest value as a relative measure and in conjunction with other objectives (e.g., how do changes in policies, services and processes impact customer satisfaction?). Data often comes from a variety of sources: outbound calls, mail surveys, email surveys, agent-assisted surveys at the end of calls, automated IVR surveys, focus groups, and other sources. Customer loyalty is usually viewed through measures of repeat business over time. See Chapters 2 and 13.

EMPLOYEE SATISFACTION: Studies have demonstrated that customer satisfaction increases as agent job satisfaction increases. Further, retention, productivity and quality often have a definable, positive correlation to agent satisfaction. Results of surveys to gauge agent satisfaction should be compared to job satisfaction levels in other parts of the organization. Data is captured via written or online surveys, focus groups or one-on-one interviews. See Chapters 14 and 17.

TURNOVER: Retention is an increasingly important objective as call centers become more complex and as agent and management skills and experience requirements escalate. Reductions in turnover typically can be translated into financial savings, overall improvements in quality and productivity, and higher levels of strategic contribution. Turnover reports are often produced monthly (calculated on an annualized basis), and should be categorized as voluntary (natural) or involuntary (unnatural). Data is captured via entries in HR records and/or a WFMS, and results are typically manually calculated or reported from the WFMS. See Chapter 14.

STRATEGIC VALUE: Measures and objectives related to the call center's strategic value seek to identify, quantify, track, improve and communicate the call center's return on investment (ROI) and impact on other business units. These measures are often related to:

- Customer satisfaction and loyalty
- Improved quality and innovation
- Leveraged marketing initiatives
- More focused products and services
- Efficient delivery of services
- Supporting self-service systems
- Minimizing potential legal issues
- Contributions to revenue/sales

These measures are appropriate in all environments. While revenue- and profit-related measures will not apply to non-commercial organizations (e.g., government and not-for-profit), the call center's impact on things like innovation, quality and customer satisfaction apply in any environment. Reports are generally a synthesis of samples and analysis, and data comes from a variety of sources. See Chapter 13.

OTHER MEASURES

There are literally hundreds of additional measures, combinations and derivatives we could add. The list is a starting point — let your needs, objectives and imagination contribute other possibilities for consideration (see section on reporting, Chapter 10).

Which Measures Are Right for Your Organization?

Given the sheer number of possibilities — and the constant change in the business environment — many managers are looking for clear-cut guidance on objectives and standards. Where do we stand? What are others doing? What performance is good enough? What will satisfy customers? What is "world class"?

Those are reasonable questions, and you should be asking them. But let's start with a basic truth: Ultimately, you will need to establish measures and objectives that are *right for your organization.* That involves learning all you can about the process of establishing call center objectives and how variables are interrelated; developing a solid customer access strategy and tying it to your organization's overall strategic objectives; and then establishing the measures and objectives that make sense for you.

"Not everything that can be counted counts, and not everything that counts can be counted." — **ALBERT EINSTEIN**

"OK," some will say, "We agree with the notion of choosing objectives that are right for our organization. Still… help us to get started. Which measures absolutely positively must be in place?"

Fair enough. There are some measures that should be in place in every customer contact center, whether commercial or government, sales or service. They include:

STRATEGIC VALUE. What contributions is the call center making to other business units, and how are they favorably impacting revenues, marketing initiatives, product innovations and other primary business objectives (see Chapter 13)?

CUSTOMER SATISFACTION AND LOYALTY. Customer loyalty may not directly apply in environments where customers do not have other alternatives; but customer satisfaction is always a necessary and appropriate measure.

EMPLOYEE SATISFACTION. Employee satisfaction clearly influences — even drives — customer satisfaction and is an essential measure in any environment. (see Chapter 17)

QUALITY AND FIRST-CALL RESOLUTION. Quality is the link between call-by-call activities and the organization's most important high-level objectives. First-call resolution is essentially an extension of quality — a tangible result of getting quality right.

SERVICE LEVEL AND RESPONSE TIME. If calls don't get to the right places at the right times, then little else can happen.

FORECAST ACCURACY. If you don't have an accurate prediction of the workload coming your way, it's almost impossible to run an effective, efficient center.

SCHEDULE ADHERENCE. Having the right number of properly skilled people in place at the right times is another important enabler to everything else you're trying to accomplish.

Many organizations also track average handle time — which is essential for forecasting, and for gauging the impact of process improvements and relative efficiency. But many are wisely moving away from establishing AHT as a strict agent standard (see discussion, Chapter 14).

Other measures and objectives should be driven by your organization's and call center's mission and objectives. For example, many customer service environments focus on customer satisfaction, efficiency issues and cost measures. Sales environments often base key objectives on revenue, cross-sell, upsell and customer retention activities. And encouraging the use of self-service systems and preventing contacts before they happen (e.g., by working with other business units to simplify features, fix glitches or improve manuals) are important objectives in many technical support environments.

As you home in on the right objectives, keep your eyes on the prize:

maximum strategic value. As Keith Dawson, editorial director for *Call Center Magazine*, puts it, call-handling stats are "very comfortable" metrics. "But do they really tell a deep story of what a call center represents to an organization? No, for that you need to measure things like customer satisfaction and revenue generated. How many customer calls were turned into sales opportunities, or even chances to get simple feedback on what your center is doing?"

FOCUS ON WHAT REALLY MATTERS

In recent years, there has been a lot of attention on call center "optimization." To many, optimization is synonymous with driving costs out of the business — moving contacts to lower-cost channels (e.g., self-service), reducing human contact with the customer, and driving down handling times.

"This is all wrong," says consultant Mary Murcott in her book, *Driving Peak Sales Performance in Call Centers*. "This is not optimization; this is driving a distorted view of efficiency even further down the current wayward road." According to Murcott, true optimization means optimizing business outcomes like customer loyalty and revenue. Significant performance improvement requires moving away from "ancillary measurements," such as cost per call, and instead focusing on channel profitability and loyalty.

In an era when products and services quickly become commodities, customer contact services represent significant differentiation and value-add opportunities. Do you and the rest of your team realize the potential of your customer contact services?

Building a Supporting Culture

As you establish measures, track performance and work toward achieving important objectives, it is essential that your team understands what measures are really saying. And that requires understanding how call center dynamics work. For example:

- Maybe your first-call resolution rate is lower than what similar organizations say they are achieving; but you may be measuring it more rigorously and working to prevent easy-to-handle contacts at the source.
- Your center's average handling time (AHT) may be higher than the usual, and yet if you are using that time to prevent repeat calls, improve processes and capture information that can improve products and marketing, your total call load (AHT x number of calls) along with associated costs may, in fact, be far better than the norm.
- Your service level or response time objectives may be more modest than others in your industry. But you may actually be doing better — if you hit them increment after increment, day after day.

To drive the right performance, sometimes you'll need to take steps that may initially feel like a leap of faith. For example, Independent Blue Cross in Philadelphia removed the "average talk time" statistic from its reward and recognition program, as did Boston Coach with its "number of calls handled per shift" metric. Instead, both organizations have put more emphasis on quality and process improvements. Sharp Electronics tied its agents' compensation and promotions, in part, to how well they used the organization's knowledge-management software (which was developed and built inhouse by the agents). Aetna U.S. Healthcare went so far as to advertise its focus on first-call resolution in newspapers and online ads (see the box on facing page). In these and many similar cases, organizations report better overall results when they focus on the things that matter most.

It's often said that "what gets measured gets done." I believe that's an over-simplification. I've seen organizations measure lots of things, yet not make sustained improvements in those areas. I am convinced that it's a matter of, not only measuring the right things, but also focusing on them, working on them, building a culture that understands and contributes to them, and ultimately, building processes and ensuring that day-to-day activities and decisions support them.

AETNA PUTS TEETH IN FIRST-CALL RESOLUTION

When Aetna U.S. Healthcare introduced a formal first-call resolution program, they publicized their commitment to the new initiative by telling customers about the change via whole-page newspaper and online ads. The ads highlighted "Aetna's First-Call Resolution program. Answering the call to solve your problems," and explained that the company would "measure customer service by the number of problems solved, not just the number of calls answered."

Let customers in on a bold, new service strategy, and you'd better make good on your word. Aetna apparently has. Since the program's inception, the insurance provider's customer service centers have experienced reduced call volumes and a lower ratio of calls per member, which, according to Tanis Sugden, service center head of Aetna's Thousand Oaks, Calif. operation, "can be attributed, in part, at least, to our efforts to resolve members' issues on the first call." In addition, Aetna reports a 10 percent improvement in customer satisfaction (as measured by post-call surveys).

Source: *Call Center Management Review*

Everyone Counts!

Which performance objectives are established — and how they are applied — tend to vary significantly from one organization to the next. However, one principle is universal: Every position — indeed, every person — plays a part in helping the call center to achieve high-level objectives.

Unfortunately, the nature of overlapping responsibilities can leave individuals feeling like there is little connection between what they do and what the call center is trying to achieve. Nothing could be further from the truth. The following table provides a summary of the connections between roles and key objectives. While not every possible position/role is included, the table illustrates the diverse but shared contributions those in a variety of roles make to overall results.

Key Objectives	Responsibilities for Accomplishing Objectives
Quality	**Agents:** Have a direct impact on call-by-call quality, which contributes to overall quality, first-call resolution, and a low rate of errors and rework. **Supervisors:** Contribute to quality objectives by ensuring that individuals in their teams have the resources, coaching and feedback they need to handle each contact with quality. The experience supervisors have in handling frontline work, as well as their proximity to it, make them invaluable in quality improvement initiatives. **Quality Specialists:** Manage a centralized repository of quality data captured contact by contact (by the quality specialist or by supervisors). Analysis of this information leads to process, system, training and coaching improvements. **Workforce Planners:** Impact quality by forecasting the call center's workload accurately and ensuring that schedules match requirements (resulting in the right contacts going to the right places at the right times). They also are responsible for identifying the best times for people to work on quality initiatives and training. **Technical Support (IT):** Enable quality by equipping the call center with appropriate tools and technologies. For example, information systems that provide agents with accurate, real-time data on customers, products, services and policies contribute enormously to call quality and first-call resolution. Similarly, capable systems that are thoughtfully programmed ensure that the right contacts are routed to the right places at the right times. **Managers/Director:** Contribute to quality and accessibility first and foremost by ensuring that agents, supervisors, planners and others have the training, skills, tools and processes that enable them to be successful in their positions. They ensure that the call center is an inherent part of organizationwide processes (e.g., marketing and product development). They also are generally responsible for cultivating a culture that values quality from top to bottom.

Accessibility	**Agents:** Contribute to accessibility by being in "the right places at the right times, doing the right things." **Supervisors:** Contribute to accessibility by ensuring that individuals are in the right places at the right times, doing the right things. They help to resolve adherence problems and often serve as liaison between real-time workforce managers and teams. **Quality Specialists:** Are inherently close to processes that impact handling times and other key accessibility drivers. **Workforce Planners:** Accessibility is a primary workforce management responsibility. Workforce planners impact accessibility by forecasting the call center's workload accurately and ensuring that schedules match workload requirements. **Technical Support (IT):** Enable accessibility by ensuring that systems are structured well, responsive and support real-time call-handling requirements. IT also has the responsibility to ensure that systems are up and running and that technical problems are quickly resolved. **Managers/Director:** Contribute to accessibility by ensuring that the call center's priorities — and supporting operational decisions — support accessibility. They see that employees have the resources they need, and that processes and systems support consistent accessibility. They ensure that departments across the organization that may impact the call center's workload collaborate with call center planners.
Efficiency	**Agents:** Contribute to efficiency objectives, not only by how they handle contacts, but by how they code work. E.g., when they use talk time, after-call work and other work modes consistently and accurately, they contribute to more stable, reliable data for forecasting, scheduling and other objectives. Agents also have a direct impact on adherence to schedule. **Supervisors:** Ensure that work is being handled as required,

(continued next page)

Efficiency *(continued)*	which leads to stable results and reliable data for planning purposes. They also usually serve as coordinators/liaisons for planning meetings and when schedules are adjusted to accommodate changing workload requirements. They have a key role in coaching agents to achieve adherence results. **Quality Specialists:** Have a responsibility not just for quality, but for associated efficiencies. E.g., if it takes one agent seven screens to do the same thing another can do in three, quality specialists can drive relevant training and coaching improvements. **Workforce Planners:** As with accessibility, objectives related to efficiency are primary workforce planning responsibilities. Accurate forecasting, staffing and scheduling, as well as competent real-time adjustments contribute enormously to efficiencies. **Technical Support (IT):** Contribute to efficiency by ensuring that workload tracking tools are correctly programmed and that trainers and supervisors teach agents their proper use. They also have a role in providing and supporting systems that provide reports and data essential to the planning process (e.g., routing systems, reporting tools, etc.). **Managers/Director:** Impact efficiency not only by ensuring that the center has the right tools, methods and training in place, but also by establishing a culture of collaboration — and one that emphasizes the importance of accurate and comprehensive planning. And, as with accessibility, ensuring that data, information and plans that other departments have are shared with the call center.
Cost Performance	**Agents:** Have an indirect but significant impact on cost performance objectives. By doing the right things at the right times and handling contacts with quality, they contribute to accessibility and quality, which, in turn, have a direct bearing on cost performance. Also, in revenue-producing environments, sales skills significantly impact revenue results.

Cost Performance *(continued)*	**Supervisors:** As with agents, supervisors have a significant impact on cost performance objectives. By enabling their teams to do the right things at the right times and handle contacts with quality, they contribute to accessibility and quality, which, in turn, have a direct bearing on cost performance. Coaching and monitoring should also support overall budget and revenue objectives. **Quality Specialists:** Important aspects of quality include those things that lead to revenue and cost performance objectives (e.g., efficient processes, seeing cross-selling opportunities, etc.). **Workforce Planners:** Virtually every cost performance objective is impacted by the accuracy of workforce planning and effectiveness in carrying out those plans. E.g., forecasts and schedules that are improved by just 1 or 2 percent can translate to thousands of dollars of daily savings in medium to large call centers. Appropriate schedules reduce overtime costs, and accurate planning ensures that contacts are going to the right agent groups at the right times — which impacts revenue and cost results. **Technical Support (IT):** The technologies available to the call center — their functionality and how they are programmed and used — have a significant impact on cost performance objectives. This is true both for customer-facing systems (e.g., to what degree will they use self-service channels?), information systems agents use to handle contacts with quality, and reporting systems used by management to leverage call center efficiencies and effectiveness. Efficiency of systems, uptime, and technical support response times all contribute to cost objectives. **Managers/Director:** Have primary responsibility for identifying budgetary requirements and ensuring that the call center gets the resources necessary to fulfill its mission. They also have a significant impact on cost performance by

(continued next page)

Cost Performance *(continued)*	ensuring that the right people, processes and technologies are in place and working in sync.
Strategic Impact	**Agents:** Contribute to customer satisfaction (and subsequent loyalty and repeat business) through their contributions to accessibility and quality on a contact-by-contact basis. But agents also have a much larger strategic impact; for example, the information captured during contacts — assuming it is complete and accurate — becomes the basis for product and service improvements and innovations, better marketing campaigns, and quality improvements (inside and outside the call center). Agents are also key in educating customers on the availability and use of self-service access channels. **Supervisors:** Contribute to the call center's strategic impact by helping to facilitate their teams' success. Supervisors are also frequently involved in projects and initiatives to identify, measure, track, improve and communicate the call center's impact on the organization (e.g., through data analysis teams and as liaisons between other groups/departments and frontline activities). **Quality Specialists:** Typically, quality specialists are involved in assembling information captured during contacts, analyzing it and getting it to other departments for which it would be useful. Quality specialists also are responsible for recommendations on process improvements that would contribute to higher levels of customer satisfaction and agent support. **Workforce Planners:** Have a similar impact on both customer satisfaction and employee satisfaction. For example, when the call center is accessible, due to accurate forecasts and schedules, customers are happier because they can reach the services they require quickly and easily. Similarly, good service levels mean occupancy levels that are not too high, giving agents the chance to "breathe" in between contacts and to work with callers who aren't angry

Strategic Impact *(continued)*	from waiting in a long queue. Again, accurate planning matches right resources with right contacts, enabling the highest quality services and customer satisfaction. **Technical Support (IT):** Technologies impact customer satisfaction first at the user interface — e.g., are customer-facing systems (IVRs, Web, etc.) easy to use, and do they enable customers to accomplish what they want? "Back-end" systems also have a huge role; e.g., do agents have the information and support they need? Are capabilities in place to capture data from contacts that can be used to improve products, services and marketing, as well as to better understand customers? The answers to these questions impact customer satisfaction, employee satisfaction and the call center's overall ROI. Technical support also has a key role in developing and maintaining disaster-recovery plans. **Managers/Director:** Ensure that the culture, environment, tools and resources are in place to support a high-value environment. They also work with managers across the organization to use data captured during call center contacts to improve the organization's overall effectiveness in meeting the needs of customers. They ensure that call center staff remain focused on the vision of the organization and that behaviors are within company guidelines and support the company's brand and direction.

In short, every role has an impact on overall results. Consequently, it is essential that you take steps to ensure that the interrelated nature of call center objectives and responsibilities is understood at all levels.

Establishing the right measures and objectives is one of the most important and challenging responsibilities in leading and managing a call center. However, objectives and standards will have little positive impact unless the call center is also making fundamental improvements to call center processes. When robust process-improvement efforts are coupled with sensible objectives and accountabilities for individuals and teams, the call center is in a position to achieve results that create real value for customers and for the organization. We'll pick up with these subjects in the next two chapters.

Points to Remember

- Although terms such as measure, objective, goal and target are often used interchangeably, they have different meanings when specifically applied.
- Common call center performance measures can be broadly divided into categories that include quality, accessibility, efficiency, cost performance and strategic impact.
- There are literally hundreds of possible performance measures and objectives from which to choose.
- Key measures — e.g., those related to strategic value, customer satisfaction, employee satisfaction, quality and first-call resolution, service level and response time, forecast accuracy and schedule adherence — should be in place in every customer contact center.
- Other measures will be unique to your environment — you will need to establish objectives that are right for your organization.
- Each person in the call center, whatever his or her role, has an impact on overall results. Consequently, it is essential that the interrelated nature of call center objectives and responsibilities be understood at all levels.

CHAPTER 13:
Improving Call Center
and Organizationwide Performance

It will not suffice to have customers who are merely satisfied.
W. EDWARDS DEMING

This first decade of the 21st century has been, in many ways, a challenging season for the management teams of call centers. In many cases, resources remain tight even as workloads continue to grow. And other factors have also added to the pressure, e.g., customer expectations continue to climb, upper-level management demands ever-better returns on investments and contacts are becoming more complex.

In a sense, call centers represent a subset of the demands that are being put on organizations in general in today's competitive environment: Find ways to make service delivery faster, better and more cost effective, year after year. That requires working smarter, not necessarily harder. It means consistently making improvements to call center processes and services — and applying these principles across the broader organization.

Five principles (see box) are significantly transforming the most forward-thinking call centers. And when applied beyond the call center, they are exponentially more powerful.

FIVE IMPORTANT PRINCIPLES

- Quality is built around customer expectations
- Quality and service level work together
- The process is where the leverage is
- Find and fix root causes using appropriate quality tools
- Skills, knowledge and leadership will make the difference

Quality and Customer Expectations

The imperative to identify and address customer expectations stems from a widely accepted principle: Satisfied customers will lead to increased customer loyalty, retention and revenue. That is why the customer access strategy must be based on an understanding of the 10 customer expectations (see Chapter 2).

THREE ESSENTIAL QUESTIONS

- What are customer expectations?
- Are you meeting them?
- Are you using the fewest possible resources?

A lesser-known but similarly powerful principle is also at work: Meeting customer expectations often translates into higher levels of service that are delivered at lower costs. Yes, more loyal customers save the organization oodles of marketing dollars. But there's more to it than that.

Take the issue of being courteous — in today's environment that means such things as don't make customers repeat the same information, don't transfer them around and don't make them go over their account history again. Customers don't know the extent that these guidelines require processes and systems that deliver relevant information to the right agent at the right time. To them, it's simply a matter of courteous service. To the organization, however, meeting this expectation almost always translates into service that is more cost-effective to deliver. Being responsive, handling contacts right the first time, relaying to customers what to expect —

everybody wins, including customers, employees and shareholders.

Three key questions that should always be part of your decision process are: What are customer expectations? Are you meeting them? Are you using the fewest possible resources? Don't guess at what your direction should be. Rather than create decisions based on what your executive team "believes" customers expect, get your information from the source. Ensure that your customer surveys are frequent and detailed enough to provide the specifics related to each of the 10 expectations — and how you're measuring up to them (see Chapter 2).

CUSTOMER FEEDBACK DRIVES LYNKSYS' IMPROVEMENT INITIATIVES

Linksys (a division of Cisco Systems, Inc.) recently launched a comprehensive customer feedback process to drive improvement initiatives throughout their Technical Assistance Center. The management team of the 24x7 multisite international call center, which handles customers' inquiries about and problems with the company's wireless products, routers, network cards and USB adapters, wanted to ensure that process-improvement efforts were focused on the things that matter most. "We, like all companies, have limited resources, so targeting initiatives of the greatest value to our customers is key to maximizing the value of our investment," says Steve Gordon, vice president of services.

The approach includes a concise online survey focused on areas where industry studies have shown customers have reported the most challenges. "Many of the studies in our industry show that customers value above all else the proper diagnosis and resolution of an issue in a timely manner," says Gordon. "If you can reliably solve the issue quickly and correctly, you'll delight your customer base. So we targeted a survey that focused on these common customer concerns using a statistical approach."

The online survey is sent to all Linksys customers (following an interaction with the call center) via an email invitation. The survey contains 12 focused questions that pertain to both the nature of the customer's problem/inquiry and their perception of the service provided by the call center. "The intent is to collect not only customer feedback on our service,

(continued next page)

but to follow the data back to the product, customer location, language and specific call center so that we can track our operation at a fairly granular level," Gordon explains. "This gives us the opportunity to clearly identify problem areas and allows us to target specific fixes." Agents are also very much involved and, according to Gordon, their input is taken just as seriously as customer feedback.

Since implementing the initiative, the company has seen notable improvements in how customers rate the "quality of the experience" [during an interaction with the call center] and, specifically, in the "problem-resolution" category. In addition to improvements in service and technical support, Linksys has also made numerous enhancements to products based on the collective customer feedback it receives. "We've worked closely with our engineering team using customer feedback... to focus on improvements in our products."

Source: *Call Center Management Review*

Quality and Service Level

Service level and quality tend to be inextricably associated with, and complementary to, each other. As discussed in Chapter 4, service level is an enabler. As service level deteriorates, more callers will verbalize their criticisms when calls are finally answered. Agents spend valuable time apologizing to callers. Call-handling time goes up. Morale, turnover and burnout take a hit — as can recruitment and training costs.

Further, when you consider the components of a quality contact (see box), the complementary relationship becomes clear. These items apply almost universally. Take a few minutes to study the list and think through how each item applies in your environment. What if data is not entered correctly? What if the caller doesn't have confidence the call was handled correctly? What if you didn't capture useful information from the transaction? These problems contribute to repeat calls, escalation of calls and complaints to higher management. The problems also entail callbacks and rework, further reducing service level.

WHAT IS A QUALITY CONTACT?

- Customer does not get a busy signal when using telephone or "no response" from Web site
- Customer is not placed in queue for too long
- Agent provides correct response
- All data entry is correct
- Agent captures all needed/useful information
- Agent has "pride in workmanship"
- Contact was necessary in the first place
- Customer receives correct information
- Customer has confidence contact was effective
- Customer doesn't feel it necessary to check up, verify or repeat
- People "down the line" can correctly interpret the order
- Customer is not transferred around
- Customer doesn't get rushed
- Customer is satisfied
- Unsolicited marketplace feedback is detected and documented
- Call center's mission is accomplished

Upshot: quality suffers and costs go up. When service level is low because agents are overworked due to constant congestion in the queue, they work less accurately and can become less "customer-friendly." Callers tell them in no uncertain terms about the tough time they had getting through. And agents tend to make more mistakes. These errors further contribute to repeat calls, escalation of calls and diversion of agents to activities that should be unnecessary. Poor service level becomes a vicious cycle.

Just as service level and quality are linked, so, too, are quality and response time. For example, if customers don't receive a reply to an email as quickly as expected, or if they don't receive the correct or expected response, they may send another. This can be the start of a similar cycle.

If response time is bad, what began as a fax or email can turn into a phone call: "I'm calling to check up on an email I sent to you. I haven't heard a reply yet, and am wondering..." If the original customer transaction hasn't yet been handled, agents likely won't have the information necessary to deal with these calls without duplicating efforts for both the call center and the caller. Again, costs go up.

To visualize the relationship between accessibility and quality, it's useful to view the implications through the lens of a staffing table (see figure). What portion of average talk time, average after-call work or call volume is due to repeat calls, or waste and rework? What could have been prevented? How about staff — e.g., how many agents are involved in creating or fixing waste and rework? Looking at these relationships in this way can quickly dispel the notion that accessibility and quality are at odds and must be "balanced." They work together. And driving both in the right direction often has a positive impact on costs.

REVISITING SERVICE LEVEL

Input

Average talk time (sec.) = 180
Average after-call work (sec.) = 30
Calls per half-hour = 250
Service level objective (sec.) = 20

?

Output

Agents	ASA	Service Level	Agent Occupancy	Trunk Load
30	209	24%	97%	54.0
31	75	45%	94%	35.4
32	38	61%	91%	30.2
33	21	73%	88%	28.0
34	13	82%	86%	26.8
35	8	88%	83%	26.1
36	5	92%	81%	25.7
37	3	95%	79%	25.4
38	2	97%	77%	25.3
39	1	98%	75%	25.2
40	1	99%	73%	25.1

?

Errors and rework are often part of a downward cycle. They consume valuable staff time, which can lead to insufficient staff to handle the workload. Insufficient staff then leads to a low service level/response time, high occupancy, unhappy customers and increased stress. Those things contribute to errors and rework, completing the cycle. So reducing errors and rework has a positive impact on service level/response time, morale, customer satisfaction and costs.

IMPACT OF REDUCING DEFECTIVE CONTACTS

- Quality up
- Production of good contacts up
- Capacity up
- Lower costs
- Profit improved
- Customers happier
- Agents happier

EXAMPLES OF COSTS WHEN QUALITY IS LACKING

- Escalation of calls and complaints to higher management
- Repeat contacts from customers
- Callbacks to customers for missing or unclear information
- Cancellations
- Cost of closing accounts
- Handling product returns
- Unnecessary service calls
- Wrong problems get fixed
- Calls to customer relations
- Negative publicity from angry customers
- Diversion of agents to activities that should be unnecessary
- Agents taking the heat for mistakes made by others
- Bad moves, adds and changes
- Shipping expenses to reship, express mail
- Inaccurate inventory status
- Loss of referrals

The Call Center Process

Another basic tenet of the quality movement is continuous process improvement. The best call centers make the effort to understand their processes and are working to improve them.

A process is a "system of causes." (Note: In the context of quality and process improvement, "system" refers to the system of causes or processes — not a technology.) The call center is part of the organization, which is an expansive system of causes. An agent group is a system of causes within the call center. And each call is comprised of a system of causes. The call center itself is a process, a system of causes.

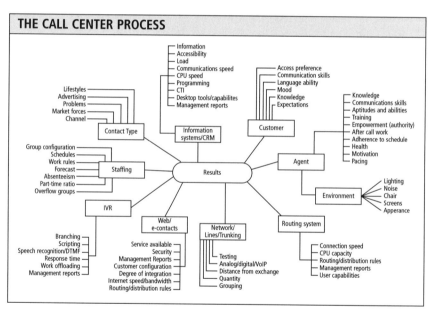

The central focus of the process illustrated in the figure can be any high-level measurement. Note that most of the items are the responsibility of management, not the agents. Also notice that just about everything is interrelated, so the causes of performance problems are often difficult to isolate and measure. The diagram is only one of many ways to depict the call center process.

276

This picture leads to a conclusion that is at the heart of the modern quality movement: There is little use exhorting agents to improve quality without making improvements to the system itself. Most of the things that contribute to quality are out of their hands, such as having good training, the right tools, accurate information and a logical work flow. The system of causes — the process — is where the leverage is. Some call center managers try to force change by setting strict standards for agents. But that will not improve underlying processes and is usually detrimental.

So where do you begin? One place to start is to look at the most important performance indicators (see Chapter 12), and ask some key questions. What are customers complaining about? What are customers suggesting? Where are you making mistakes? What do you want to raise or lower the level of? But tracking results won't inherently improve them. To make improvements, you have to work on the factors that cause these outputs to be where they are. In other words, you have to work at a deeper level — the root causes.

Opportunities for Improvement

Without appropriate tools, identifying the root causes of quality problems in a call center is a significant challenge. Consider a recurring problem, such as providing incomplete information to customers. Maybe the cause is insufficient information in the database. Or a need for more training. Or maybe a lack of coordination with marketing. Or carelessness. Or agent stress from a chronically high occupancy rate. Or a combination of any of these factors, coupled with 1,001 other things!

If the problem is to be fixed, you need to know *what* to fix. Then you can take the necessary corrective actions. The tools that the quality movement has produced over the years are necessary to understand processes and locate the root causes of problems. If you've had any quality training, you are probably well-versed in their use. My purpose here is to summarize ways in which they can be applied in the customer contact environment.

277

FLOW CHART

A flow chart is a "map" of a process used to analyze and standardize procedures, identify root causes of problems and plan new processes. Flow charts are also excellent communication tools, and can help you to visual-

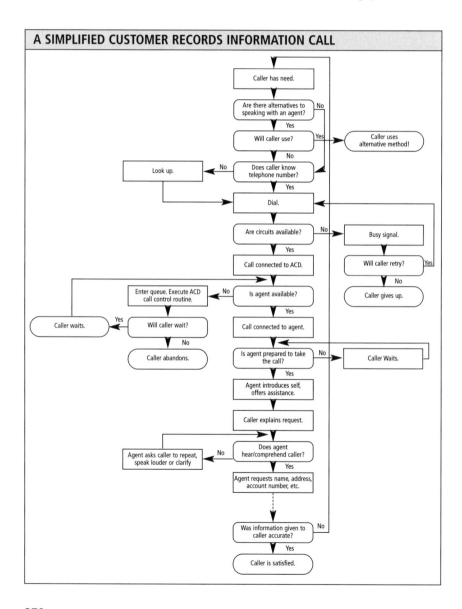

A SIMPLIFIED CUSTOMER RECORDS INFORMATION CALL

ize and understand the flow of a process.

One of the most useful applications for a flow chart is to analyze the specific types of transactions you handle. When most of us think of a "call," we think of a rather simple, singular event. Not so! Even a simple transaction consists of many steps. To really understand a transaction, especially the more complex variety, it is necessary to chart what happens, step by step.

If you haven't charted your contacts by type, give this task to a few of your agents. In fact, put them in a conference room for a couple of hours. Give them a stack of index cards and have them write each step in a typical contact on individual cards, then lay out the cards in order on a large table. In a relatively short period of time, they should be able to tell you where there are procedure inconsistencies, database deficiencies and bottlenecks in the process. Notes on a wall or flow-charting software work well, too. You will eventually want to invest more than a couple of hours in this activity, but this will get you started.

Sometimes a sweeping analysis of all the activities required to handle contacts is in order. With top management support and direction, representatives from the call center, billing and credit, fulfillment, marketing, information systems and other departments can map out interdepartmental and interorganizational processes to identify areas that need overhaul.

Example Applications:

- Contacts, step by step
- The planning and management process
- IVR and ACD programming
- Key procedures

CAUSE-AND-EFFECT DIAGRAM

In 1943, Dr. Kaoru Ishikawa of the University of Tokyo first developed the cause-and-effect diagram, alternatively called a "fishbone diagram" because of its shape. It has since become recognized and used worldwide. The chart illustrates the relationships between causes and a specific effect

279

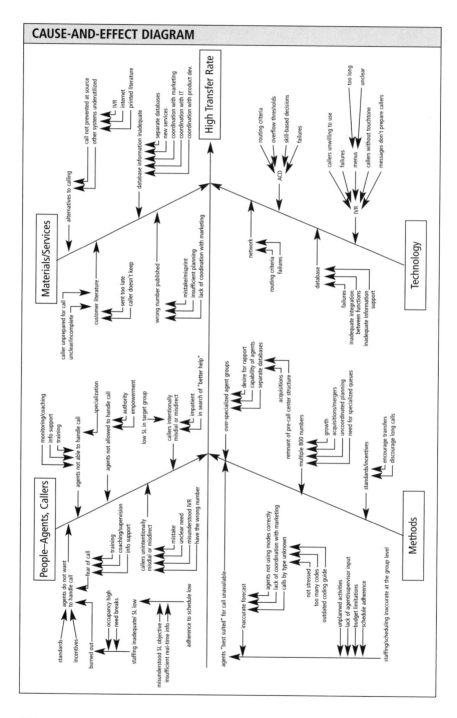

CAUSE-AND-EFFECT DIAGRAM

you want to study. Preparing a cause-and-effect diagram is an education in itself. Everyone who participates will gain new understanding of the process.

The traditional cause categories used in these diagrams are often referred to as the 4Ms: manpower, machines, methods and materials. A variation on these categories — people, technology, methods and materials/services — works better for call centers. However, these labels are only suggestions; you can use any that help your group creatively focus on and think through the problem. Possible causes leading to the effect are drawn as branches off the main category. The final step is to prioritize the causes and work on the most prevalent problems first.

There is no one right way to make a cause-and-effect diagram. A good diagram is one that fits the purpose, and the shape the chart takes will depend on the group (see example).

A "production process classification" diagram is a variation on the traditional cause-and-effect diagram, and the cause categories follow the production process. In the transfer rate example, production categories would include: caller develops the need to call, caller dials and directs, call is routed, call is answered, need is identified by the agent, and so on.

Example Applications:

- Long calls
- Repeat calls
- Poor adherence to schedule
- Inaccurate forecast

SCATTER DIAGRAM

A scatter diagram assesses the strength of the relationship between two variables, and is used to test and document possible cause and effect. The diagram of average handling time in Chapter 6, page 103, is an example.

If there is positive correlation between the two variables, dots will appear as an upward slope. If there is a negative correlation, the dots will appear as a downward slope. The closer the pattern of dots is to a straight line, the stronger the correlation is between the two variables.

Example Applications:

- Average handling time versus experience level
- Average handling time versus revenue generated
- Service level versus error rate
- Experience level versus quality scores

PARETO CHART

Vilfredo Pareto (1848-1923) was an Italian economist whose theories have had widespread impact. One of the better-known results of his work is the Pareto chart, which is a bar chart that ranks the events you are analyzing in order of importance or frequency. For errors by type, you can create two more Pareto charts: cost to fix and time to fix. The Pareto principle dictates that you should work first on the things that will yield the biggest improvements.

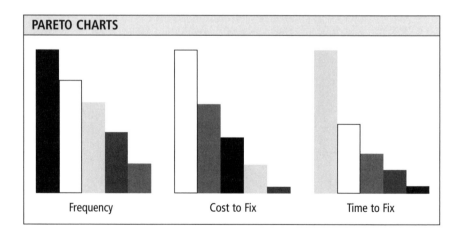

PARETO CHARTS

Frequency   Cost to Fix   Time to Fix

Example Applications:

- Contacts by type
- Errors by type

- Contacts by customer demographics
- Responses to customer surveys

CONTROL CHART

One of the reasons that quality problems in the call center are challenging and often confusing is because they are a part of a complex process, and any process has variation from the ideal. A control chart is a tool that provides information on variation. There are two major types of variation: special causes and common causes. Special causes create erratic, unpredictable variation. For example, an agent with degenerative hearing loss, unusual calls from unexpected publicity, or a computer terminal with intermittent problems are special causes. Common causes are the rhythmic, normal variations in the system.

A control chart enables you to bring a process under statistical control by eliminating the chaos of special causes. You can then work on the common causes by improving the system and thus, the whole process. Special

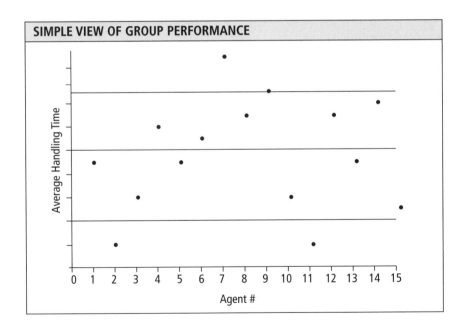

SIMPLE VIEW OF GROUP PERFORMANCE

causes show up as points outside of the upper control or lower control limits, or as points with unnatural patterns within the limits.

A control chart cannot reveal *what* the problems are. Instead, it reveals *where* and *when* special causes occur. Once special causes are eliminated, improving the system itself will have far more impact than focusing on individual causes. Improvements to the system will move the entire process in the right direction.

In short, control charts can:

- Control and reduce variation
- Prevent you from chasing the wrong problem
- Give early warning of changes in the process
- Improve predictability
- Improve planning

There are numerous books and seminars on statistical process control. And for a more philosophical discussion of quality control and insight into the colorful life of the late W. Edwards Deming, read his pivotal work, *Out of the Crisis* (Massachusetts Institute of Technology, Center for Advanced Engineering Study).

Example Applications:

- Average handling time
- Percent adherence
- Percent defective calls (from monitoring)
- Requests for supervisory assistance (transfers)

BENCHMARKING

While many of these tools focus on improvements from within, the idea behind benchmarking is that breakthrough ideas often come from the outside. Benchmarking is the process of measuring your products, services and procedures against those of other organizations.

Keep some cautions in mind: Organizations are different enough, even within a given industry, that universally accepted standards are usually not defensible. Things like labor rates, customer demographics, customer tolerances, trunk and network configurations, hours of operation and the mix of part- and full-time agents vary widely.

Further, organizations often interpret performance measurements differently. What is most important is knowing how the results were achieved, not just what the results are.

With these cautions in mind, a disciplined, focused benchmarking effort can produce the information necessary to make significant improvements in areas such as customer satisfaction and retention, costs and revenues, management processes, metrics used and others. A general approach to benchmarking can be summarized as follows:

DEFINE PROCESSES AND COLLECT PERFORMANCE DATA: This involves getting agreements on processes to be compared and measurements to be used.

ANALYZE COLLECTED DATA AND IDENTIFY BEST PRACTICES: This includes normalizing the raw data for differences, such as currencies, hours of operation, etc., and then identifying the best performers from each category.

PREPARE RECOMMENDATIONS: This entails preparing specific recommendations, based on findings.

APPLY FINDINGS: This involves developing a plan to implement improvements and track results.

Benchmarking, like other aspects of quality improvement, should be an ongoing effort. As the industry improves, what were once cutting-edge practices become the norm. As best practices become generally accepted, they can no longer be considered "best practices."

TOOLS ARE JUST TOOLS

With any of these tools and methods, there is a danger of getting caught up in the tool itself and not moving on to problem resolution. Ensure that

285

DON'T FORGET THE OBOES

A popular trend in process improvement is the effort to correlate specific call center activities to overall customer satisfaction. For example, some consulting organizations have been convincing clients to lower service level objectives because their scatter diagrams demonstrate minimal correlation between overall service level and customer satisfaction results.

The effort to understand how specific activities and measures influence overall results is laudable. But it can be reckless to claim that you've figured out just how much a specific variable impacts customer satisfaction. The late Peter Drucker often used an orchestra analogy to remind us that a manager has the task of creating a whole that is greater than the sum of its parts. "A conductor must always hear both the orchestra and the second oboe," he said. "Can you hear the second oboe?"

There's a fine line here: We need to understand how specific activities impact overall results; but we are being irresponsible if we cut oboes or add trumpets simply because this or that study shows they have X and Y impact on customer satisfaction. As any coach, conductor or artist knows, there's more to it than that.

the tools do not become an end in themselves. Once you identify problems to tackle, you will need to assign clear responsibilities, provide necessary resources and track progress. Results are what matter.

Skills, Knowledge and Leadership

Lasting changes require leadership and management know-how throughout the organization, coupled with a focused set of continuous improvement activities that follow a disciplined problem-solving approach. Making continuous innovations and improvements that lead to services that are faster, better and cheaper is an ongoing process that must be an inherent part of the organization's culture and outlook.

I believe the following points encapsulate the critical factors required to create the organizational understanding and approach necessary for substantial and ongoing improvements. Although you can't boil leadership and culture change down to a simple checklist, there is something powerful about consistently focusing on the things that matter most. (These points were inspired by the well-known work of the late Dr. W. Edwards Deming and, more recently, ICMI Founder Gordon MacPherson, Jr., now enjoying retirement. My hat is off to both of these great thinkers.)

- Develop a global view of your organization's mission and principles. Identify the "big picture" in terms of the organization's mission and direction and how the call center supports overall objectives. Then take steps to ensure that every person understands the "why" behind what they are doing, and how these principles apply to day-to-day tasks and responsibilities.

- Know your job. Analyze and understand every facet of your role and responsibilities. Then do the same for every position in the call center (and the broader organization).

- Recognize that everybody's "best efforts" or just trying harder isn't enough. Look for problems and innovation opportunities in processes. Processes are where the most leverage will be.

- Fully training people to do their jobs is non-negotiable, and comes before everything else. This responsibility cannot become victim to busyness and shifting priorities.

- Use statistical and analytical methods to understand and improve the performance of individuals, the call center and the organization. Don't make decisions based on assumptions — insist on having and using accurate and timely data.

- Ensure that the call center's performance optimizes the good of the organization as a whole, not just of individual projects or departments.

- Remember that those who know processes and customers best are those closest to the work (agents and supervisors). Actively seek their ideas and input, and create an atmosphere of trust and open communication.

- Use performance measurements, monitoring and coaching as a means of learning and improvement at the process level (as well as for individuals). Make decisions based on data and knowledge, not just assumptions.

- As a general rule, don't wait to make sweeping changes all at once. Instead, as possible, make smaller improvements regularly and continuously.

- Encourage maximum personal development of the whole person (e.g., in terms of thinking, analysis, understanding the organization's overall objectives, etc.). This is just as important as job-specific training.

- Strive for and expect never-ending improvements. Build this perspective into the culture.

"This very slight change had worked a revolution. This very slight change had in fact reduced the price of the raw material enormously, and this had rendered it possible, first, to raise the wages of the laborer — a benefit to the country — secondly, to improve the quality of the goods — an advantage for the consumer — and thirdly, to sell them at a lower price even while making three times the profit — a gain for the manufacturer."

VICTOR HUGO, *LES MISERABLES*, 1862

Some will correctly point out that many of these points could form the framework of a Six Sigma initiative (pioneered by Motorola in the early 1980s) or a total quality management (TQM) program (popularized in the late 1980s/early 1990s). Yes, in many ways they could. But be cautious of labels — the most popular management movements (e.g., TQM, reengineering, CRM, etc.) tend to eventually collapse under their own weight. But many of the core methodologies and principles behind these movements are useful and have staying power (see the excerpt from *Les Miserables*). Stick with the principles that are truly useful, inculcate them into your culture, instill them into your plans and thinking.

Building Strategic Value

Recall from the first chapter that customer contact centers have the potential to create value on three distinct levels: efficiency, customer satisfaction and business unit value (strategic value). Level three — working with other business units — is where you can truly begin to leverage the call center's potential to deliver strategic value to the organization.

As a primary customer touch point, the call center has significant potential to provide other business units with valuable intelligence and support. This can include input on customers, products, services and processes — information that, when captured, identified, assimilated and turned into usable knowledge — can literally transform an organization's ability to identify and meet customer expectations and demands.

The table, "Potential Contribution to Other Business Units," summarizes key benefits and support that the call center can provide to other business units. Many of these issues involve capturing, disseminating and using the information captured in the course of interacting with customers.

The benefits can be significant — and varied. For example, consider the impact when the call center:

- Helps operational areas or manufacturing units pinpoint and fix quality problems, which boosts customer satisfaction and repeat purchases, reduces costs associated with warranties and repairs and prevents unnecessary contacts to the call center.

- Helps marketing develop more effective campaigns. For example, having a better understanding of what customers need and want, and ensuring that marketing efforts target best prospects can improve response rates, reduce relative marketing costs, and even help the organization boost market share.

- Serves as an early warning system of potential legal troubles. Product defects, reactions to food or prescription drugs, security holes discovered in a firm's Web site, inaccuracies in warranty statements or customer invoices — the list could go on for pages, and the call center is often first to hear of these issues. Having strong, collaborative ties to other areas of the organization is a prerequisite to handling them as quickly and effectively as possible.

- Helps research and development (R&D) identify customer needs and the firm's competitive advantages and disadvantages. In many ways, focus groups, market research and traditional broad-based surveys are no match for the intelligence the call center can capture through interactions with hundreds or even thousands of prospects and/or customers. This input can ultimately help the organization focus on providing better products and services to better defined customer segments — favorably impacting costs, revenues, marketshare and even the organization's reputation and brand.

- Enables the organization to improve self-service systems, based on the specific assistance the call center provides to customers who opt out of or need help with these systems. This not only lowers the costs of providing customer service — it can also boost customer satisfaction and ensure that the call center has the capacity to focus on issues that really require or benefit from agent involvement.

In short, when the call center has an eye on the larger implications of quality and innovation, it will positively impact the *entire organization's* workload, productivity and quality.

POTENTIAL CONTRIBUTION TO OTHER BUSINESS UNITS	
Business Unit	**The Call Center Provides These Benefits...**
Marketing	• Provides detailed information on customer demographics • Tracks trends (purchases, customer service and support issues, etc.) and response rates • Enables permission-based, targeted marketing • Supports segmentation/branding • Provides customer input on competitors • Provides customer surveys and feedback
Financial	• Captures cost and revenue information by customer segment • Contributes to the control of overall costs • Serves as an early warning system (positive and negative) • Is essential to successful mergers and acquisitions • Contributes to shareholder value through strategic value contributions • Is essential in establishing budgetary strategy and priorities
HR/Training	• Contributes to recruiting and hiring initiatives • Contributes to skill and career path development • Contributes to coaching and mentoring processes and expertise • Helps foster a learning organization (e.g., through systems, processes and pooled expertise on products and customers) • Contributes to training and HR expertise and processes
Manufacturing/ Operations	• Pinpoints quality and/or production problems • Provides input on products' and services' usability and clarity • Contributes to manuals and procedures • Highlights distribution problems and opportunities • Facilitates communication related to capacity or production problems

(continued next page)

Research & Development (R&D)/Design	• Provides information on competitive direction and trends • Highlights product compatibility issues and opportunities • Provides customer feedback on usability • Differentiates between features and benefits from the customer's perspective • Identifies product and service differentiation opportunities
IT/Telecom	• Furthers organizationwide infrastructure development • Furthers self-service usage and system design • Provides a concentrated technology learning ground • Provides the essential human bridge between diverse processes and systems • Is a key driver in IT/Telecom investments
Legal	• Enables consistent and accurate customer communications and policies • Serves as an early warning system of quality problems • Identifies and addresses impending customer problems • Provides a rapid response to news/media reports • Contributes to internal communication • Serves as a training ground for customer service policies

Some organizations have made this level of contribution a priority for years. For example, the GE Answer Center has been, since the mid-1980s, capturing information in the call center and using it for everything from product improvements to targeted marketing campaigns. Similarly, Amazon.com, for years now, has referred to their call centers as "R&D machines," providing information useful for continuously improving services, processes and self-service capabilities. Intuit, a leader in financial management and accounting software for small businesses and consumers, has a long history of developing products that are based in large part on the input of customers and agent feedback. Sallie Mae, the United States' largest provider of financial loans, has improved everything from self-service capabilities to the clarity of correspondence with customers through the help of the call center. Some government agencies and others in non-commercial environments (e.g., not-for-profit organizations) discovered long ago that they, too, can benefit enormously from the call center's potential to help streamline processes and services across the board and enable the organization to stretch limited resources.

Even so, I believe that the call center profession is only beginning to discover the powerful contributions that are possible. And those furthest along are the first to point out that there's a lot more potential to discover. The processes, technologies and human know-how behind capturing, deciphering, communicating and using intelligence from customer contacts are works in progress.

How do you leverage the potential your call center has? A number of key lessons are emerging:

- Seek first to understand. Develop good working relationships with the individuals who run other areas of the organization. Learn about their goals and objectives and how the call center might best support their needs.

- Build an understanding of the call center's role and potential. Ensure that the prevailing perspective is that the role of the call center is to serve, not to point out flaws — while that may be obvious to those in the call center, you'll want to emphasize it from the start.

- Build a team that is focused on capturing, analyzing, sharing and using value-added information across the organization. A suggested ratio is that you need one business analyst for every 30 to 50 agents — that will depend on many factors, of course, but the right ratios and resources will become more clear once you get the ball rolling.

- Ensure that quality at the point of customer contact is given the broadest possible definition — e.g., that coaching, monitoring and objectives at the agent level support these major strategic opportunities.

- Footnote assumptions and unknowns in reports and data. Ensure that everyone understands where the data came from and what considerations are present. Strategic decisions based on misinterpreted reports can be worse than if there were no reports at all.

- Get the best tools you can. Analytics capabilities and performance management systems can help you analyze content, detect trends and causal factors, and identify improvement opportunities. Get started, even if you don't have these capabilities — but work toward acquiring and building supporting technologies, as feasible.

- Ensure the information is useful and usable, based on an ongoing commitment to understand business requirements and how to turn mounds of call center data and "call center-esque" codes into actionable information.

- Don't get overwhelmed. There is an infinite amount of information that you could provide to each business unit. Instead of focusing on quantity (by trying to ensure that everything that may be valuable is shared) concentrate on providing just the information that is likely to be most useful.

Every customer contact your center handles provides implicit and/or direct insight into processes, products, policies, services, customers and the external environment. You have the opportunity to play a central role in building a stronger organization with better services and products across the board — but it's a role that must be earned.

This is not a new area of call center management — but then neither is improving customer loyalty or building innovative products and services. Contributing valuable information to strategic business units will remain on the forefront of call center management because the contacts we handle today represent the latest read on our customers and how well we're serving their needs in an ever-changing external environment.

Shhhh... The Real Secret

What's the real secret to improving call center performance? Instilling the principles covered in this chapter into your organization, and *sticking to them* — day after day, month after month, year after year. It's a never-ending journey — and an exciting one, because it prepares your organization for the unknowns ahead even as it delivers better results today.

Points to Remember

- Quality is built around customer expectations. Since customer expectations are constantly evolving, the definition of quality must also evolve.

- Quality and service level/response time work together. Over the long term, good quality improves service level/response time by reducing waste and rework. And a good service level/response time provides an environment in which high quality can be achieved.

- The process is where the leverage is. There is little use in exhorting agents to improve quality without making improvements to the "system of causes," or process.

- Use the tools to find and fix root causes. Flow charts, cause-and-effect diagrams, scatter diagrams, Pareto charts and control charts are especially useful for identifying the root causes of quality problems in a call center.

- Your employees are the most important source of call center success, now and in the future. Lasting changes require leadership and management know-how throughout the organization.

- Call centers have enormous potential to deliver strategic value to the organization, through information and intelligence that can be shared with and applied in other business units.

CHAPTER 14:
Boosting Individual Performance

It's a self-fulfilling prophecy — if a leader really believes that people can do more, they'll begin to expect more from themselves.

ROBERT TOWNSEND IN *REINVENTING LEADERSHIP*

The subject of measuring and managing the performance of individuals has always been hotly debated among call center professionals. Since performance measurements are usually tied to behavioral expectations and standards, many issues enter the discussion — e.g., fairness; which measurements are truly under an individual's control; individual capabilities, drives and motivators; and the efficacy of the processes they are working within. Few subjects elicit such strong and varied opinions.

As a result, there are numerous sets of performance measurements and standards in place, even among call centers with similar functions. But there are also consistent principles at work in call centers that are getting the best results. In this chapter, we'll look at the issues behind several distinct trends, and discuss how the right performance measures and expectations encourage the right behaviors and ensure that the entire team is moving in the same direction.

Agent Performance Measures

Number of contacts handled (e.g., calls per hour or calls per day) used

297

to be an almost universal productivity measurement in call centers. In fact, many call center managers viewed contacts handled as virtually synonymous with productivity. While there always have been concerns about sacrificing quality for quantity, contacts handled has been the preferred benchmark for establishing productivity standards, comparing performance among agents and groups, and assessing the impact of changes and improvements to the call center.

But as a measure of performance, contacts handled is (and always has been) problematic, for several reasons. First, as is often pointed out, when the number of contacts handled is overemphasized, quality can suffer. Agents may even trick the system to increase their call count in order to achieve a standard or incentive.

Second, many of the variables that impact contacts handled are out of agents' control. These include call arrival rate, contact types, customers' knowledge, customers' communication abilities, the accuracy of the forecast and schedule, and the adherence to schedule of others in the agent group.

Further, several mathematical realities are also at work that are not within agents' control. As discussed in Chapter 9, small groups are less efficient (have lower occupancy) than larger groups at a given service level. Since the number of calls is changing throughout the day, so are the calls-per-hour averages for a group or individuals within a group.

As a measure of performance, contacts handled is (and always has been) problematic.

Some call center managers convert raw calls handled into normalized calls handled (sometimes called "true calls handled") — an adjusted measurement that can be more fair and meaningful. For example, occupancy, which is not within the control of an individual, can be neutralized by dividing calls handled by percent occupancy. Using the numbers in the table, 5.6 average calls per agent divided by 65 percent occupancy (first row) is 8.6 normalized calls, as is 6.7 calls divided by 78 percent, 7.7 calls divided by 90 percent, and 8.1 calls divided by 94 percent. Other managers go a step further and develop statistical control charts to determine whether the process is in control, what it's producing, and which agents, if any, are outside of statistical control.

Calls in Half-Hour	Service Level	Agents Required	Occupancy	Avg. Calls Per Agent
50	80/20	9	65%	5.6
100	80/20	15	78%	6.7
500	80/20	65	90%	7.7
1,000	80/20	124	94%	8.1
Assumption: Calls last an average 3.5 minutes.				

However, even with these efforts to ensure fairness, contacts handled begins to lose meaning as multiple contact channels, skills-based routing, call blending and other capabilities proliferate, resulting in increasingly sophisticated and varied types of interactions.

QUICK QUIZ ON AGENT CONTROL OVER CONTACTS HANDLED

Check the boxes next to items over which agents have real control.
- ❑ Adherence to schedule (their own)
- ❑ Number of staff scheduled to answer calls
- ❑ Average talk time (their own)
- ❑ Number of calls coming in
- ❑ Distribution of long calls and short calls
- ❑ Distribution of easy calls and difficult calls

299

For managers who have depended on contacts handled as the basis for performance measurement, this has left a vacuum: How can you measure productivity in an increasingly varied and complex environment? For a growing number of call centers, the answer is a combination of adherence to schedule and qualitative measures.

Adherence and Qualitative Measures

Adherence to schedule is a measurement of how much time during an agent's shift he or she is handling contacts or available to handle contacts For example, if adherence to schedule is expected to be 90 percent, each agent should be available to handle contacts .90 x 60 minutes, or 54 minutes on average, per scheduled hour.

Adherence consists of time spent in talk time, after-call work, waiting for calls to arrive, and placing necessary outgoing calls. Lunch, breaks, training, etc., are not counted as time assigned to handle contacts, and are not factored into the measurement. (Be sure to differentiate the terms "adherence to schedule" and "agent occupancy." They are two different things. In fact, when adherence to schedule goes up, service level will go up, which drives occupancy down. See Chapter 9.)

Adherence and qualitative measurements make a powerful pair. They can effectively replace contacts handled, average call-handling time and other measures of output.

Adherence can also incorporate the issue of timing — when was a person available to take calls? This is sometimes called "schedule compliance." The idea is to ensure that agents are plugged in not only for the amount of time required, but when required.

Adherence to schedule should be established at levels that are reasonable and that reflect the many things that legitimately keep agents from the phones. It should also be flexible (e.g., adjustable downward) when the workload is light.

A primary advantage of adherence factor is that it is a reasonably objective measurement. Agents cannot control how many calls are coming in, how grouchy or nice callers are, the types of calls they will handle, how accurate resource planning is, and so on — but they are (in most situations) in control of being in the right place at the right time.

Agents at long last feel they are being assessed on the two things they can control: being in the right place at the right times and handling contacts that come their way with quality.

Enter the issue of quality. In most call centers, qualitative criteria continue to become more refined and specific. An important and developing aspect of quality is that agents take the necessary time to handle contacts correctly. This, of course, means not rushing calls. But it also means not spending time on calls over and above what is required to satisfy callers and handle transactions completely and correctly. (Remember the three essential quality questions from Chapter 13? Quality is identifying, then meeting, customer expectations, using the fewest possible resources.)

If agents have the skills to effectively manage and control calls, and qualitative measurements are refined enough to measure whether or not agents are doing this proficiently, then adherence and qualitative measurements make a powerful pair. They can effectively replace contacts handled, average call-handling time and other measures of output.

By focusing on adherence and quality, other measures — such as average handling time, number of calls taken, percent of time spent in talk time and percent of time spent in after-call work — tend to take care of themselves. Case in point — if you want to increase the number of contacts agents are handling, that will take you right back to: a) their availability to take contacts; and b) how they handle the contacts that come their way.

301

The number of contacts they take will be a byproduct of those two factors. Similarly, if you want to impact average handling time, you will need to go back to the way agents are handling contacts and the processes they are working within.

When quality and adherence to schedule objectives replace other performance standards that are outputs, agents' energies are focused on the factors that they directly control. Instead of worrying about this number looking good and that number lagging, they can focus on doing their job. (Besides, there are plenty of ways agents can trick the system, just as there are numerous ways managers can tinker with call center reports to relay just about any message they want.)

WAYS AGENTS CAN TRICK THE SYSTEM

- Call other agents
- Hit available, click off the call
- Let "phantom calls" look like they are handled
- Remain available, then hit unavailable to go to back of queue
- Don't disconnect after caller is gone
- Put caller on hold without saying "hello"
- Instead of completing a transfer, remain silently on line
- Park call on somebody else's extension
- Tell caller system is down when it isn't
- Using logon code for a group with lower productivity
- "Hello, hello… I can't hear you. Please call back."
- When lots of calls are waiting, hit available twice to get credit for two calls

---

Assuming adherence and quality objectives are implemented fairly and appropriately, agents will feel they are being assessed on the two things they can do something about: being in the right place at the right times and handling contacts that come their way with quality. (Notice the parallels between individual objectives and the two themes that come out of the def-

> **KEEP IT SIMPLE**
>
> I am seeing efforts in many call centers to streamline and simplify agent performance standards. In many cases, they have become too complex — weighted averages, percent time in this and that mode, formulas that would take a mathematician to figure out. Yes, if I'm one of your agents, I need objectives on being in the right place at the right times (schedule adherence), and doing the right things (quality). Beyond that, give me an understanding of your business, the unique environment I'm part of, and the importance of my contribution. I'll produce good numbers and, more importantly, I'll produce good business results. As Dee Hock, founder and former CEO of VISA, once put it, "Simple, clear purpose and principles give rise to complex and intelligent behavior; complex rules and regulations give rise to simple and stupid behavior."

inition of call center management introduced in Chapter 1: Get the right resources in the right places at the right times, do the right things.)

Many managers still believe that tracking production outputs, such as contacts handled or average handling time, is necessary. And there's an important distinction — tracking these measures at a management level for trending and process control efforts *is* recommended — but that's a far cry from setting performance standards at the agent level. The trend is clear: Well-defined qualitative measurements, coupled with measures of adherence to schedule, are supplanting standards that are mere after-the-fact outputs.

Of course, focusing on adherence and quality is not feasible in environments where these measurements are vague and indeterminate. They must be implemented fairly, and with foresight and care.

Using Adherence Measurements

The main objective of adherence to schedule is to ensure that agents are in the right place at the right time, doing the right things. In principle, it's a fair standard. But it must be implemented judiciously, or it can backfire in a *big* way.

TERMINOLOGY

Many call center managers define adherence to schedule differently, and the terms used can vary. Adherence to schedule is a general term that can refer to either (or both) of the following:

1. *The amount of time* in the course of a shift that agents were available to handle contacts. Alternative terms include "availability" and "plugged-in time."

2. *When* agents were available, during their shift. Alternative terms include "schedule compliance" or just "adherence." (I often use the term adherence interchangeably with adherence to schedule — in other words, in the general sense.)

Virtually all call centers that have adherence-to-schedule objectives track the amount of time agents are available, and many also incorporate the issue of timing. Further, there's some latitude for using different variables or activities that qualify as adherent.

Average adherence should be determined individually and for each agent group. Sometimes individuals need specific coaching or training that is not necessary for the whole group. And tracking adherence as an average for the group reveals how well management is doing in creating an environment in which appropriate adherence objectives can be achieved.

Be sure to include after-call work as a part of adherence, along with talk time and the time agents spend waiting for contacts to arrive. After-call work, when defined appropriately, is a legitimate part of handling time (see Chapter 6). Putting a ceiling on it can be detrimental to quality. If you feel it is too high, you should investigate what is causing it to be where it is, and make appropriate process improvements, or adjustments to training.

GETTING GOOD RESULTS

Real-time schedule adherence monitoring capabilities are available in many workforce management systems. With this capability, the software collects real-time information from the routing system(s), compares it to the work schedule and reports variations. Exception reports are based on user-defined thresholds. For example, if an agent is supposed to be back from break at 10:15, and you set a five-minute grace period, your screen will highlight that person's name at 10:20 if he or she isn't back, ready to handle calls.

Some managers view real-time monitoring systems as *the answer* to the adherence issue. And workforce management vendors sometimes push them hard. But that perspective can be incompatible with the circumstances in a modern contact center. Empowered agents with high levels of skills and training are increasingly more common in today's environment. Monitoring their comings and goings can be reminiscent of strict industrial-era standards.

I am not suggesting that you shouldn't use adherence-monitoring technology. But it is best utilized as a tool to provide information to the supervisory team. That's where adjustments are best made. The alternative is to have strict mandates and tracking at a level above supervisory teams, and have your supervisors spend valuable time filling out "exception reports."

So, how *do* you get good adherence to schedule? I believe there are a number of important prerequisites:

1. Train each agent on how much impact he or she has on the queue, and therefore, the importance of adherence to schedule (see Chapter 9).
2. Establish concrete service level and response time objectives that everybody knows and understands (see Chapter 4).
3. Educate agents on the essential steps involved in resource planning so that they understand how schedules are produced.
4. Develop appropriate priorities for the wide range of tasks that your agents handle.

5. Provide real-time service level information to agents and back it up with training on how to interpret the information, and what the corresponding actions should be.

6. Track and manage schedule adherence at the supervisory group (team) level, as conditions dictate.

7. Track schedule adherence for the entire agent group for planning purposes and to assess how well management has created a process that enables appropriate schedule adherence.

In summary, adherence to schedule is an important objective. But setting strict standards and watching every move individuals make is generally not the best way to get good results.

Measuring Quality

Most call centers use some form of call evaluation, typically monitoring (e.g., silent, with a beep tone, side-by-side or, increasingly, record-and-review), to evaluate the qualitative aspects of call handling, and to identify training and coaching needs. But there is at least some ongoing controversy surrounding the subject of monitoring. (Understandably, many managers don't like the term either, preferring alternatives such as "quality assurance.")

Here is ICMI's take on the subject (and, we suspect, the view of most call center managers):

- Monitoring is not inherently good or evil.
- Whether or not monitoring results are useful or meaningful depends on why and how it is conducted.
- Intentional and unintentional abuses of monitoring do occur, which everyone in the call center management profession should condemn and work to prevent.
- Managers have a responsibility to review the quality of service that agents provide to customers.

ICMI'S RECOMMENDED MONITORING PRACTICES

- Inform job candidates of the monitoring process.
- Cover the monitoring program in detail during agent orientation, and allow new-hires to monitor and assess contacts using the monitoring form.
- Determine whether or not to tell agents when they are being monitored, in accordance with individual preferences.
- Advise agents that the call center's business lines will be monitored, and where to find unmonitored lines for personal calls.
- Monitoring equipment should only monitor what is said on the line, not what is said by the agent between calls at his/her workstation.
- Permit only qualified personnel to monitor for quality or to evaluate the results of monitoring.
- Clearly inform agents about the purpose of monitoring, how it is conducted and how the results are used. Post the organization's written monitoring policies for all employees to see, and have them sign off on it when they are hired.
- Do not publicly post monitoring results by name or other data that could identify an individual.
- Do not single out an individual agent for unsatisfactory performance detected by monitoring when the unsatisfactory performance is common to the group.
- Use standardized and consistently applied evaluation forms and monitoring techniques.
- Use objective criteria in evaluation forms and techniques.
- Monitor all agents periodically to determine where the performance level of the group is centered. This level is management's responsibility. New-hires, agents whose performance indicates a need for more training and coaching, and agents who request it should be monitored more frequently.
- Give feedback promptly.
- Conduct regular calibration sessions to ensure consistency and fairness.

(continued next page)

> • Permit only personnel with a legitimate business need to monitor calls
> for orientation purposes. Examples are: new call center personnel who
> will be involved with call handling, consultants working on
> improvements and visitors approved by management who are studying
> the call center's operations.

RATING SYSTEMS

Monitoring results can be numerically evaluated in a variety of ways. Basically, the methods can be categorized into one of three groups: 1) scores based on pass or fail; 2) scores based on weighted values for each item; and 3) scores based on the proportion or number correct or incorrect.

Pass/fail is a relatively cut-and-dried approach, assuming the criteria are not overly subjective. If agents score above a set threshold, they pass. If not, they fail. Passing would be equivalent to meeting the minimum expectations of the call, or just "good enough." Some pass/fail advocates take a hard line, and declare that if an agent fails on just one item, the entire contact must be rated defective. Others take a much more lenient (and potentially less effective) approach and look at the overall result.

Proponents of the second method — scores based on weighted values for each item — believe the pass/fail method is inappropriate because it doesn't take into account how different items impact quality. For example, getting correct information from the customer might be much more important than using his or her name several times during the call. With weighted values, management can produce reports that track quality levels in individual performance categories, beyond simply tracking defective calls.

With the third scoring method, the number of items correct or incorrect is expressed as a proportion of the total possible number of quality criteria. Incorrect items are called defects. Some carry this approach a step further and categorize failures or defects as critical or fatal (e.g., not entering an order quantity correctly) or non-critical (e.g., misspelling a name). Those who argue against this method say that it doesn't recognize the degree of contribution each item makes to quality. But proponents point out that it's much better than an overall pass/fail system, and more objective (and potentially easier to manage) than a method that assigns values to each criterion.

There is room for opinion, and we've seen all three methods work well — or poorly. But we generally prefer that score results be based on the proportion of defects. The pass/fail method doesn't provide enough information about calls and trends to guide you in making improvements at the individual and process levels. And methods that assign a value to each item are, too often, overly subjective.

ALTERNATIVES TO MONITORING

Here are some of the alternatives that call centers are using to supplement traditional monitoring efforts:

- Provide name at the beginning of the call, establishing a sense of accountability.
- Provide opportunity for callers to take short IVR surveys or leave record messages about their experience, after the call.
- Managers walk the floor and observe the "agent side" of calls. This gives only one side of the conversation, but does provide a feel for what is happening.
- Managers sit down and plug in with agents, to catch them "doing things right."
- Agents simulate calls and role-play situations in training.
- Incentives are provided at the team level, making each agent accountable for others in the group.
- "Mystery shoppers" from outside firms pose as customers and provide a report on their experiences.
- New-hires or agents who are struggling are seated next to top performers.

LEVERAGING THE EFFORT

As qualitative measures become increasingly important, it is essential to get good results from your monitoring efforts. The following are some important steps you can take.

INVOLVE AGENTS IN THE PROCESS. Without exception, call centers that have the most effective monitoring programs are those that involve agents in the process. Some call centers use peer monitoring, where agents take turns evaluating each other's calls. Others use reverse monitoring, where agents monitor supervisors or team leaders. Others have agents monitor and score their own recorded calls. Many call centers incorporate monitoring into their training programs, and have groups of agents independently score recorded calls and discuss results.

> **GETTING GOOD RESULTS FROM MONITORING**
>
> - Involve agents in the process
> - Refine qualitative criteria
> - Check the process
> - Take a good sample
> - Fix problems at the group level
> - Correlate monitoring results to other key measures

Putting agents into your shoes, so to speak, taps into two phenomena. First, the better your agents understand and buy into the quality criteria, the easier it will be for them to excel. Second, agents will become their own in-process inspectors, correcting problems before they happen. Agents buy into the monitoring process to the degree that it helps them identify areas that need improvement, and recognizes and rewards them for the things that are going well. And, as the quality movement has stated so clearly, those closest to the work understand it best.

REFINE QUALITATIVE CRITERIA. In some call centers, agents get coaching only when there is a serious problem. Further, neither agents nor supervisors can identify specific, agreed-upon components of a quality call — they just "sort of know" when a call goes as it should. Because most

FROM "BIG BROTHER" TO THE "GOOD GUYS" AT STARBUCKS

Want to transform your QA team "from big brother to the good guys?" That's how Beverly Stryker, quality assurance and training manager at Starbucks Coffee Company, describes the enormous changes that took place at Starbucks' customer contact center after they involved their representatives in developing a new program.

One of the first responsibilities of the newly assembled task force — which included representatives from all three business areas that the center supports (Starbucks Card, Warranty Services and Starbucks Customer Relations) — was to develop a QA mission statement, which includes the following:

- Define individual and team training needs to improve and recognize competencies and to relay non-restrictive flow of information
- Improve efficiencies and customer satisfaction through effective partner tools and resources
- Conduct timely and consistent coaching, done with respect and dignity with the goal of instilling and maintaining confidence and empowerment
- Assure correct, clear and professional interactions with customers to increase confident and satisfying relationships.

The team also created new scoring forms and helped to establish expectations for each group. These and other aspects of the initiative — e.g., developing a strong partnership between the QA department and the supervisors (who do the coaching at the agent level), focusing on development versus "catching them doing things wrong," and acquiring a quality monitoring system that saves time and improves consistency — have won the support and commitment of agents throughout the center. As one of the warranty services representatives puts it, "I feel comfortable knowing that every customer will receive the legendary service they've come to expect from Starbucks."

agents produce reasonably good calls most of the time, few get positive reinforcement on things that are specifically going well or additional guidance on things that can use some work.

One way to identify more specific and useful monitoring criteria is to create a flow chart of the major types of calls you are taking (see Chapter 13). The flow chart will identify aspects of the call-handling process that need improvement.

CHECK THE PROCESS. Does your monitoring program reflect, in a consistent and unbiased way, what is really going on in the call center? To find out, conduct a simple experiment. Have those who do the evaluations independently score five recorded calls. Then, compare the results. If the scores are significantly different, take the system back to the shop for a tune-up or overhaul. Until you do, you'll be getting mixed results and wasting time and effort. Or worse, you'll be alienating agents who don't trust the results and who aren't getting the recognition and help they need.

TAKE A GOOD SAMPLE. Since monitoring is a sample and does not provide a 100 percent check of every call, it is important to get a representative sampling that accurately reflects activity. You have a responsibility to gather enough observations to obtain useful information, spot trends and provide meaningful feedback to your agents. Monitoring takes time, and often only gets done when things aren't so busy; e.g., when service level is decent and there aren't a zillion calls stacked up in queue.

Of course, the call center atmosphere and the way contacts are handled can take on a different tone when service level is low, occupancy is high and the pressure is on. That's when you really need a good sample, so be sure to include samples from busy periods.

Another requirement to get a good sample is to monitor everyone consistently, including the most experienced agents and the top performers. This is necessary to determine where the group's performance level is centered. New-hires and poor performers may need extra monitoring and coaching, but set an objective for the minimum number of times you monitor every agent. According to ICMI surveys, many call centers monitor around four to six contacts per agent, per month — a figure that I tend to

THE HIRING, TRAINING AND COACHING TRIFECTA

As is often pointed out, the best call centers do a great job of hiring, training and coaching. But the point that is sometimes understated is the degree to which these processes depend on and benefit each other.

Consider hiring. An effective recruiting and hiring process ensures that your call center will have the right people for the job. Without it, you'll be placing a huge burden on training and coaching — and those processes will, most likely, be focused on the bare essentials. With it, you'll be assembling a team that, with the right training and support, can work together effectively, support and further the organization's culture, and adapt and change as the customer contact environment evolves.

Some underlying trends have resulted in training becoming increasingly important in the customer contact environment. One that is likely obvious to most is that the environment is becoming more complex, requiring robust training that provides a strong and effective base of know-how for employees. A more subtle trend is that many call center managers are placing greater emphasis on finding agents who support and further the culture of the organization and then training them on appropriate skills — rather than finding those with the right skills but who may not fit as well into the culture and environment.

Effective coaching is in-the-trenches, hands-on and directly focused on specific problems, solutions and opportunities. There's no hiding from the details, no glossing over the issues at this level. Coaching provides valuable insight into the hiring process by helping to identify the traits and makeup of employees who perform best. And it can and must be a primary feeder of training — identifying improvement opportunities, gaps that must be addressed, practical lessons-learned, and other issues that are leveraged when they are addressed at the group (not just individual) level.

In short, hiring, training and coaching are interrelated aspects of an overall effort. They work best when they are viewed and managed as such.

believe is too low in many cases. But suffice it to say, this figure varies widely depending on the purpose of the program and the resources available.

Automated monitoring systems can be a big help. These systems electronically record and store calls automatically, eliminating the need for real-time agent monitoring. Contacts are captured based on business rules that dictate which agents to monitor, when and how often. The recordings are accessed and reviewed according to the monitor's schedule.

FIX PROBLEMS AT THE GROUP LEVEL. It's essential, of course, to tie coaching activities to monitoring results. However, in too many cases, monitoring tends to be overly focused on individuals: "Joe, you're doing a great job. You were helpful; you identified the caller's need correctly. Just a couple of things to work on..." However, this method may be inefficient and erratic, as it fixes problems that may be common to the whole group — one agent at a time.

An infinitely more powerful way to leverage the monitoring process is to have a mechanism for getting the assessments back to someone who can analyze results for the entire group. Problems common to many agents can be addressed more efficiently at the group level through process improvement; e.g., group training, restructuring system tools, identifying skill issues or other improvements.

Begin analyzing group assessments by ranking the most common errors in order of frequency. This will identify training and improvement priorities.

You may also benefit from creating a statistical control chart of the group's scores and plotting each person's performance on the chart (as discussed in Chapter 13). Agents outside the control limits will need individual attention. But if they are within the limits, it's a problem common to the group that requires a solution at the group level.

CORRELATE MONITORING RESULTS TO OTHER KEY MEASURES. An important part of leveraging your quality-improvement efforts is to compare monitoring results to other key call center measures. For example, compare monitoring scores to:

• Customer input and satisfaction surveys

- Service level
- Average handling time
- Experience level

Is there a correlation? In what way? Some call center managers have discovered that when service level drops significantly, quality scores begin to fall. Others have noticed that scores improve during agents' initial months with the call center, and then begin to plateau. You will gain new insights by investigating these correlations.

USING AGENT-LEVEL CUSTOMER FEEDBACK

Unbeknownst to them, customers are becoming coaches. While, historically, call centers have relied solely on supervisors and/or quality assurance specialists to rate contacts and provide agents with feedback, Hilton Reservations, Wells Fargo Banker Connection and other progressive centers are going straight to the source to find out just how a particular agent performed on a call, email, chat session or other type of contact.

Gathering agent-level customer feedback typically involves a brief survey (usually around five to 10 questions) that focuses on a specific transaction that took place between an agent and a customer, and that seeks to find out how satisfied the customer was with that contact and/or agent. These surveys typically include questions that are related to the key criteria also included on the call center's monitoring form. Common survey methods include outbound calls, IVR surveys or Web/email surveys.

One of the main reasons why such feedback is a hit in call centers is that it is a hit with *agents*. Most find it much easier to accept an assessment of their performance that includes feedback from the person who was directly involved in the contact, rather than from a third-party observer alone. And the more palatable and trusted a performance assessment is, the more likely an agent is to accept it and to strive to improve.

Terri McMillan, a senior vice president with Wells Fargo Banker Connection, points to the connection between customer feedback and a

(continued next page)

---

stronger QA program overall. "The management benefit of tying customer surveys directly to QA evaluations is the enhanced calibration between the customer experience and QA, and the added confidence it gives our specialists in the QA program," she says. "The real bonus is in sharing customer survey scores and verbatim comments with specialists to reinforce coaching, incorporate into performance measurements and spotlight specialists through recognition!"

OTHER JOB ROLES

What about assessing performance for those in other positions, e.g., analysts, trainers and managers? How does the reality of overlapping responsibilities (discussed in Chapter 12) translate into performance standards for individuals and teams? On one hand, every person has a bearing on call center performance objectives. On the other, is it fair to set performance standards on things that are outside the direct control of an individual?

In principle — and in practice — the answer is fairly simple. Managers are inherently responsible for achieving results through other people. Consequently, the senior-level call center managers/director are generally held responsible for the full repertoire of call center performance objectives that the organization establishes. Of course, they shouldn't be held accountable for objectives that are in conflict or that are mutually exclusive. And they can only accomplish what is possible within the context of the resources they have to work with. But, by nature, they answer for overall results.

Managers and analysts in supporting roles are in a similar situation; however, with more specific responsibilities, accountabilities are generally associated with the areas in which they have primary responsibility. For example, the workforce manager in charge of forecasting and scheduling is generally accountable for the accuracy of the forecast (among other things) even though it is influenced by many variables, people and departments outside of their immediate control. Even so, if the forecast is way off the

TWO APPROACHES TO SETTING PERFORMANCE STANDARDS

Since performance standards impact everything from pay and promotions to training and coaching, they must be chosen carefully. It is important not to focus on average performance when setting performance expectations at the job level. For one thing, average performance may or may not meet the objectives of the call center. Further, by nature, about half of a group will be performing above average and about half below — regardless of the actual proficiency with which the group is performing. Instead, you should generally use one of the following two methods to set individual performance objectives:

1. Minimum standard: Determine the minimum performance standard that will achieve call center objectives. Then, use this method for establishing objectives.

2. Acceptable range: Determine a range of acceptable performance. The range then becomes the guide to establishing objectives. Training or other actions will be necessary for individuals who fall below the acceptable range. Those above the range are either shortchanging the process, or are role models for training and process improvement efforts that can be applied to the rest of the group.

mark, they need to have answers as to why — and recommendations on how it can be improved.

Given overlapping responsibilities in call centers, high-performance centers put much more emphasis on processwide improvements than strict output quotas (e.g., handling X contacts or keeping handling time under N seconds). They work hard to educate everyone on the interrelated nature of processes and the impact each person has on results. They also establish key areas of accountability.

As you establish accountabilities (see table, next page), keep your eye on the prize. What is the call center's mission? Which activities best support the mission? How can you best align expectations to drive the right activities and, in turn, further the call center's mission?

EXAMPLE EXPECTATIONS BY JOB ROLE

Agents
- Adherence to schedule
- Quality (contact by contact), including:
  - Identify and handle customer inquiries
  - Apply customer service policies
  - Perform business retention activities
  - Resolve customer problems
  - Educate customers on products and services offered
  - Match product benefits with customer needs
  - Enter coding and tracking information completely and accurately

Supervisors
- Team adherence to schedule
- Quality of the team
  - Ensure team meets quality objectives
  - Provide monitoring and coaching to individuals
  - Work with management to identify systemic quality problems
- Effectiveness of performance reviews and team meetings
- Performing the work of the agents during peak periods (as applicable)
- Representing team on special projects/initiatives

Quality Specialists
- Leading and managing monitoring processes
- Ensuring consistent calibration
- Synthesizing monitoring input and preparing timely reports
- Identifying individual and process improvement opportunities
- Tracking and analyzing monitoring results vs. customer satisfaction measures

Workforce Planners
- Creating accurate workload forecasts
- Organizing schedules that fit well for workload and agent requirements
- Assessing budgetary needs and implications of resource requirements
- Taking the initative to coordinate plans with other departments
- Ensuring proper use of work modes (e.g., after-call work, auxiliary modes, etc.)
- Presenting key performance results to executive management

Technical Support Managers
- Maintaining existing systems with minimum downtime
- Addressing usability issues (e.g., configuration, programming, etc.)
- Updating call-routing tables and systems as required
- Troubleshooting technical problems
- Recommending system improvement opportunities

Call Center Managers and Directors
- Ensuring that the call center meets key objectives related to:
  - Quality
  - Accessibility
  - Efficiency
  - Cost performance
  - Strategic impact
- Establishing clear objectives for employees
- Maintaining morale
- Preparing budgets, illustrating budgetary tradeoffs
- Overseeing hiring and training efforts
- Aligning call center objectives with enterprise and customer objectives
- Maximizing the call center's return on investments

Understanding and Managing Turnover

Turnover (attrition) is a fact of life in any organization. Some call centers operate with annual rates of less than 5 percent, while others see rates exceeding 30 percent (and in some cases, far more).

Excessive turnover costs an organization in many ways — higher recruiting and training costs; a lower average experience level leading to higher handling times, more transferred calls and lower service levels/response times; the need for more coaching and supervision; and the impact on everyone's morale when key people leave.

But turnover can also bring benefits — e.g., if employees leave for other positions within the organization, the call center gains experienced advocates in other departments. Turnover may also reduce structural costs (assuming new employees are brought in at lower pay scales) and create the means for the call center to bring in additional employees with needed skills and fresh insights.

The causes and costs/benefits will vary by type of turnover — e.g., voluntary external turnover is more of a detriment to the organization than planned internal turnover. For better or worse, turnover will have an impact on your call center. Since the cost of low quality and productivity can be significant, it is important to track and manage turnover as aggressively as other important performance indicators.

CALCULATING YOUR TURNOVER RATE

To measure turnover correctly, you'll need to calculate an annualized turnover rate, which provides a consistent basis for comparison and trending. An annualized number does not require 12 months' worth of data. The calculation is as follows:

EXAMPLE: INPUT FOR TURNOVER CALCULATION		
	Number of agents exiting the job during the month	Average number of agents on staff during the month*
January	2	104
February	1	103
March	4	101
April	0	101
May	3	109
June	5	106
July	2	105
August	3	103
Total/Average	**20**	**104**

* The average number of agents on staff during the month is often calculated by taking an average of the counts at the end of each week of the month. Alternatively, an average can be taken of the trained staff count at the beginning and end of the month.

Turnover = (number of agents exiting the job ÷ average number of agents during the period) x (12 ÷ number of months in the period)

Using the data from this example, the calculation yields the following: (20 ÷ 104) x (12 ÷ 8) = 28.8%. So, the call center has an annualized turnover rate of about 29 percent.

While an overall annualized turnover rate is a useful number, it is of more value to further break down the number into internal/external, and voluntary/involuntary categories. Internal turnover refers to employees who leave the call center, but stay within the organization. External turnover refers to employees who leave the organization entirely. Since the causes are usually different than those for internal or involuntary turnover, the manager can prepare an action plan accordingly.

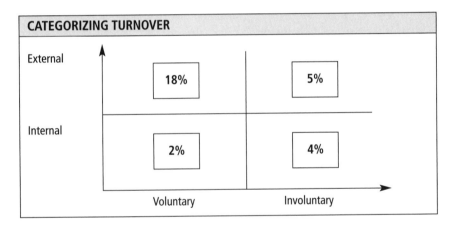

WORKING ON ROOT CAUSES

Leading call centers are continually working on the root causes of turnover. Many of the problems are by-products of a poor planning process, so they continually assess and address resource issues. They are also broadening the responsibilities that agents have and opportunities to learn, grow and advance (see Canadian Tire Financial Services example, Chapter 15).

I've also noticed a shift in perspective on internal turnover (people leaving the call center for other opportunities within the organization). In many ways, it's a good thing — the time people spend on the front lines with customers gives them a healthy perspective that they carry into other departments. But there has to be a balance. Losing people too soon can cost the call center — and the organization — dearly.

Consequently, a growing number of call center managers are working to expand the time agents spend in the call center before moving elsewhere, (e.g., they are working with their colleagues in other parts of the organization to encourage agents to stay longer). They are also helping agents to see the enormous impact the call center can have on the organization and customer base, as well as the exciting future ahead as the information/communication-oriented economy changes and develops.

COMMON CAUSES OF TURNOVER

(Not listed in any specific order)
- Better opportunities within or outside the organization
- Pace of effort required
- Repetition
- Over-regimentation
- Sense of powerlessness to make a difference
- Frustration of not being allowed to do a good job
- Unrelenting attention necessary
- Being "tied to a desk"
- Feeling of being excessively monitored
- Feeling of not being appreciated
- Handling complaints or problems all day
- Odd work hours
- Insufficient pay
- Lack of proper tools and training
- The demand for increased skills from agents who do not want to perform those skills or who are not equipped to perform them

Points to Remember

- Contacts handled is problematic as a productivity measurement. Too many variables are outside of agents' control.
- Adherence to schedule and qualitative measurements can effectively replace other measurements that are merely after-the-fact outputs.
- Qualitative measurements have become more focused, as they've become more important in today's environment.
- For the best results, involve agents in establishing and maintaining the monitoring and coaching program.
- Given shared responsibilities for achieving many call center results, it's important to establish the right accountabilities, both for those in individual job roles and for the overall team.
- Don't leave turnover to chance — track it, manage it, and take steps to fix it.

CHAPTER 15:
Building a More Effective Organization

Every organized human activity — from the making of pots to the placing of a man on the moon — gives rise to two fundamental and opposing requirements: the division of labor into various tasks to be performed, and the coordination of those tasks to accomplish the activity.

HENRY MINTZBERG

Like the road network in a community or the design of the hull on a boat, the forces of organizational design are constantly at work. A well-designed organization will enable the call center to be flexible, fast and efficient. When structured poorly, it will hamper communication, create barriers to performance and lead to unpredictable and inefficient workarounds.

In this chapter, we'll look at some of the most important aspects of building an effective organization, including:

- The principles of effective structure
- Job roles and responsibilities
- Spans of control (e.g., agent to supervisor ratios)
- Cultivating good communication

An important theme runs through these subjects: Successful organizations design their structures to fit their unique and evolving situations. Don't let your organizational structure become stagnant. It can and must change as your services develop.

325

The Principles of Effective Structure

There is a paradox at work in many organizations, related to organizational structure. On one hand, the organizational design is constantly exerting its forces as it channels communications, shapes protocol and establishes lines of authority. It is one of the most influential and "visible" aspects of any enterprise. Most managers can draw their organization charts in their sleep. And yet, it is an issue that, in the daily hubbub, somehow becomes assumed — almost outside the realm of managerial consciousness.

While any call center is undergoing constant change at the agent group level as the organization evolves to meet variable workload demands, bigger questions remain. Stop and think: Is your organization working for you?

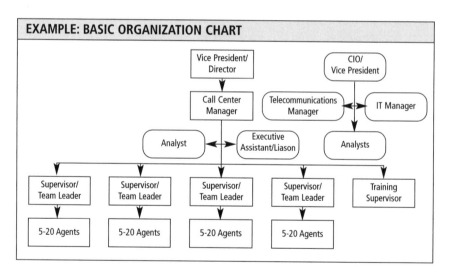

EXAMPLE: BASIC ORGANIZATION CHART

Although some aspects of organizational design are similar from one call center to the next — e.g., the components illustrated in the figure are present in most organizations — there are about as many unique organizational structures as there are organizations. Even so, there are solid, consistent principles behind any effective design. These include the following.

THE ORGANIZATION'S MISSION AND STRATEGY DRIVE THE STRUCTURE.
Organizational design is a strategy to help the organizaztion reach its objectives; design helps translate strategy into operations. Answers to major questions, such as the call center's role, to whom the call center reports and how the call center will be positioned vis-à-vis other service delivery methods (e.g., the sales force, retail operations and online services), must flow from the highest levels of strategy. In a common example of how strategy drives structure, many call centers are now handling all types of customer contacts (e.g., email, Web-initiated contacts, support calls related to self-service systems, etc.) as organizations focus on consolidating related

---

THE IMPACT OF ORGANIZATIONAL DESIGN

Organizational structure (also called organizational design) provides the alignment of roles and responsibilities for business units, departments and individuals. There are many reasonable definitions of organizational structure, but almost all refer to both the division of labor and the coordination of responsibilities and tasks. Major issues defined or impacted by organizational design include:

- The call center's position in the larger organization
- The call center's significance to the organization; e.g., versus other channels of service delivery (retail locations or direct sales/service)
- The call center's overall mission and responsibilities
- Specific job roles and responsibilities
- Lines of communication and authority
- Political protocol
- Agent group structure
- Analyst and support positions
- Ratios (e.g., staff to supervisor)
- Number of sites and level of integration
- Process, technology and facility requirements
- Budget allocations

services in order to provide cohesive access channels.

The culture and environment of the organization tend to play a large role in determining structure. For example, more formal, bureaucratic organizations tend to have formal structures, while less formal organizations often choose flatter structures with dispersed responsibilities.

INFORMAL AND FORMAL STRUCTURES ARE WELL-ALIGNED. The formal structure is the one defined by organization charts and in position and process descriptions. The informal structure is... well, how things *really* function. I recall working with a call center that had grown ad hoc training and technology support functions (e.g., "Hey, Joanne can do that... let's ask her") because they weren't getting timely support from those areas.

Organizations are complex, and there will always be some degree of informal communication and workflow. But if an informal structure grows topsy-turvy, it's time for management to address the root causes of these developments. Just as great sports teams define positions around natural talent and abilities (e.g., quarterback), formal structures should reflect efficient flows, natural lines of authority and earned responsibilities.

CURRENT AGENT GROUPS FORM THE FOUNDATION OF CALL CENTER STRUCTURE. Once the call center's place in the larger organization is defined, the call center should be built from agent groups upward. (Recall from Chapter 6 that agent groups share a common set of skills and knowledge, handle a specified mix of contacts and can be comprised of hundreds of agents across multiple sites. Supervisory groups and teams are often subsets of agent groups.)

The ideal agent group is one in which each person is proficient at handling every type of contact, through any channel, speaks all required languages, and can maintain the company's branding and image for every customer segment. That, of course, is not realistic in most environments — thus, the tiered groups, network configurations, overflow parameters, skills-based routing and other alternatives that we use to get the right call to the right place at the right time.

ARE YOUR AGENT GROUPS TOO POOLED? TOO SPECIALIZED?

There is no ideal formula for deciding how pooled or specialized agent groups should be. However, the symptoms of groups that are too pooled or too specialized are usually evident.

Symptoms of agent groups that are too specialized:

- Small groups with low occupancy and/or erratic service level/response time results
- An overly complicated planning process
- Many calls are not handled by the intended group (due to overflow)
- Agents become frustrated with narrow responsibilities

Symptoms of agent groups that are too generalized:

- Calls have a higher average handling time than necessary as agents grapple with a broad range of issues
- There is a high number of transferred calls
- Training time is long
- Quality often suffers
- Agents are frustrated with too much to know

Here's the point: Everything — hiring, training programs, supervisory and management responsibilities, analyst activities, quality standards, workforce planning, you name it — is based on agent group structure. But as agent group requirements evolve, the larger organization built on those groups can become obsolete. This is an issue that requires constant review. Has the superstructure become obsolete even as agent group requirements have moved on? Think through those agent groups. Redefine the responsibilities of that expanding analyst area. Bring supervisor ratios into sensible alignment. Rethink your training programs.

DIVISIONS AND RATIOS ARE SUPPORTED BY THE HIGHEST PRIORITIES. Any defined team, agent group, functional area or location (unless networked seamlessly to other sites) is defined by dividing lines, and divisions should be justified by the highest priorities. It's important to constantly review any divisions.

For example, a governmental organization recently combined dozens of local call centers into a few consolidated regional centers. They decided that consistent overall service to clients was a higher priority than satisfying the interests pushing to keep the jobs in each local community. In another case, a computer company with 24x7 technical support combined several daytime groups into a pooled group at night equipped to handle a broad range of transactions; although handling time is higher, quality remains consistent with daytime service. The organization decided that the ability to reach an agent — albeit one who may need a bit more time handling the contact — wisely wins out over maintaining small, specialized groups at 3 a.m.

REPORTING ARRANGEMENTS ASSIGN APPROPRIATE ACCOUNTABILITIES. There are situations in which the call center is dependent on people who report to other areas that have different or even competing interests. Yes, everybody is ultimately on the same team. But when call centers are being judged on their ability to handle a changing workload, the telecom folks are intent on living within their budget this year, and marketing is being assessed on response rates... well, that's a recipe for problems.

The answer? Sit down with colleagues across divisions and identify objectives and accountabilities that may be in conflict. Maybe training needs to report to the same area as the call center, or to the call center. Maybe some expenditures that are spread across IT, marketing and customer service budgets should be combined. Perhaps some support functions ought to be brought under the call center umbrella.

SUPPORT POSITIONS ARE ENABLERS. Roles geared around ensuring compliance, establishing rules and creating exception reports are often counterproductive. Alternatively, creating better processes, facilitating collaboration and, in general, supporting and enabling the call center's highest values are support responsibilities that will contribute to overall success. Those in support roles must find a good balance between burdensome control and an organization so loosely managed that it loses effectiveness.

THE STRUCTURE FACILITATES BRANDING. The organization's desired

STRATEGY DRIVES STRUCTURE

Many call centers have been through consolidations or restructurings that are really just cleanup efforts for lack of having and using a customer access strategy. For example, I recall helping an insurance company with agent group "consolidation." Their sales team would sell an account to a major client and, if pressed by the prospect, would agree to provide a dedicated agent group. In all cases, they promised agents trained on the characteristics of the clients' accounts (e.g., small business, large business, government agencies, etc.). After each sale, the organization would roll out dedicated telephone numbers and the call center would then be left to figure out how to best support the account.

The call center pooled agent groups whenever possible, but they eventually reached the point where they were faced with the near-impossible task of managing numerous agent groups, routing plans, overflow contingencies and access numbers. The purpose of the consolidation plan was to get a handle on all of the available access numbers and routing plans, and then combine and simplify agent groups and accounts as possible. It was a painful effort necessitated by decisions that were being made in the absence of an overall plan. They are now taking steps to ensure that the call center and sales team work from a common plan.

image, how it wishes to define and serve customer segments, and the specific requirements of individual customers should comprise objectives that span the organization's marketing efforts, the products and services it provides, and the contributions of the call center. While that doesn't necessarily mean that separate divisions or agent groups within the call center are required to serve different customer segments, it does mean that divisions, groups and responsibilities should further rather than hinder branding requirements.

Job Roles — Emerging, Evolving

An important part of developing an effective organization is to identify the positions you'll need, and the responsibilities that will go along with each. The table provides a look at how job titles and responsibilities can be defined in a larger call center. (Large centers tend to have more specialized roles and provide good illustrations of how specific responsibilities can become. Smaller call centers often combine some — or many — areas of responsibility when creating positions. In some of the smallest centers, the manager may wear every hat — and yes, still serve as an agent at least part of the time.)

A glance through these roles and responsibilities underscores an important trend in today's environment: From supervisors on up, management-level job roles are becoming increasingly specialized. Consider workforce management, which is seeing the emergence of forecasting, scheduling and real-time management expertise. Similarly, quality monitoring depends on monitoring and coaching, program design, calibration and data analysis. Technology can also lead to specialization; e.g., individuals specifically assigned to support speech, desktops, networks, quality monitoring systems or workforce management applications. If you manage or support a small call center, you may assume many of these responsibilities but they are more specialized than in the past.

Interestingly, at the agent level, job requirements are often becoming more generalized. Agents must increasingly understand the access channels customers use, the interrelated nature of services the organization provides, and the breadth of needs and expectations that customers have (e.g., to identify cross-sell and upsell opportunities).

Clearly, running a successful call center is, more than ever, a team sport. The most successful call centers cultivate training and development programs at all levels that deliver specific skills and knowledge while reinforcing overall objectives. And the best leaders encourage collaboration and an

EXAMPLE JOB ROLES AND RESPONSIBILITIES (LARGE CALL CENTER)	
Job Role	**Typical Responsibilities**
Agent	• Identify and handle customer inquiries • Apply customer service policies • Perform business retention activities • Resolve customer problems • Educate customers on products and services offered • Match product benefits with customer needs • Enter coding and tracking information completely and accurately
Team Leader/ Supervisor	• Resolve agent and customer issues • Participate in new-hire interviews • Conduct performance reviews and team meetings • Help to handle the workload, if and when feasible and appropriate • Conduct monitoring and coaching sessions • Coordinate with training and quality assurance to identify systemic quality-improvement opportunities • Represent the team on special projects/initiatives
Technical Support	• Maintain existing software/hardware • Recommend technology solutions • Install technology systems and upgrades • Provide technical assistance to operations • Help to update call-routing tables and systems as needed • Troubleshoot technical problems • Plan and schedule system backup/outages to minimize customer impact
Workforce Manager	• Spearhead the call center planning process • Ensure key planning concepts are understood by the entire organization • Ensure call center and staffing models include accurate, updated information

(continued next page)

Workforce Manager *(continued)*	• Conduct meetings with relevant departments regarding forecast and workload requirements • Research and recommend vendor and software for forecasting and scheduling activities • Train team leaders, managers and trainers on the use of work-force planning tools (e.g., work modes, schedule adherence, etc.) • Provide executive management with reports on workload trends and staffing requirements
Workforce Analyst	• Develop reports on daily workload • Participate in forecasting meetings with relevant departments; develop accurate short- and long-term workload forecasts • Control master systems files with schedule information and shift preferences • Serve as initial contact point for all issues regarding schedules • Process day-off requests and update systems • Determine workforce requirements to meet service level and response time objectives • Determine agent schedules to meet call center objectives
Workforce Real-Time Analyst	• Provide intraday monitoring and reporting • Recommend real-time schedule changes and identify efficiency opportunities • Adjust schedules based on workload/forecast shifts • Update systems with real-time shift adjustment information • Develop and distribute real-time summary reports to management team
Training Manager	• Work with operations to determine new-hire and ongoing training needs • Develop or buy appropriate training courses; implement programs • Determine best methods of delivery • Create effectiveness evaluations and update/improve training accordingly

Training Manager *(continued)*	• Partner with operations on new initiatives and determine training resources necessary for support
Quality Assurance Manager	• Recommend, implement and direct monitoring program (e.g., side-by-side, silent, remote, mystery shopper, etc.) • Work with managers and supervisors/team leaders to calibrate monitoring processes and results • Research and recommend vendors for automated processes • Gather and distribute results • Align internal monitoring with external customer feedback
Call Center Manager	• Implement call center strategies and tactics • Establish agent and team objectives • Work with the workforce management team to ensure accurate staffing and scheduling • Work with supervisors/team leaders, analysts and support positions to establish and manage priorities • Coordinate with VP/director and other managers to monitor budget requirements and compliance • Conduct supervisor/team leader performance reviews and administer rewards • Provide on-the-job training and mentoring • Oversee recruiting, hiring and training processes
Vice President/ Director	• Collaborate with senior-level management to determine the strategic direction of the call center • Align call center objectives with the organization and customer objectives • Oversee implementation of strategies • Develop and manage budgets; secure required resources • Maximize and communicate the call center's return on investment • Oversee recruiting, hiring and training of managerial staff • Conduct performance reviews of managers and administer rewards • Champion the call center throughout internal and external channels

appreciation for the diverse responsibilities the call center requires while keeping everyone focused on the business results that matter most.

Creating Career and Skill Paths

ICMI's series of reports on staffing and retention have noted a host of reasons for agent turnover. The top five include:

- Better opportunities outside the organization
- Compensation issues
- Better opportunities inside the organization
- Lack of career opportunities
- Handling complaints and problems all day

These issues underscore the importance of developing opportunities for agents to learn, grow and advance. There are two basic approaches to employee advancement: career paths and skill paths. A typical career path model requires the development of job families, which are comprised of a number of jobs arranged in a hierarchy by grade, pay and responsibility; e.g., agent, team leader, supervisor, manager, senior manager, director. The career path then indicates the requirements for each job within the family; e.g., education, experience, tenure, knowledge, skills, behavioral competencies, etc.

Because the historical corporate-ladder approach to staff development can be limited for call centers (due to the finite number of supervisory and management positions available), a more effective approach may be the skill-path model. Skill paths focus on an individual's acquisition of skill sets. Individuals often receive more recognition, responsibility and (in many cases) compensation as they achieve new skill levels within their position.

Call centers require more diverse skills than perhaps any other part of the organization. Customer behavior, information systems technologies, queuing theory, forecasting, statistics, human resources management, training, written and verbal communication skills, reporting, real-time management and strategy are all an inherent part of the environment.

KEEPING THINGS INTERESTING AT CANADIAN TIRE FINANCIAL SERVICES

Few centers have done more to keep agents interested, involved and on board than Canadian Tire Financial Services (Welland, Ontario), where the average length of service is seven years. "Our formula for success is that we focus on employee satisfaction as the key driver in customer satisfaction," says Scott Williams, director of customer service. "Our average agent tenure would be longer, but we've had a lot of growth... which has brought down the average some."

Along with a culture of agent empowerment and involvement, CTFS has a skill-path approach in place where agents can increase their pay in increments after obtaining additional skills and knowledge through experience and continuous training. Eventually, they may become one of two elite corps in the center — subject-matter experts or peer coaches. According to Williams, "Both are very sought-after jobs — not just because they feature higher pay, but because they are viewed by agents and the call center as central roles." Subject-matter experts are the "go-to" agents for the rest of the staff, serving as help desk agents for colleagues who need assistance with a complex issue. Peer coaches play an equally important role — assisting supervisors with the critical tasks of monitoring and coaching frontline staff. "We feel that the best person to help somebody to become better is someone who does the job very well; someone who has experience every day on the phone and knows what it's like to be a representative," says Williams.

When asked if long stints in a call center might lead to complacency and stasis among staff, Williams says "yes" — if the call center itself is complacent and static. Fortunately, that is not a problem at CTFS. "We constantly have new opportunities coming up that people can take advantage of," says Williams. "Reps don't lose their edge, they hone their skills. Some of the best reps in the company have been with us for 25 years."

Source: *Call Center Management Review*

Developing attractive career and skill paths remains a significant opportunity for many call centers.

Span of Control

Span of control refers to the number of individuals a manager supervises. A large span of control means that the manager supervises many people. A small span of control means the manager supervisors fewer people. Span of control tends to decrease as the complexity and variability of the conditions in the environment increase.

AGENT-TO-SUPERVISOR RATIOS

In call centers, the agent-to-supervisor ratio is an especially important consideration. Effective ratios are dependent on the tasks, standards and responsibilities of both agents and supervisors. Many call centers have between 10 and 20 staff per supervisor, with 10 to 15 being the most common range.

However, there are notable differences by industry. For example, mutual funds and insurance companies tend to be on the low end of that spectrum (have smaller spans of control), while catalog companies and telecommunications services providers tend to be on the high end. Further, there can be significant exceptions; e.g., some reservations centers have a relatively large span of control, sometimes well in excess of 20 staff per supervisor. And technical support centers and other complex environments can have as few as five staff per supervisor. Even within an industry, there can be a wide variance (one well-known catalog company has 40 agents per supervisor — not a number I recommend — while another has 10).

Be careful about drawing quick conclusions based on these figures or industry benchmarks. There are no simple answers along the lines of, "If you are a such-and-such type of call center, you ought to have X staff per supervisor."

Some of today's trends are working to drive the span of control up, including:

GROWING WORKLOADS: In some environments, the call center's workload continues to increase. In those centers that struggle to keep up with growth, the span of control tends to increase.

BUDGET CONSTRAINTS: As organizations go through restructurings and/or budget cutbacks, they often must reduce the relative number of supervisors (increase spans of control). Many managers admit they would ideally adjust span of control downward, but insist that funds simply are not available for more supervisor/manager positions.

GROWTH OF TEAMS: A positive development has been the growth of team-based environments, which has challenged the traditional role of supervisors. Call centers are generally moving away from production-oriented "factories" toward organizations that are flatter and more team-oriented. Team leaders are assuming functions that traditionally have been in the domain of manager and supervisors.

LOWER TURNOVER: Another positive development is that a growing number of call centers are directly and successfully reducing turnover. As the average experience level of agents moves upward, less supervision is generally required.

Other developments in today's environment tend to drive span of control down, including:

THE GROWING COMPLEXITY OF CONTACTS: As better-applied technologies offload routine calls and as new channels of contact proliferate, agents are handling contacts that require more human "know-how." The growing complexity of the workload inherently requires more supervision, coaching and feedback.

MORE MONITORING, MORE EXTENSIVELY: Many call centers are taking larger monitoring samples today than they did five or 10 years ago. Monitoring, feedback and coaching take a significant amount of time.

MORE SMALL CALL CENTERS: This may be the biggest reason that the average ratio across the industry has moved down — there are simply more small groups in the sample. For example, if a new call center has only seven or eight agents, it will still likely have a supervisor even though that person will be able to supervise more people as the center grows.

There are potentially other factors that can confuse the issue of ratios. For example, the tasks of supervisors vary widely from one organization to the next. Some lean more toward "lead agent" responsibilities, in which they lead a team but also help to handle the workload, while others are much more involved in management responsibilities. Further, the time that supervisors spend monitoring and coaching (the most time-consuming supervisory responsibilities in most call centers) can vary by many multiples. And some organizations have set up internal help desks to field calls from agents who need help — a responsibility traditionally handled by supervisors.

Recommendations in general business literature vary from the "train them, empower them and get out of the way" school of thought on one end of the spectrum to a more structured approach on the other. In the respected book, *Executive Leadership*, authors Elliot Jacques and Stephen D. Clement mince no words: "There is more nonsense centering around the topic of span of control than around nearly any other subject in the whole field of organization and management." They go on to criticize managers who search for "easy-to-apply rules of thumb that need no thought." That is true in the call center environment; while somewhere between 10 and 15 agents per supervisor makes sense in many call centers, a 5:1 or 25:1 ratio may be equally justifiable.

SUPERVISOR-TO-MANAGER RATIOS

In terms of supervisor-to-management spans of control, ratios of between 5:1 and 12:1 are typical. Given the higher level and more complex interactions that must take place between managers and supervisors, spans of control are usually smaller than those for agents/supervisors. That underscores a principle generally true in most organizations: the higher up in the organization, the smaller the spans of control.

Cultivating Good Communication

Effective communication results in a shared understanding of what's most important. When people are aligned behind a set of compelling values, enthusiasm, commitment and significant productivity tend to follow. In that sense, effective communication is inseparable from effective leadership... leaders are only as effective as their ability to communicate.

Communication creates meaning and direction for people. When good communication is lacking, the symptoms are predictable: conflicting objectives, unclear values, misunderstandings, lack of coordination, confusion, low morale and people doing the bare minimum required.

Although cultures and communication styles vary, there are predictable and notable principles among high-value call centers. Among the most important are:

COMMIT TO KEEPING PEOPLE IN THE KNOW. Leaders of high-performance organizations are predisposed to keeping their people in the know. They actively share both good news and bad. This minimizes the rumor mill, which hinders effective, accurate communication. It also contributes to an environment of trust. It sounds simple, but just making a commitment is the first step. I know of a manager who decided to make great communication a top priority... she literally included it as an item on her daily task list — and her commitment is working wonders for productivity and clarity in the organization.

CULTIVATE A SUPPORTING CULTURE. One of the most distinguishable aspects of a positive culture is that the call center's vision, mission and impact on the rest of the organization are well-known and understood. Why does the call center exist? What is it working to achieve? What's in it for customers and for the organization? What's in it for employees? Take steps to build employee commitment to the vision. Get their input as it's being developed, then publish it, live by it — use it to guide tactical, day-to-day decisions. (See Chapter 17 for more on culture.)

ESTABLISH APPROPRIATE COMMUNICATION TOOLS. A prerequisite to an environment in which communication thrives is that individuals and teams have compatible and capable communications technologies. The usual channels apply — telephone, voicemail, email, intranet, instant messaging, and collaboration and conferencing tools offer enormous potential if they are available and compatible across the organization. Further — and this is so simple but so effective — create directories (online, print, perhaps both) of contact information for your call center and cross-functional teams. This provides necessary information, and it creates symbolism that reinforces communication and camaraderie.

DEVELOP FORMAL AND INFORMAL CHANNELS OF COMMUNICATION. Effective leaders cultivate both formal and informal channels of communication. But the mission and values being communicated remain consistent. The communication formats can include newsletters, meetings, visual displays, email, voicemail, posters, intranets and informal "hallway meetings." One of the formal means of communication between frontline workers and management is employee satisfaction surveys. As part of the process, the best call centers involve agents in addressing problems, and they close the loop by consistently communicating progress toward resolving issues.

ENSURE THAT STRUCTURE AND POLICIES SUPPORT COMMUNICATION. In general, flatter, more collaborative organizations help to foster an environment in which trust and communication flourish. Policies and procedures can also impact trust and communication. For example, monitoring and coaching programs that truly contribute to the growth and well-being of individuals and the organization help to build trust and encourage communication.

LISTEN ACTIVELY AND REGULARLY. Listening encourages diverse perspectives, enables individuals to grow and creates community within the organization. Active listening enables a culture that brings out the best in people. Further, many studies on the subjects of leadership and strategy have shown the visions of some of history's greatest leaders actually came from others in their circles. The leaders may have selected the best vision to focus on, then shaped it and communicated it to others in a compelling way, but they rarely originated the vision.

DON'T OVERDO IT. Experienced leaders are aware of an interesting paradox: too much communicating inhibits effective communication. There is an optimal level of communication beyond which more communication becomes counterproductive. Too many meetings, memos, conferences, email messages and on-the-fly discussions may be symptoms of weaknesses in plans and processes. With better tools, more focused training and appropriate levels of empowerment, the need for excessive real-time communicating can be avoided — because the communication is built into individual understanding and established processes.

Too many meetings, memos, conferences, email messages and on-the-fly discussions may be symptoms of weaknesses in plans and processes.

Meg Whitman, CEO and president of eBay, reportedly requires her leadership team to turn off all mobile devices during meetings. I'm convinced she's onto something that goes beyond just the ability to focus on a meeting.

One of the highest forms of leadership is to build an organization or team that runs smoothly without your constant involvement. If you're perpetually glued to your phone, email or mobile devices, there's probably opportunity to clarify responsibilities and improve processes and training. The alternative consists of ongoing interruptions that whipsaw your concentration and perpetuate dependencies. Can you go on vacation without checking in? That's a sign that you've probably built a team or an organization that's working. (And you deserve that vacation!)

SUCCESSFULLY LEADING DISTRIBUTED TEAMS

Information and communications technologies have spawned organizations that span geography and time. Multisite environments, cross-functional teams, and extended-hour or 24x7 operations are common call center examples. If you are a call center manager, you will likely have the responsibility of getting results from people who work in different locations, who don't report to you or who don't work the same hours.

Unfortunately, technology hasn't eliminated the natural barriers that exist between people who work in distributed environments. People who work in different places and/or at different times often have trouble seeing themselves as an integral part of a larger team.

Like leadership in general, there's no specific recipe for building a cohesive virtual team. There are, however, tried-and-true principles that will significantly increase your chances for success:

- Create a clear vision for the call center.
- Create opportunities for the people in the distributed environment to get to know each other. (I know of one call center director who had managers in distributed sites record short answers to questions about themselves — e.g., what's your dream vacation? How did you end up in the call center? She then combined the responses and sent the compiled recording to the team. Another manager set up a Web site profiling the members of a multisite team, then gave everyone a short quiz on the interests and backgrounds of the other members.)
- Look for ways to keep everyone involved. Often, some amount of expediency must be traded for the sake of fostering a collaborative environment.
- Take steps to ensure that everyone gets key information at the same time.
- Spend a disproportionate amount of time tending to the needs and relationships of the more "distant" members of the group. (Distant may mean the members who work the night shift, or those who are in a site thousands of miles away.)
- Look for ways to scrap or, at least, minimize the impact of unnecessary hierarchies and cumbersome bureaucracies, which tend to wreak havoc

on distributed teams.

- Consistently communicate progress. It's important to keep the group updated and on the same track.

The challenges of leading a distributed team are real and ongoing, but being part of an environment in which people successfully work together across distance and time is one of the most rewarding professional experiences you can have. In today's world, it is also one of the most necessary.

Points to Remember

- Your organizational structure should be unique and fit your specific environment. It can and must change as your services evolve.

- Even though organizational structures are unique from one organization to the next, there are dependable, consistent principles that lead to effective design.

- An important part of developing an effective organization is to identify the positions you'll need and the responsibilities that will go along with each — and then keep them up to date.

- Developing attractive career and skill paths that keep employees interested, engaged and productive is an important leadership responsibility.

- Sensible agent-to-supervisor ratios are dependent on the tasks, standards and responsibilities of both agents and supervisors.

- Good communication results in a shared understanding of what's most important. When everyone is aligned behind a set of compelling values, enthusiasm, commitment and productivity will follow.

Part Five:
Leadership in the Digital Age

CHAPTER 16:
Enabling Technologies, New Possibilities

CHAPTER 17:
Characteristics of the Best-Managed Call Centers

Improved management techniques, new enabling technologies, and an emerging focus on creating higher levels of strategic value are changing call centers dramatically. Forward-thinking leaders recognize the opportunities — and challenges — that these changes bring. They are moving forward with foresight and planning, and creating cultures in which positive change is welcomed.

CHAPTER 16:
Enabling Technologies, New Possibilities

We think we invent technology, but technology also invents us.

RICHARD FARSON

New management techniques coupled with emerging technologies* are changing call centers dramatically. A notable example is the shift from bull-pen style call factories of the past to environments increasingly characterized by high levels of skill, multimedia contacts, distributed resources and reports that reflect vital intelligence on customers, products and processes. The opportunities for better serving customers and delivering more value to the organization are immense.

But opportunities for

SOME OF TODAY'S COMPETITIVE PRESSURES

- Handle greater workloads
- Boost revenues
- Reduce costs
- Improve customer satisfaction
- Increase customer retention
- Improve cross-sell, upsell
- Address more complex issues
- Accelerate service delivery
- Improve consistency
- Provide more personalized services
- Offer greater choices and control
- Provide access alternatives
- Increase hours of operation
- Deliver "exceptional" service

---

*See www.icmi.com for lists of suppliers, contact information and other useful resources

349

those organizations that choose to lead rapidly morph into pressures for those struggling to keep up. The convergence of Internet, communications and computer technologies is creating new services, heightening customer expectations and multiplying the interactions between and among customers, organizations, suppliers, industry interest groups and government. Customers are informed and connected — and organizations must continually transition sales and service delivery systems to meet their expectations, or risk dissatisfying, disillusioning or driving them away.

Technology is an important driver of these developments, and can and must be part of the answer in addressing them. But new technologies are not passive — they almost always present new management and process challenges. To get good results, they must be viewed in terms of how they can support and further the organization's mission and strategy, and then must be implemented and managed with foresight and appropriate planning. To that end, we'll look at some of the major technology developments changing today's environment, along with important underlying trends and key leadership responsibilities.

Infrastructure: Change from the Ground Up

To get a sense of context, let's go back in time for just a moment — to 1858. After more than a year of enduring storms, sickness and failures on the high seas, the crew of the HMS Agamemnon had just completed running the first transatlantic telegraph cable. Investors on both sides of the Atlantic had provided the funding, and hopes for the beginnings of a new communications era were high. Unfortunately, the signals that trickled through the cable were so weak that it took 16-and-a-half hours and the most sensitive equipment available to decipher the first message of just 90 words sent by Queen Victoria. Worse, the cable's insulation failed several days later, and it never worked again. For onlookers, investors and especially the crew, this was a heartbreaking, bitter end to an immense undertaking. But the project — though viewed as a failure at the time — helped to create a vision of a more connected world.

It wasn't until almost a century later, in 1956, that the first transatlantic telephone cable, running between the British Isles and Newfoundland, Canada, was inaugurated. The crew and investors of 1858 would be amazed to see what has transpired since. High-capacity fiber optic cables crisscross oceans and continents; satellites reach many of the most remote parts of the globe; wireless services provide instant access to telephone, email, messaging, Web and other information services. And our knowledge-based economy has become driven by communications — the ability to get to knowledge when and as needed.

The stunning developments in today's infrastructure and networks depend on more than just the ability to establish connections. The other part of the equation — which is only now emerging — is the way information and services are digitally represented and transported. Consider a familiar example, digital photography: You can snap a picture on your camera or mobile phone, email it to grandma, print it for an album, edit it and even use it as a background image on your computer screen. Similarly, music can be downloaded, edited, transferred to a portable player, used as the ring tone on your mobile device, even broadcast to your car radio. Pictures and music — as well as television, movies, games and other types of media — have been forever freed from the rigid technical confines of the past.

The migration of the voice-switching infrastructure from traditional circuit-switching based on TDM (time division multiplexing) to packet-switching based on IP (Internet protocol) networks is bringing similar flexibility and change to customer contact centers. Voice over IP (VoIP) is much more than a way to economize on transmission costs. The more fundamental impact is that what were essentially two sets of technologies in call centers — one for voice, one for data — can now be integrated in a common platform. The potential advantages are many:

- **MULTIMEDIA.** All contacts can be handled by a common routing and

351

reporting system.

- **MULTISITE OPERATIONS.** Anyone tied into the network — including agents in satellite offices, home agents or other departments — can technically be part of the call center, whether routinely or on an ad hoc basis.

- **COST EFFICIENCIES.** All things equal, the costs to purchase, use and maintain IP-based systems are often lower than for TDM-based systems.

- **SIMPLIFIED MANAGEMENT.** Moving to IP architecture often results in fewer systems, licenses and maintenance agreements to manage.

- **SCALABLE.** Adding or reducing agents is simple and cost-effective, with minimum technology impact.

- **INTEGRATED REPORTS.** With activities consolidated in one architecture, reports can provide a more holistic perspective of contacts and customers across sites and media.

- **DISASTER BACKUP.** If harnessed appropriately, IP-based architecture can provide the redundancies inherent in Internet-based services.

- **OPEN STANDARDS.** Systems based on open, common standards are more readily integrated.

In the past two decades, great strides have been made in computer telephony integration (CTI) applications, which, through standards, middleware and (usually) lots of programming, can integrate the traditional computer and telephony worlds. CTI can enable screen pops (simultaneous voice and data delivery), database-driven call-routing, integrated performance reporting and a host of other capabilities. And CTI will remain alive and well until voice is fully absorbed by IP-based technologies in the coming years. But the term itself will be transitional, and will likely someday fade as "computer" and "telephony" lose distinction within IP architecture.

The future is IP-based architecture. New, creative applications will proliferate, and empowered by a common, integrated platform, organizations will increasingly design unique customer applications for their specific environments. Reports that give deeper meaning to what customers do and

BLUE CROSS BLUE SHIELD OF SOUTH CAROLINA ADOPTS CLICK-TO-TALK

Blue Cross Blue Shield (BCBS) of South Carolina is an early adopter of VoIP capabilities. In 2004, BCBS of S.C. implemented an application they call STATchat both to offer health care providers an effective and efficient e-support option and to gradually wean them from the more expensive traditional phone channel.

In the event that a provider fails to find the answer he or she seeks on the provider portal of BCBS of S.C.'s Web site, he or she can click on a button that says "STATchat" (next to the button are the words "Click here to speak to the next available agent"). A box then pops up and says, "initializing," and then "dialing." Soon thereafter, "connected" appears in the box, and the provider hears a live agent through his or her PC (provided the PC is equipped with a soundcard): "Hello, this is [agent's name]. Thank you for calling Blue Cross Blue Shield of South Carolina. How may I help you?"

The center uses priority queuing to give Web callers quicker service, and the majority of provider inquiries now come in through the click-to-talk application. With so many providers moving online, BCBS of S.C.'s savings have been substantial. "Those who call using STATchat cost our call center a fraction of what traditional callers do," explains David Boucher, assistant vice president of Health Care Services.

Boucher was confident that the organization could steer providers to the Web by promoting the fact that they'd be able to speak to a live agent online with little to no wait and no IVR hassle. He also knew that many providers, once on the Web site, would at least try to get the information they were seeking without live assistance — thus freeing agents to handle only the most complex provider inquiries.

BCBS of S.C. initially began trials with a small set of subscribers. After working out a few technical glitches (e.g., screens not populating with claims data and poor audio) and receiving much provider praise, the call center rolled out STATchat to all provider organizations already registered to use BCBS of S.C.'s interactive Web site services.

Source: *Call Center Management Review*

experience will develop further. Computer databases, which include information on customers, products and services, and processes will become more involved in handling contacts — e.g., in how and where they are routed, the people and information that are involved, and how insight from them is captured and reported. And increasingly, thinking of computers and telephones as separate technologies will fade.

"A plate of silver and one of zinc are taken into the mouth, the one above, the other below the tongue. They are then placed in contact with the wire, and words issuing from the mouth are conveyed by the wire."
— 1854 NEWSPAPER, DESCRIBING HOW THE YET-TO-BE INVENTED TELEPHONE MIGHT WORK

Is making the switch from TDM to IP something you can run out and do tomorrow if you haven't begun the transition? Hardly. Changing out systems can be costly, and what you have may be working just fine. Your network has to be ready or you'll run into quality problems. You'll need to look at all of the systems capabilities you have now, and consider how or even whether or not they can make the transition to the new environment. You'll want to revisit the technology strategy for the larger organization — being part of an overall transition plan usually makes the most sense. Reliability and voice quality are essential in the call center environment, and you'll need to prepare accordingly. And yes, you'll need to take stock of your organization's readiness — in terms of IT support, vendor relationships, budgets, growth plans and culture — to embark on what will amount to a pretty dramatic change. In short, you'll need a sensible migration strategy that considers your current situation, where you want to go, and how best to get there in coming months and years.

There are billions of dollars worth of TDM-based systems installed across the globe, and this transition will take years. But it's already well under way. And it's changing call centers from the ground up.

354

Getting the Right Contacts to the Right Places at the Right Times

The efficiencies call centers can bring to an organization have always stemmed largely from how contacts are routed and distributed. Prior to call centers, the "clientele approach" was prevalent. Customers tended to ask for and talk to the same representatives, whom they reached through a switchboard operator or by dialing a direct number. It was not very efficient. When automatic call distributors (ACDs) came along in the early 1970s, they challenged existing thinking. Rather than send calls to individuals, the idea was that they could be automatically connected to a group of agents cross-trained to handle a variety of contacts. Shared computer sys-

---

IDENTIFYING CUSTOMERS AND/OR WHAT THEY NEED

To implement customized routing and contact-handling routines (e.g., skills-based routing), you'll need to know who your customers are and/or (especially) what they need when they contact the organization. Common identification methods include:

- Caller-entered information (e.g., into an IVR or speech system), which can be matched to services desired or specific customer records.
- ANI (automatic number identification), the billing number the call originated from, which can often be matched to customer records in a database.
- DNIS (dialed number identification services), the telephone number the caller dials, which can indicate the reason for the call, language preferred, etc.
- Email addressed to, subject line, sender's address or customer entered data, which can be matched to services desired or customer records.
- Text included in a document (e.g., sent by fax or mail), which can be interpreted and processed through optical character recognition (OCR) or related technologies
- Web URL, cookies or customer entered data, which can be matched to services desired or customer records.

---

tems and information also played important roles in enabling pooled groups of agents. In short, the "powerful pooling principle" became — and still is — the essential core of call center efficiency (see Chapter 9).

The pooling principle is only powerful if agents are truly cross-trained to handle the variety of contacts that come their way. Most organizations have more than one agent group — sometimes many — geared around specific call requirements and areas of specialized expertise. In the early days of ACDs, agent groups and other parameters were rigidly defined. You might be able to move an agent from one group to another based on keyboard command, or make various other changes (e.g., to overflow parameters), but the systems themselves didn't do much to help. Then along came "dynamic reconfiguration" in the late 1970s, which enabled ACDs to automatically change system thresholds based on real-time circumstances (the term was coined by designers at Rolm, now part of Siemens). It was a precursor to the intelligent-routing capabilities we have now, which go far beyond these pioneering efforts.

Today, routing and distribution software is based on "if-then" programming logic, which has enabled system managers to design flexible and sophisticated call-handling routines: "If the queue is backed up beyond eight callers in group A, then…" You can specify routing, priority, announcements and information-access alternatives for each call, based on many criteria. And skills-based routing, which entered the market in the early 1990s, makes it possible to route individual contacts to specific agents on a call-by-call basis (see Chapter 7).

Advanced network services can extend routing, distribution and other call-handling variables to distributed call centers that include sites across the globe or even home-based agents. Originating area code or prefix, time of day, day of week, workload conditions and many other parameters can be part of routing and distribution criteria.

And yet, as advanced as routing and distribution capabilities have become, they are predominantly telephone-centric. CTI can include database and caller-entered information in call-routing and handling routines — but, again, it involves integrating what are essentially separate voice and data systems. The vision — one that is in the early stages of being applied — is that one routing application can and should seamlessly handle all types of contacts across your customer contact operations.

A single routing engine does not mean that you must use universal agents (sometimes called "super agents") to handle every type of contact and every contact channel — that's for you to decide. Instead, criteria you define dictate how contacts are delivered and handled. The degree to which your call center is pooled or specialized depends on the business rules you establish. Applied well, these capabilities can deliver quicker, more effective service for customers, and efficiencies for the organization.

Boosting Productivity and Quality

In recent years, there have been many developments in systems that can improve call center performance. Again, the underlying themes include architecture based on open standards, ready integration with other systems, flexibility and maximum user control. Examples include:

QUALITY MONITORING SYSTEMS. At a basic level, quality monitoring systems record calls to provide a record of transactions and enable supervisors to review them with agents for quality improvement purposes. Many systems can be set up either to record all calls or to just take samples. Return on investment is usually defined in terms of reductions in errors and rework, improved first-call resolution and the time that is saved by being able to quickly find and review any contact. But the benefits can go far beyond those associated with recording and reviewing calls. Both voice and screen activities can be recorded in many cases, and, increasingly, all contact channels can be included. Supervisors can insert voice annotations into original recordings for training purposes and managers can include specific contacts in reports that go to others, e.g., for "voice of the customer" purposes. Integration with other systems can provide rich, three-dimensional reports on activities, help with coaching and training, and even link to technology-based training modules that are geared around individual performance evaluations. And reports that reflect information picked up in the QA process can be used across the organization for improving products, services and processes.

WORKFORCE MANAGEMENT TOOLS. At a basic level, workforce management systems can provide automated tools for forecasting, staff calculations, schedules and tracking/reporting. In recent years, applications have become ever better at handling these core processes. For example, forecasting and scheduling for the full range of contact channels, skills-based scheduling and user-defined reports that integrate with other systems have paralleled the needs created by the emerging multichannel environment. Real-time adherence monitoring software can highlight discrepancies between actual and planned schedules (see Chapter 14) and account for a wide range of activities. Administration tools have become much friendlier, enabling everything from automated shift-swaps and vacation approvals to integration with payroll and financial systems. And one of the most useful developments has been improvements in modules that enable "what-if" analysis for budgeting and resource decisions. Integration with quality monitoring systems and training tools will become even more robust, enabling seamless forecasting, scheduling and real-time management of virtually any kind of call center activity, including those that are not immediately related to handling customer contacts.

CUSTOMER RELATIONSHIP CAPABILITIES. There are many tools that can help you establish and build better relationships with customers. For example, contact management technologies enable you to log contacts, view customer profiles and access a consolidated history of all contacts customers have had with the organization through any media — face-to-face, phone, email, Web, etc. Salesforce automation tools enable you to track contacts and leads with prospects or existing customers, provide scripts, schedule follow-up contacts and, in general, manage sales interactions. Fulfillment tools can manage the delivery of products, services and materials. Help desk capabilities or support systems can assist you in tracking and managing incidents that require support or problem resolution. Other tools enable you to access account histories, as well as information on billing, shipping, services delivered and related activities. Products suites and open systems can help you pull together the pieces that make the most sense for your organization and customers, and business rules enable you to define how it's all going to work.

ANALYTICS AND PERFORMANCE MANAGEMENT. Many organizations are realizing that their data is the proverbial gold mine, and are turning to increasingly sophisticated tools for gathering, storing, analyzing and reporting. Data analytics tools can help you find, pull together and analyze information from many sources — e.g., who's buying what, what are the trends, where are the opportunities? Speech analytics systems can explore the content of recorded calls, search for key phrases or expressions (e.g., competitor names, or red flags such as "cancel"), and even detect and provide insight into caller emotions. And performance management tools — sometimes referred to as dashboards or scorecards — can integrate data from many systems with goals and objectives, to help guide decisions at many levels of the organization (see box, "Better Tools and a Higher Level Focus = Better Results").

KNOWLEDGE MANAGEMENT TOOLS. Knowledge management systems enable you to cultivate and benefit from the knowledge gained through handling customer interactions and supporting the organization's processes, products and services. The main objective of knowledge management is to create, leverage and reuse resources so people will not spend time "reinventing the wheel." Whether home-grown or off-the-shelf, these systems can be a boon to first-call resolution, efficient handling times and customer satisfaction.

DESKTOP CAPABILITIES AND RELATED TOOLS. The agent desktop has been major area of development in recent years, providing access to systems, information and media through a familiar browser-based interface. Document imaging and on-screen retrieval can boost the number of calls

BETTER TOOLS AND A HIGHER LEVEL FOCUS = BETTER RESULTS

The biggest development in call center technology is a change in priorities, explains Joe Fleischer, chief technical editor for *Call Center Magazine*. "Rather than focusing only on how to make communication more efficient, call centers will rely on technology to help them better understand customers."

An important tool enabling this shift in focus is performance management software. "Performance management tools reveal the ways that different efforts within your call center — including how you hire, train, schedule, evaluate, coach and route calls to agents — affect one another. This kind of information allows you to bring about improvements not only in terms of individual metrics, but also to your company's understanding of customers," says Fleischer.

"Until a few years ago, the primary function of these tools was to enable call center supervisors or dedicated quality assurance staff to document whether agents followed certain rules of behavior, like using the right words when greeting callers. But managers have since come to recognize that metrics that only emphasize operational efficiency or adherence to procedures aren't always the best indicators of a call center's performance."

Today's tools do much more, says Fleischer. "For example, they allow call centers to account for intervening issues outside of an agent's control that may be affecting outcomes of calls. And some performance management suites enable companies to incorporate customers' feedback as part of their evaluations of their call centers."

The end result? "Call centers gain more responsibility in relation to their ability to understand, retain and earn revenue from customers. Call center managers who can effectively apply tools like performance management systems to help their companies achieve these aims are in the best positions to make the leap from managers to leaders."

you handle on the first attempt dramatically. The ability to send real-time information on call center performance to the desktop helps agents stay abreast of trends and developments. Auto-greetings allow agents to pre-record their introductions and provide them in digital clarity at the beginning of calls — starting every contact with the right greeting and a chipper voice. Communications tools such as instant messaging (IM) can help agents access information and assistance during contacts. Telephony features themselves provide increasingly customizable work states, call coding options and call handling capabilities (e.g., one-click transfers or requests for assistance, etc.). And in today's world, these features can be provided on a telephone (TDM or IP) or through a PC-based "softphone."

IVR CAPABILITIES. The proliferation of interactive voice response (IVR) technology and its impact on call centers for self-service and call-routing has been nothing less than phenomenal. When coupled with databases and routing systems, IVR systems enable callers to provide and access information through keypad input or speech recognition. For callers, IVR systems have become a way of life, along the lines of bank ATMs. Speech recognition, a high-end IVR capability that is becoming widely used, has improved dramatically in recent years. By enabling a more natural interface, well-designed systems greatly extend application opportunities (it's a lot easier to say "Rancho Cucamonga, California" than to try to enter it on a keypad). And well-designed and personalized applications (see Chapter 2) tend to attract customers who would not otherwise successfully complete self-service transactions. Speech engines and algorithms have become increasingly robust, recognizing accents, colloquialisms and expansive vocabularies. IVR technologies have also provided other performance-boosting goodies — e.g., post-call surveys can prompt callers through questions that capture information which can be tied back to specific transactions and agents. And development standards have enabled speech systems to leverage and use Web-based architectures and programming, attracting a broad base of programmers working on new applications.

WEB-BASED APPLICATIONS. The Internet continues to open up new ways for organizations to deliver services, add value and communicate with customers and suppliers. From the simple FAQs (frequently asked questions) that became common a decade ago to today's powerful multimedia appli-

THE HOSTED SOLUTION ALTERNATIVE

Lori Bocklund, president of the consulting firm Strategic Contact, cites the potential advantages of hosted solutions:

- Rapid implementation — hosted solutions can be in place in weeks, not months, and can therefore deliver return on investment more quickly
- State-of-the-art technology — both at the time of implementation and ongoing, the solution is state-of-the-art as the provider continuously upgrades and evolves technologies to meet market and customer needs
- Best-practices applications — the vendor brings expertise to the initial applications implementation, as well as ongoing tuning as they apply new insights to optimize customer solutions
- Operations cost rather than capital cost — the structure of a periodic fee for services is attractive to many financial managers
- Little cost to prove value — hosting minimizes upfront costs, including internal resource costs, so that the return on investment can be proven without great cost or risk
- Usage-based pricing — users can vary the number of ports, licenses or transactions with business peaks and valleys
- Reliability — the provider delivers a highly-redundant system to serve all its customers
- Scalability — the provider delivers a fully scalable solution, enabling users to ramp up quickly
- Fewer support resources — the resource demands are lower, both those required upfront for implementation, integration and application development, as well as ongoing for operations and maintenance
- Consistent applications across multiple sites — a hosted solution is oblivious to where your agents or infrastructure reside, and provides a consistent application for all users

"Hosted applications can help you get more out of your center quickly," Bocklund says. "They are an option worth considering for centers that need additional functionality but have limited technical resources, or too many things on their plate to take on deployment of another complex technology. Mature hosted applications include CRM and IVR (speech). Full hosted contact center solutions and specialty applications for things such as proactive alerting are offered as hosted options, as well."

cations that enable everything from financial trading to real-time flight tracking, the Web is changing the way we work and live. In many cases, the Web is enabling both callers and agents to tap into the same tools and information, improving the consistency and cohesiveness of services. And the important role of search capabilities — which cannot be overstated — has turned a vast unnavigable universe of content into a source of immediately accessible information, content and solutions. Web-based applications have created an interesting shift in customer attitudes, creating a large percentage of customers who choose to use them whenever possible, and who have developed loyalties and expectations of them.

HOSTED SOLUTIONS. Hosted solutions are provided by a vendor who is responsible for hardware and software applications, and charge for usage on a fee basis. Although many came and went with the boom and bust of the late 1990s, hosted solutions are back — and, in general, they're much more viable and, in the right environments, can be a great alternative for rolling out technology solutions quickly and cost-effectively (see box).

CUSTOMER CAPABILITIES. When discussing customer contact technologies, it's easy to forget what's happening on the customers' end. And yet, the information, services and tools that they use are, of course, the other side of customer contact equation. As I work on this chapter, crews are installing fiber optic cables throughout the neighborhoods in my community. And it's a scene being played out in many parts of the world — whether by fiber, cable, phone line, mobile or other type of access (even power lines can be used to carry digital information) — broadband services are conquering "the last mile." And access to information continues to be redefined — think of vehicle telematics (communications capabilities in autos, which can be used for calls, remote diagnostics, paying tolls, automatic collision notification and a host of other purposes); mobile devices providing ubiquitous access to SMS messaging, pictures and video, electronic currency, and a growing variety of communications and media; smart products that self-heal and automatically upgrade; online communities, forums and interest groups; and information from countless sources. As communication hubs, call centers must accommodate the many ways customers can provide and access information — no small feat. Of course, forward-looking organizations are turning this challenge into a competitive opportunity.

Seven Key Trends

These advances all sound very positive, right? But what do we really make of them? What should we — rather, must we — prepare for? While there are many trends that have emerged, I believe that the following seven are especially important. These are not predictions — they have already been set in motion and are changing the customer contact landscape significantly and rapidly.

SEVEN KEY TRENDS

1. Customers are better informed and have higher expectations
2. You'll always need agents — but for different reasons
3. Agent-assisted services are being rationed
4. Call center employees require increasingly high levels of skill
5. Call center structures are being redefined
6. Yet-to-be imagined services will emerge
7. Clear business thinking is more important than ever

1. CUSTOMERS ARE BETTER INFORMED AND HAVE HIGHER EXPECTATIONS

The proliferation of wireless and broadband services, Internet-based information, sophisticated search tools and ever-changing cultural expectations have created a better informed, more empowered and more savvy customer base. As consultant Gordon MacPherson put it a decade ago, "A new breed of technology-sophisticated consumers is demanding a choice of how they will be served. They often know what the choices could be, and they will become increasingly critical if you do not offer the choices they think you should offer." It's up to you to open up and develop the alternatives as technologies and expectations evolve.

You also must make access choices clear to customers. "I can't find your tech support number on your Web site." "I got trapped in the system." "I can't seem to figure out how to reach a real person." These complaints are indicative of a fundamental misunderstanding of the value of customer relationships and of the call center's potential to contribute strategic value (see Chapters 12 and 13).

All channels have a place. A call center agent won't suffice when the customer needs to download software. Speech recognition doesn't illustrate a graph of movement in a financial market. Web-based services don't come close to matching the proficiency of an experienced technical support representative, nor can they cross-sell and upsell in the personalized manner of a seasoned sales representative. Your customers and their specific situations will dictate the best channels to use in each case.

Heightened customer expectations also add a sense of context, even urgency, to the quality- and performance-boosting technologies that are becoming available. The contacts that require agent assistance have to go well — you can and must deliver value on all three levels — efficiency, customer loyalty and business unit contributions (see Chapters 1 and 13).

2. YOU'LL ALWAYS NEED AGENTS — BUT FOR DIFFERENT REASONS

I recall having a lunch meeting with an executive of a company based in New York City. After meeting in his office that morning, we walked to a restaurant for lunch — about four short city blocks away. It was high noon, and there was a throng of people on the sidewalks and crossing intersections — literally hundreds at each corner. I found myself fixated on just how many people were using their mobile phones or thumbing through email and other information. (I've since found myself making the same observation in cities around the world; it's a strange pastime, I admit, but it puts faces — lots of them — on industry stats).

After lunch, we continued our discussion. "Our plans are for customer calls to go away," he told me. "Any transaction we can get onto the Web is going to be cheaper for us and better for them [the organization's customers]." I couldn't help but smile at the contrast between his strategic initiative and what we had just seen on the street below. "You mean the masses of people we just saw making calls and sending email are all going to hang up and use self-service when they contact your company?"

Many industry pundits predicted in recent years that self-service capabilities would dramatically reduce reliance on agent-assisted services across the industry. Some were convinced that we would need fewer agents, period. But the variable missing in much of the analysis is that communications capabilities help create new kinds of services and grow the economic pie. Many organizations are finding that total contact workload often — not always, but often — increases as new customer access channels are added. And that's true in general — the widespread use of email, for example, has not led to a commensurate drop in phone calls or in-person travel; at best, it has slowed the growth of other channels. By opening access alternatives, we seem to be encouraging customers to contact us more often. Contacts will happen — and that puts a premium on ensuring that we squeeze maximum value out of them (Chapter 13). Get used to that reality now, and you'll be better positioned to open all forms of channels and encourage —

not force, encourage — optimum use of self-service.

3. AGENT-ASSISTED SERVICES ARE BEING RATIONED

Here's the tricky part of predicting that you'll always need agents: Many of the contacts being handled today can be, will be and should be handled by self-service channels in coming years. Consider the travel sector. Every time a long-established airline closes a call center somewhere, journalists jump on the story — "Is the call center industry in decline? Is this represen-

---

THE CALL CENTER'S ROLE IN BUILDING SELF-SERVICE CHANNELS

Many organizations are learning firsthand that call centers can play a central role in encouraging and supporting low-cost access channels. For example, the call center can provide a wealth of information on which contacts can be automated and what can be done to improve customer acceptance. Further — and paradoxically — providing agent assistance when and as needed encourages customer confidence in self-service systems.

Here are some things you can do to further the call center's opportunity to build self-service channels:

- Equip agents to educate customers on self-service options. Agents should be trained on the advantages and use of self-service systems so that they can encourage customers to use these options when appropriate.
- Collect and analyze data about calls currently handled in the call center. Look for opportunities to provide self-service features that callers will want to use. Improved speed of access and around-the-clock availability are often at the top of the list.
- Observe agents handling contacts, step-by-step. Your best call center agents really know how to serve customers; watching them work can present many opportunities for developing and improving self-service systems. In many ways, self-service systems can be modeled after effective agent practices.

(continued next page)

- Involve agents in system design. Call center agents should actively serve on project teams responsible for building self-service systems, and can help monitor and test systems and interpret customer behavior and feedback.
- Integrate self-service and call center systems and developments. Integrated systems can enable agents to use the information captured in self-service applications when assisting customers.
- Capture customer feedback about self-service systems. The nature of input is that you'll get a lot more of it when things go wrong than when they go right. Even so, customers who share their dissatisfaction represent the tip of the iceberg; in most cases there will be many more who were dissatisfied but who did not bother to tell you. This information is essential to improving system design.
- Enable customers to easily reach agents. If callers can't reach an agent when necessary, they will often resent the need to use self-service systems. Support may take many forms, such as:
  - A clearly identified way to exit an IVR application
  - Prominently displayed telephone numbers on your Web site
  - Text-chat, click-to-talk or co-browsing capabilities
  - Email addresses and Web templates for questions, comments and other input
- Track data from all support modes and analyze it for improvement opportunities; specifically, why do customer contacts happen? Which do you want to encourage and which do you want to prevent (as possible)?

Self-service systems must be an integrated part of your customer access strategy. If they are perceived primarily as replacements for call center agents rather than complementary access channels that free agents to do more high-value work, then call center employees will be less enthusiastic about helping to improve them and encourage their use. But by keeping the focus on cultivating better ways to serve customers, self-service systems become an essential part of building valuable, cost-effective services.

tative of what's happening across the board?" (The fact that they even care is indicative of the kind of employment numbers call centers post.) Short answer: no. Those interactions needed to be automated. Most of us are simply not calling airlines as much as we used to — we're seeing the advantages of booking online and checking in by Web or kiosk.

Historically, that kind of displacement has been going on for decades. For example, when telephone companies automated switching centers, there were marches on the streets to protest the hundreds of thousands of lost operator jobs. The fear was that there would simply not be enough jobs to go around. Sound familiar? That was over a half-century ago.

Forward-thinking organizations are taking tangible steps to establish self-service alternatives and encourage customers to use them. And leading call centers are taking a proactive role in this effort (see box, "The Call Center's Role in Building Self-Service Channels"). They are ensuring that their highly trained, highly paid agents are handling transactions that really require the human touch. In other words, they are rationing live answer.

4. CALL CENTER EMPLOYEES REQUIRE INCREASINGLY HIGH LEVELS OF SKILL

As self-service technologies offload relatively simple or well-defined contacts and products and services grow increasingly diverse and complex, agents face a number of challenges. In addition to handling more difficult transactions, they must serve increasingly well-informed and varied customers; adjust to rapid changes in products, services and technologies; operate in a time-sensitive, multimedia environment; communicate quickly and accurately in both verbal and written form; and understand Web- and IVR-based applications and help customers use those alternatives.

At the management level, the traditional "jack-of-all-trades" call center manager role is being divided among specialists doing everything from data analysis to scheduling, quality monitoring and coaching. Evolving technologies are powerful and enormously flexible, but they are contributing to the emergence of technology managers who require specialized expertise to understand, manage and maintain them.

And an undeniable trend adding complexity to call centers is the emergence of new contact channels. While the core principles of effective call center management are timeless and universal, the operational specifics vary from one channel to another — e.g., staffing for text-chat is different than staffing for calls or email (see Chapter 7). And requirements at the agent level vary, even though the products and services being supported from one channel to the next are the same.

5. CALL CENTER STRUCTURES ARE BEING REDEFINED

Many organizations are restructuring so that all channels of contact with customers are under the same management umbrella. This is causing enormous internal structural change that involves IT, marketing, HR and virtually every other department. Whatever the final structure, all contact channels must be planned and operated cohesively — each impacts the others.

Many call centers are also becoming more distributed. Multisite call centers and agents based at home, in other departments or even in other organizations have proliferated rapidly in recent years (see Chapter 8). Virtually any place with up-to-spec communications technology and a skilled and flexible labor force is a candidate for regional, national or international-oriented call centers. The call center as a "place" will, in many cases (certainly not all), fade.

Job roles are changing along with organizational structures. As discussed in Chapters 13 through 15, it will be increasingly important for call center managers to cultivate and broaden the skills of agents and supervisors, and for organizations to provide attractive skill and career paths for them.

6. YET-TO-BE IMAGINED SERVICES WILL EMERGE

As advanced as technologies have become, many are in still in their infancy. Multimedia will prevail and the distinctions between calls, text-chat, browsing and even video will blur — they'll just be interactions. The single-channel, monomedia environment will fade as richer forms of communication that combine all of these elements emerge.

Multimedia appeals to the way we are wired up. We communicate best when our senses work together. Think about these ingredients, and ponder ways they can be combined:

- Digital
- Virtual
- Telephone
- Television
- Broadband
- Software
- Mobile
- Television
- Computer
- Interactive
- Information
- Entertainment
- Multimedia
- Networks
- Communities
- Currency

In coming months and years, these components will be mixed and harnessed in numerous, yet-to-be-imagined ways. And the latest technology won't be on customers' minds. They just want things to work as they should. If they're browsing your Web site and need further help, they want a knowledgeable agent a click away — or perhaps another customer, user forum or knowledge network. And if they end up in a queue — queues will still happen — they'll expect a reasonably short wait time. They expect processes to be integrated and thoughtful. And they will expect to reach professional, competent agents. In short, they want services that are reliable, intuitive, accessible — even enjoyable — to use.

7. CLEAR BUSINESS THINKING IS MORE IMPORTANT THAN EVER

New technologies are not passive — to get good results, they must be implemented with foresight and good planning. Take, for example, skills-based routing. Remember how it was supposed to solve scheduling and staffing problems? And yet, many call centers have taken a few steps back from the most involved types of skills-based routing, having been unable to achieve the efficiency and effectiveness they had with pools of cross-trained agents. It turns out that it's like hot pepper sauce — a little bit goes a long way, and the use and context must be precise.

Similarly, open systems offer wonderful flexibility and customization, but they need to be programmed to do what you want them to do. Clarification and definition of the underlying business rules is an ongoing challenge for any organization. And that has a lot more to do with clear business thinking than a specific technology capability. The late Peter Drucker contended that the most important impact of information technology is not the capabilities of the technologies themselves, but that these systems force you to organize processes and information more logically.

Good Leadership Is Essential

Effective leadership in this environment requires a multifaceted approach, and a few important recommendations come to mind:

1. Keep your eyes on the prize: The purpose of any new technology should be to support the governing principles and mission of your organization. Keep it simple — don't over-complicate applications to the point that they are ineffective or unmanageable. When complexity begins to throw things off course, go back to the basics (see box, "As Much as Things May Change..."). Stay focused on what really matters.

2. Remember that new capabilities both depend on and dramatically impact training, policies, planning, budgeting, other systems and many other issues. Those who take a systemic approach to planning and imple-

AS MUCH AS THINGS MAY CHANGE...

Jay Minnucci, VP of ICMI's Consulting Division, agrees that the emerging multichannel environment can get complex. "One common thread weaving its way through the discussions on multichannel customer access is complexity," he says. "That's not always the point of the discussion, but the conversation gets so full of technological possibilities, customer behavior issues and process requirements that the overall theme winds up drifting toward complexity."

And therein lies the opportunity, he says. "There is no value in allowing people at any level, in any department, to be mired in such complexity that it chokes growth opportunities. Instead, constantly remind everyone of the basics that are here today, and will continue to be here tomorrow." And what are those basics?

- Quick, friendly service wins. Time and time again, in every survey in nearly every industry, customers verify the fact that their purchasing decisions are based on such "emotional" issues as the availability and friendliness of a service representative.
- Good service has a far greater impact on revenue than on expenses. Before getting hung up on the cost of installing and supporting new service channels, consider the impact of not having them.
- Customers have been embracing (and paying for) convenience for the last three decades. There is nothing to indicate that will change anytime soon.

"In short, when confusion reigns supreme, bring people back to the basics," advises Minnucci. "Convenience counts. Good service pays for itself many times over. Quick, friendly service is a differentiator. These things aren't changing anytime soon, no matter what the future brings."

menting systems, and who put adequate thought into process- and people-related issues earn the highest returns on technology investments.

3. Recognize that just about any technology can be viewed as the proverbial "double-edged sword." For example, monitoring capabilities can be

© 2003 Ted Goff

"This plan will be much easier not to implement than the last plan we didn't implement."

Reprinted with permission.

great sources of stress for agents. Or they can be used to identify improvement opportunities and coach agents to higher levels of performance. Similarly, technology that gives managers outside the call center access to call center information may bring unwanted attention. Or it may be a boon to the interest level and support the call center receives. Ensuring that others have an understanding of technologies and how they will be used is key.

4. It's essential to develop a sound customer access strategy and use it to guide decisions (see Chapter 2). As you view technology possibilities though the lens of your customer access strategy, some key questions will likely surface; e.g., which technologies best support your plans and direction? How will processes need to change? How will agent requirements be impacted, both in number and skills required? How will your cost structure — expenses and revenues — be impacted? How will overall service be improved? How technologies are implemented, supported and used is every bit as important as the capability of the technologies themselves. The answers to these and related questions will help you make wise investments, and ensure that technology is being led by your mission and direction — not the other way around.

5. Inaction is the worst action you can take. Given the pace of change, it's important to begin planning your call center's migration into the next era now.

Points to Remember

- Advanced call center technologies are creating enormous opportunities for better serving customers, empowering agents and increasing efficiency in the call center.
- These technologies are not passive, and they are changing caller behavior, leading to significant reallocations of resources, and changing the responsibilities of agents and managers.
- New capabilities must be implemented with foresight and care, and must support the organization's mission.
- The key trends that have been set in motion provide a framework for understanding the changes taking place and preparing your call center for tomorrow's environment.
- New capabilities both depend on and dramatically impact training, policies, planning, budgeting and many other issues. Effective leadership is essential to getting the most out of your technology investments.

CHAPTER 17:
Characteristics of the Best-Managed Call Centers

A vision without a task is but a dream; a task without a vision is drudgery; a vision and a task is the hope of the world.

CHURCH INSCRIPTION, SUSSEX, ENGLAND 1730

In some call centers, you can feel the energy as soon as you walk in the door. It takes many forms: pride of workmanship, a feeling of community, good planning, coordination and the willingness to make the "extra

CHARACTERISTICS OF THE BEST-MANAGED CALL CENTERS

1. They produce high levels of value.
2. They have a supporting culture.
3. They know that their people are the key to success.
4. They build plans and services around evolving customer expectations.
5. They have an established, collaborative planning process.
6. They leverage the key statistics.
7. They view the call center as a total process.
8. They use technology to support and further their mission.
9. They get the budget and support they need.
10. They build an effective organization.
11. They are willing to experiment.
12. They see the possibilities.

effort." Everybody knows what the mission is and everybody is pulling in the same direction. The call center "clicks."

While there are a myriad of factors that go into creating this sort of environment, there are 12 overarching and interrelated characteristics that emerge in call centers that consistently outperform others.

1. They Produce High Levels of Value

Great call centers have an incessant focus on creating high levels of value for their organizations and customers. Far too many organizations are still focused primarily on one level or one dimension of call center value — e.g., to "deliver services efficiently," "improve revenues" or "boost

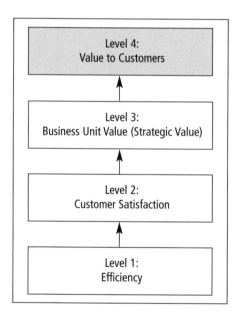

customer satisfaction." The best align their resources, strategy and culture to deliver maximum value on all three levels (see Chapters 1 and 13): efficiency, customer satisfaction and loyalty, and business unit value (strategic value).

By doing so, they create a fourth level of value, one that could never be sufficiently measured, but is as real as any of the others: the ultimate value these services provide to customers. What really happens when customers can access the services they need and want — seamlessly, easily? What is the impact on their economic situation? Their peace of mind? Their families? Society in general? Because call centers are so central to the delivery of services that so many organizations provide, call centers — and all who are part of them — can *make a difference.*

2. They Have a Supporting Culture

Culture — the inveterate principles or values of the organization — tends to guide behavior, and can either support and further or, as some have learned the hard way, ruin the best-laid plans for organizational change. While there is no guaranteed formula for creating a supporting culture, many seasoned call center managers agree that shaping culture — or, more correctly, enabling it to flourish — is a primary leadership responsibility. As a result, they spend an inordinate amount of time understanding the organization and the people who are part of it.

How do leading call centers create high-performance cultures? How do they communicate their mission and values in a way that gets buy-in and alignment? There are some notable characteristics that stand out:

- They have a people-first perspective (see next characteristic).
- They are committed to effective communication (see Chapter 15).
- They have — and use — an up-to-date customer access strategy, which ensures that everyone is "on the same page" (Chapter 2).
- They cultivate a collaborative planning process so that their operations run smoothly, enabling them to focus on higher level issues that matter most (see the fifth characteristic).
- They ensure that everyone across the call center and larger organization has an understanding of the call center's contribution to the organization (see the first characteristic).

3. They Know that Their People Are the Key to Success

Cultures vary dramatically from one organization to the next. You'd likely notice some hairstyles that you don't see everyday at Virgin Mobile's Customer Care center. Nintendo has a break room (yes, with video games) that puts most others to shame. Wells Fargo Banker Connection (see box) has a somewhat more formal, polished atmosphere — expected and fitting in the banking environment. But in each case, a "people-first" philosophy is evident. Virgin Mobile's Nancy Tichbon, director of customer experience, puts it this way: "It just makes sense to us: If our people are happy and motivated, our customers are going to have a great experience. And it goes without saying that if our customers are satisfied, our shareholders will be delighted. Thus, if we live by this value... ultimately, everyone wins."

The most important implication of the trends discussed throughout the book, and particularly in Part Four (Chapters 12 through 15), is clear: Your people are your key to success.

FIRST (AND LASTING) IMPRESSIONS AT WELLS FARGO BANKER CONNECTION

The following is an excerpt of a speech given at ICMI's ACCE conference by Vanita Vik-Ohlgren, who is with Wells Fargo Banker Connection, a multisite center with locations in Fargo, ND and Billings, MT. Vik-Ohlgren, who is based in Fargo, N.D., is a Banker Connection manager — that's the title the organization uses for those who supervise teams of agents. Banker Connection is a past recipient of ICMI's Global Call Center of the Year award.

Do you remember the anticipation you felt before starting a new job? You're so excited and nervous that you probably planned out what you were going to wear a week in advance. And then the first day came and you were hidden away in a room somewhere filling out paperwork and forms. How dull and boring! And that's the way it used to be at Banker Connection, except we topped it off by following the new-hire paperwork with hours of computer-based self-training.

First impressions are lasting, and we didn't want new-hires to perceive that we (or their new jobs) were going to be dull and boring. So we made an effort to transition from a lackluster and unwelcoming environment to one where our new team members would go home at the end of the day and say, "I made a great choice when I accepted their offer."

How did we do that? Here are some of the ways:

- A "welcome" sign is signed by the management team prior to day one and hung on the new team member's cube.
- A "welcome to the team" greeting card is signed by every team member on the new person's team, and is mailed to them before they even start.
- The hiring manager greets the new-hire(s) at the front door.
- A "welcome" gift kit is presented to each new-hire on day one.
- We provide a "welcome to Banker Connection" manager tour.
- The team member is welcomed by a senior manager.
- We review our vision/values, Wells Fargo and Banker Connection history, and an overview of our business and community involvement.
- We conduct a "getting to know you" exercise.
- Lunch is on us!

Besides the welcoming atmosphere, we also focus on that first (and lasting impression). We have developed a couple of programs that we feel are essential to successful on-boarding and retention. The first is the "buddy program," where the new-hire is paired with a seasoned team member who acts as their "buddy" while in training and for one month following their skills assessment.

The second is our "team member connection activities" program, which includes weekly interaction and activities designed to build relationships between new-hires and their managers while they are in training. This ensures a successful transition from training to becoming part of their new team on the floor.

Once we've attracted talented employees, we work hard to keep them. As part of that effort, we've developed the "Manager's On-Boarding Guide," a unique and effective approach to welcoming new team members in all job categories during their first six to 12 months. Carefully orchestrated events and activities help to engage team members from day one, and ensure that new team members get signed up for their benefits and get paid on time, instill a sense of enthusiasm, and help managers set the stage for development in an inclusive, positive work environment.

4. They Build Plans and Services around Evolving Customer Expectations

One of the most critical — and difficult — aspects of managing a call center in coming months and years will be to provide services that satisfy changing consumer demands. Those who fall behind will pay a brutal price: dissatisfied customers, insufficient support from the organization and low morale in the call center. But those who stay ahead of the curve will enjoy strong customer loyalty and the many benefits that come with it. The stakes are high.

Many call center managers are discovering first-hand a basic reality of customer psychology. When you improve your service, customers rather quickly progress through four distinct stages:

1. They appreciate it.
2. They get used to it.
3. They expect it.
4. They demand it.

Consequently, continually improving services to meet evolving customer expectations is a mandate in today's environment. In leading call centers, the 10 customer expectations (see Chapter 2) are an important part of the call center's development and culture. The list is sometimes plastered to the wall — literally — and works its way into everything from strategy to process design to day-to-day planning and coaching activities.

In short, the best-managed call centers have an incessant focus on evolving customer needs and expectations. They are continually redefining plans and reshaping services around those expectations (see Chapters 2 and 13). They know that what worked yesterday will not necessarily work tomorrow.

5. They Have an Established, Collaborative Planning Process

Effective planning is a central theme in Part Two and Part Three of this book. A major objective of good planning is to get the right number of skilled people and supporting resources in place at the right times, doing the right things.

But systematic planning accomplishes more than that. It also improves communication and culture by: creating a body of information that wouldn't otherwise be available; forcing people to look into the future and see their work in the context of a large framework; and necessitating communication about values — issues such as resource allocations, budgeting and workload priorities.

Perhaps most important, systematic planning necessitates communication about values on issues such as resource allocations, budgeting and workload priorities. In summary, it forces the kind of communication that the call center requires.

Largely due to effective planning, great call centers work so well that they are almost transparent. The teams concentrate on delivering the organization's services, and on building the organization's value and brand — not on running call centers, per se. *The call center just works.* As a result, higher levels of value are possible.

6. They Leverage the Key Statistics

As discussed in Chapters 12 through 14, measurements are plentiful — and it's easy to get buried in information. The call centers that get the best results from using their reports and information have several things in common:

- They focus on a relatively small number of measures and objectives that support their mission and direction. They know that trying to focus on too many things is counterproductive.

- They ensure that measurements are as accurate, complete and unbiased as possible. They are aware of how easily statistics can be misinterpreted. They view reports in light of how they relate to each other. They know that a single report, outside the context of the others, can lead to erroneous conclusions.

- They understand that simply tracking high-level measurements won't inherently improve results. Instead, they work on the factors — the root causes — that cause these outputs to be where they are (see next characteristic).

7. They View the Call Center as a Total Process

Call centers that consistently get the best results view the call center as a total process. That has been a major theme in this book, and it takes many forms:

- Ensure that everyone in the call center and those with key supporting roles outside the call center have a basic understanding of how call centers operate (encourage them to read Chapters 9 and 10!).

- Recognize the process to be where most quality problems occur — and also where the opportunities for improvement in services and reductions in costs reside (Chapter 13).

- Develop an effective, collaborative planning and management process.

- Take the initiative in coordinating with other departments.

- Be prepared to respond to changing conditions.

- Understand how the call center supports the organization's direction.

The days of the call center existing as an island unto itself — "That's the call center over there, and they handle sales and customer service" — are gone. The reality is that the call center is an important part of a much bigger process.

8. They Use Technology to Support and Further Their Mission

As discussed in Chapter 16, new technologies are not passive — they are changing caller expectations, causing reallocations of resources, creating power shifts in call centers, and changing the responsibilities of agents and managers. The best call centers identify the technologies that further the mission of the organization, and they implement them with the necessary foresight, planning and training.

They also recognize that an important (according to the late Peter Drucker, *the* most important) impact of technology is not the capabilities of the technologies themselves, but that they require you to organize your processes and information more logically. Their systems are supported by processes that ensure that information on customers, products, processes and services is current and accurate.

For example, their knowledge management systems work because they make entering and updating knowledge a priority at the point of contact. Their quality monitoring systems are valuable because they have clearly defined quality and what needs to happen to support the organization's highest-level objectives. Their reporting systems provide essential support for making sound business decisions because they produce accurate information on the right things, delivered to the right people at the right times. Their workforce management systems work well for them because they understand and apply sound underlying principles of planning and management.

In short, they respect what technology can do but they know that it's of little use without supporting processes and a clear direction. Some have the latest capabilities, other don't — but what they have, they use to support their mission and most important objectives.

9. They Get the Budget and Support They Need

Far too many call centers are operating under the auspices of, "OK, here are the resources we're willing to give you, and here's what we want you to achieve..." That is the proverbial cart before the donkey.

Consider an analogy. Airlines couldn't possibly operate a flight without a tangible connection between the results they want to achieve and the supporting resources they need. They start with an objective — fly 300 people from Washington to London. The objective is not a wishful goal — it is a specific predetermined outcome supported by carefully calculated resources.

Similarly, the best call centers first decide on the objectives they want to achieve. They then allocate the resources necessary to support those objectives, through informed calculations and disciplined planning (as discussed in Chapters 4 through 10).

10. They Build an Effective Organization

Successful call center leaders design an organizational structure that facilitates collaboration among and across job roles and business units. They tap into the principles of good organizational design (covered in Chapter 15) and revisit their structure often. They continually work on identifying positions they need and defining the responsibilities that go along with each. They gauge whether agent-to-supervisor and supervisor-to-manager ratios are working as they should, and adjust them as needed.

Above all, successful leaders know that communication is the glue that holds the whole thing together. They work hard to maintain effective communication, including across distributed teams. They understand how communication creates meaning and direction for people, and are committed to keeping a common vision at the forefront of the culture and daily activities.

11. They Are Willing to Experiment

The most successful call center teams continually review and reassess how they do things and the results they are achieving. What can be improved? What should be scrapped? What assumptions no longer make sense? What can be done differently? They would agree with the advice of management consultant Dr. Ichak Adizes, who reminds us, "You don't know what you don't know until you know it. ...the right solution is a continuous search for the right solution."

An idealist believes that the short run doesn't count. A cynic believes the long run doesn't matter. A realist believes that what is done or left undone in the short run determines the long run.

— SIDNEY J. HARRIS

---

12. They See the Possibilities

The call center industry has come a long way in recent years. Customer expectations are high — and for good reason. For the most part, call centers have learned how to deliver. Collectively, they have invested billions in equipment, networks and software. They have spent untold hours training and equipping people. They have learned the nuances of forecasting, staffing and the behavior of queues. They continue to improve processes and find new and better ways to get things done. And, they have identified evolving customer needs, and are constantly changing to meet those needs.

But things are changing fast, and some call center managers view the future with apprehension. They fear the impact and uncertainties that new technologies will bring. They are concerned about ever-heightening competition. They contemplate the increasingly diverse interactions their call center will handle. They wonder how they're going to keep up in an envi-

387

ronment that changes *so quickly, so persistently.*

It's important to remember, though, that the very things that are bringing uncertainties are also bringing new opportunities. More than ever, organizations need professionals who can help them sort through the changes and make sound business decisions. Professionals who see the possibilities ahead.

Where to from Here?

Clearly, customer contact operations are becoming increasingly complex to operate. The proliferation of wireless and broadband services, Internet-based information, search tools and ever-changing cultural expectations is creating a better-informed and more savvy customer base. Automated services (Web-based self-service, IVR, speech applications, et al.) are offloading more straightforward contacts, leaving call centers with more complex work. And many organizations are restructuring so that all channels of contact with customers are managed under the same umbrella; this is causing internal structural change that involves virtually every part of the organization. I firmly believe that if you know and practice the principles covered in this book, you will have a big head start.

In so many ways, we are all pioneers in creating the next generation of services — services our customers will come to expect, our organizations will depend on and our economy will require.

We are becoming a communication-oriented economy. Ours is often called a knowledge-based economy, and knowledge is essential — but it has no value unless you can *get to it when you need it.* Call centers are right in the middle of that development. In so many ways, we are all pioneers in creating the next generation of services — services our customers will come to expect, our organizations will depend on and our economy will require.

We've got more opportunity right now than at any time in the history of the call center industry.

I often hear various pundits and observers talk about how advanced customer contact centers are today. I think we're just getting started. I believe we're going to see more development in the next five to 10 years than we've seen in the last three decades. And the opportunities are there for the taking — it will truly be *call center management on fast forward.*

Thank you for joining me on this journey!

Notes

CHAPTER 1

Puvis de Chavannes quote, source: Brooks, John. *Telephone, the First Hundred Years*, Harper and Row, 1976, page 118.

John Brooks quote, source: Brooks, John. *Telephone, the First Hundred Years*, Harper and Row, 1976, page 117.

Call Center Definition, source: ICMI's *Essential Skills and Knowledge for Effective Call Center Management* seminar, 1990-2006.

Planning steps, source: ICMI's *Essential Skills and Knowledge for Effective Call Center Management* seminar, 1990-2006.

CHAPTER 2

AAMC Consumer Health Line, source: *AAMC*, Spring 2006, p. 16.

Ten customer expectations, source: ICMI's *Essential Skills and Knowledge for Effective Incoming Call Center Management* seminar, 1990-2006.

CHAPTER 3

Three driving forces (random call arrival, visible and invisible queue, and seven factors of caller tolerance), source: ICMI's *Essential Skills and Knowledge for Effective Call Center Management* seminar, 1990-2006.

Three types of traffic arrival, source: J. Jewett, J. Shrago, J. Gilliland, B. Yomtov. *Traffic Engineering Tables: The Complete Practical Encyclopedia*, Telephony Publishing Corporation, 1980.

WordPerfect reference, source: *Call Center Management Review*, July 1994.

British Airways case study, source: *Call Center Management Review*, April 1997.

Virtual queuing citations, source: Virtual Hold Technology and interviews with ICMI staff.

CHAPTER 4

Service level and response time examples, source: ICMI surveys.

ASA and delay calculations, source: ICMI's QueueView staffing program based on Erlang C.

Incremental Revenue (Value) Analysis, source: ICMI.

CHAPTER 5

Georgia Power, source: Levin, Greg. "Top Agents as Teachers: Using Experienced Staff to Optimize Coaching and Training," *Call Center Management Review*, January 2006.

Mountain America Credit Union, source: Mayben, Julia. "Call Center Manager Spotlight," *Call Center Management Review*, September, 2002.

Eddie Bauer, source: reference from first edition of book.

CHAPTER 6

Breaking down a forecast, source: ICMI's *Essential Skills and Knowledge for Effective Incoming Call Center Management* seminar, 1990-2006.

Worksheets used throughout chapter, source: ICMI.

Armstrong, J.S. (Editor). *Principles of Forecasting — A Handbook for Researchers and Practitioners*, Springer, 2001.

Forecasting study (10 common problems), source: ICMI.

CHAPTER 7

W. Edwards Deming quote, source: Deming, W. Edwards. *Out of the Crisis,* Massachusetts Institute of Technology, 1986.

Staffing and delay examples, source: ICMI's QueueView staffing program.

Mike Hills reference, source: reference from first edition of book and HTML Technologies.

Skills-based routing case, source: Original example produced by Martin A. Prunty.

Text-chat examples, source: Jay Minnucci, ICMI Consulting Division.

Traffic Engineering Tables and Formulas, source: Jewett, J., J. Shrago, J. Gilliland, B. Yomtov. *Traffic Engineering Tables: The Complete Practical Encyclopedia*, Telephony Publishing Corporation, 1980.

CHAPTER 8

Rostered staff factor (shrink factor) illustrations, source: ICMI's *Essential Skills and Knowledge for Effective Call Center Management* seminar, 1990-2006.

AMVESCAP source: Levin, Greg. "Call Center Manager Spotlight," *Call Center Management Review*, January 2006.

Vanguard example, from first edition of book.

People's Bank, source: Levin, Greg. "A Look at Call Centers Doing Big Things in Key Areas," *Call Center Management Review*, May 1999.

Met Life example, from first edition of book.

Day-Timers Customer Contact Center and Accor Reservations Center staff sharing arrangement, source: Hash, Susan. "Opposite Peak Seasons Attract: A Staff-Sharing Partnership Helps to Ease Seasonal Scheduling Dilemma," *Call Center Management Review*, November 2004.

JetBlue Airlines, source: Levin, Greg. "Extreme Telecommuting," *Call Center Management Review*, March 2005.

WillowCSN, Alpine Access, Working Solutions, source: Levin, Greg. "Homesourcing Hits Its Stride," *Call Center Management Review*, March 2005.

Service level graphs, source: ICMI

CHAPTER 9

Immutable laws, graphs, tables and examples, source: ICMI's *Essential Skills and Knowledge for Effective Call Center Management* seminar, 1990-2006.

CHAPTER 10

In the section on what senior level managers should understand, some points are adapted from a booklet by Gordon Mac Pherson, Jr. Source: MacPherson, Jr. Gordon F.: *What Senior Management Needs to Know About Incoming Call Centers*, ICMI, 1988 through 1996.

BT Americas, source: Levin, Greg. "Call Center Manager Spotlight," *Call Center Management Review*, August 2005.

Staffing budget example, source: ICMI's Consulting Division. Examples prepared by Jay Minnucci and Dan Rickwalder, of ICMI.

Stephanie Winston quote, source: Winston, Stephanie. *The Organized Executive: The Classic Program for Productivity — New Ways to Manage Time, Paper, People and the Electronic Office, Revised Edition (Paperback)*, Warner Business Books, 2001.

Laurie Solomon quote, from first edition of book.

CHAPTER 11

"Due to our inability to staff…" (cartoon), source: Kathleen Peterson, quote, from first edition of book.

Real-time management graphs and examples, source: ICMI's *Essential Skills and Knowledge for Effective Incoming Call Center Management* seminar, 1990-2006.

Apple Computer, source: ICMI Call Center Insight Tour at Call Center Demo & Conference, Austin, Texas, February 2006.

CHAPTER 12

Keith Dawson quote, source: Dawson, Keith. "Editor's Page," *Call Center Magazine*, January 2005.

Mary Murcott quote, source: Murcott, Mary. *Driving Peak Sales Performance in Call Centers*, ICMI Press, 2005.

Boston Coach and Independent Blue Cross (Philadelphia), source: Harps, Leslie, Hansen. "Use Incentive Programs to Link Desired Behaviors with Rewards," *Call Center Management Review*, April 2001.

Sharp Electronics, source: McGregor, Jena. "High-Tech Achiever: Mini USA," *Fast Company*, October 2004.

Aetna U.S. Healthcare, source: Levin, Greg. "Focusing on First-Call Resolution," *Call Center Management Review*, April 2005.

CHAPTER 13

Linksys, source: Levin, Greg. "Call Center Manager Spotlight," *Call Center Management Review*, October 2004.

What is a Quality Contact, source: ICMI's *Essential Skills and Knowledge for Effective Call Center Management* seminar, 1990-2006. Also published in *The Best of Service Level Newsletter — Volume 1*, ICMI, 1990.

Costs When Quality is Lacking, source: ICMI's *Essential Skills and Knowledge for Effective Call Center Management* seminar, 1990-2006.

Quality tools, examples: ICMI

W. Edwards Deming quote, source: Deming, W. Edwards. *Out of the Crisis,* Massachusetts Institute of Technology, 1986.

Peter Drucker quote, source: Drucker, Peter, F. *The Daily Drucker*, Collins, 2004.

Victor Hugo quote, source: Hugo, Victor. *Les Miserables*, originally published in 1862.

CHAPTER 14

Dee Hock, quoted in: Decarlo, Douglas. *eXtreme Project Management: Using Leadership, Principles, and Tools to Deliver Value in the Face of Volatility*, Jossey-Bass, 2004, p. 28.

Recommended monitoring practices, source: ICMI.

Starbucks, source: presentation by Beverly Stryker at the ICMI ACCE conference, Seattle, Washington, September 2005.

Using agent level customer feedback, sources: Levin, Greg. "Elevate Quality Assurance and Performance with Agent-Level Customer Feedback," *Call Center Management Review*, December 2005. Also, author interview by email with Terri McMillan, June 2006.

CHAPTER 15

ICMI reports on staffing and retention, source: ICMI.

Canadian Tire Financial Services source: Levin, Greg. "Call Center Manager Spotlight," *Call Center Management Review*, April 2005.

Elliot Jacques and Stephen D. Clement quote, source: Jacques, Elliot and Stephen D. Clement. *Executive Leadership*, Blackwell Publishing, Inc., reprint edition May 1994.

CHAPTER 16

H.M.S. Agamemnon, source: Russell, W.H. *The Atlantic Telegraph*, Nonsuch Publishing, 2005.

"Plate of silver…" reference, source: Brooks, John. *Telephone, the First Hundred Years*, Harper and Row, 1976, p. 36.

Blue Cross Blue Shield of South Carolina, source: Levin, Greg. "Contact Centers Voice-Enabling E-Support," *Call Center Management Review*, August 2005.

Joe Fleischer, source: from author interview and text provided by Joe Fleisher, June 2006.

Lori Bocklund, source: from author interview and text from white paper by Lori Bocklund, June 2006.

Gordon F. MacPherson, Jr. quote, source: MacPherson, Gordon F., Jr. "The New Forces of Change," *Best of Service Level Newsletter — Volume 4*, *Service Level Newsletter*, 1997, p. 460.

Jay Minnucci, source: from author interview and text from article by Jay Minnucci posted on icmi.com, June 2006.

CHAPTER 17

Virgin Mobile, source: From interview conducted by Greg Levin.

Wells Fargo Banker Connection, source: presentation by Vanita Vik-Ohlgren at the ICMI ACCE conference, Seattle, Washington, September 2005.

Dr. Ichak Adizes quote, source: Dr. Ichak, as quoted in *Manage*, Jan 1993, p. 14.

Sidney Harris, source: widely quoted. Sidney J. Harris (1917-1986) wrote the syndicated column, "Strictly Personal," from 1944-1986.

Acronyms

ACD	Automatic Call Distributor
ACW	After-Call Work
AHT	Average Handling Time
AHT	Average Holding Time on Trunks
ANI	Automatic Number Identification
ASA	Average Speed of Answer
ASP	Application Service Provider
ASR	Automatic Speech Recognition
ATA	Average Time to Abandonment
ATB	All Trunks Busy
CCR	Customer-Controlled Routing
CCS	Centum Call Seconds
CDR	Call Detail Recording
CED	Caller-Entered Digits
CIS	Customer Information System
CLEC	Competitive Local Exchange Carrier
CLI	Calling Line Identity
CLID	Calling Line Identification
CMS	Call Management System
CO	Central Office
CPE	Customer Premises Equipment
CPU	Central Processing Unit
CRM	Customer Relationship Management
CSR	Customer Service Representative
CTI	Computer Telephony Integration
DID	Direct Inward Dialing
DN	Dialed Number
DNIS	Dialed Number Identification Service

DTMF	Dual-Tone Multifrequency
ERMS	Email Response Management System
ERP	Enterprise Resource Planning
EWT	Expected Wait Time
FCR	First-Call Resolution
FIFO	First In, First Out
FTE	Full-Time Equivalent
FX	Foreign Exchange Line
GOS	Grade of Service
HTML	Hyper-Text Markup Language
HTTP	Hyper-Text Transport Protocol
IM	Instant Messaging
IP	Internet Protocol
IS	Information Systems
ISDN	Integrated Services Digital Network
ISP	Internet Service Provider
IT	Information Technology
IVR	Interactive Voice Response
IWR	Interactive Web Response
IXC	Interexchange Carrier
KM	Knowledge Management
KPI	Key Performance Indicator
LAN	Local Area Network
LEC	Local Exchange Carrier
LWOP	Leave Without Pay
MIS	Management Information System
MM	Multi-Media
NCC	Network Control Center
NOC	Network Operations Center

NPA	Numbering Plan Area
OJT	On-the-Job Training
PABX	Private Automatic Branch Exchange
PBX	Private Branch Exchange
PCP	Post-Call Processing
PDA	Personal Digital Assistant
PRI	Primary Rate Interface
PSN	Public Switched Network
PSTN	Public Switched Telephone Network
PTT	Postal Telephone & Telegraph
QM	Quality Monitoring
QOS	Quality of Service
RFI	Request for Information
RFP	Request for Proposal
RFQ	Request for Quote
RNA	Ring No Answer
ROI	Return on Investment
RSF	Rostered Staff Factor
SALT	Speech Application Language Tags
SBR	Skills-Based Routing
SFA	Sales Force Automation
SL	Service Level
SLA	Service Level Agreement
SOHO	Small Office Home Office
TCP/IP	Transmission Control Protocol/Internet Protocol
TDM	Time-Division Multiplexing
TSF	Telephone Service Factor
TSR	Telephone Sales or Service Representative
TTS	Text-to-Speech

UCD	Uniform Call Distributor
URL	Uniform Resource Locator
VDT	Video Display Terminal
VoIP	Voice Over Internet Protocol
VPN	Virtual Private Network
VRU	Voice Response Unit
VXML	Voice Extensible Markup Language
WA	Wide Area Network
WFMS	Workforce Management System
WWW	World Wide Web
XML	Extensible Markup Language

Glossary

Abandoned Call (Inbound). Also called a lost call. The caller hangs up before reaching an agent. Related terms: Abandoned Rate (Outbound), Caller Tolerance, Service Level.

Abandoned Rate (Outbound). In a predictive dialing mode, this is the percentage of calls connected to a live person that are never delivered to an agent. Related terms: Abandoned Call (Inbound), Caller Tolerance, Dialer.

Activity Codes: See Wrapup Codes.

Adherence to Schedule. A general term that refers to how well agents adhere to their schedules. The two terms most often associated with adherence include availability (the amount of time agents were available) and compliance (when they were available to take calls).

After-Call Work (ACW). Also called wrap-up, post call processing, average work time or not ready. Work that is necessitated by and immediately follows an inbound call. Related terms: Average Handling Time, Talk Time.

Agent. The person who handles incoming or outgoing contacts. Also referred to as customer service representative (CSR), customer care representative, telephone sales or service representative (TSR), rep, associate, consultant, engineer, operator, technician, account executive, team member, customer service professional, staff member, attendant or specialist.

Agent Group. Also called split, gate, queue or skills group. An agent group shares a common set of skills and knowledge, handles a specified mix of contacts (e.g., service, sales, billing or technical support) and can be comprised of hundreds of agents across multiple sites. Supervisory groups and teams are often subsets of agent groups.

Agent Out Call. An outbound call placed by an agent.

Agent Performance Report. An ACD report that provides statistics for individual agents (e.g., on talk time, after-call work and unavailable time).

Agent Status. The mode an agent is in (e.g., talk time, after-call work, unavailable, etc.). See Work State.

All Trunks Busy (ATB). When all trunks are busy in a specified trunk group. Generally, ATB reports indicate how many times all trunks were busy (how many times the last trunk available was seized), and how much total time all trunks were busy. They don't reveal how many callers got busy signals when all trunks were busy. Related Terms: Erlang B, Trunk Load.

Analog. Telephone transmission or switching that is not digital. Signals are analogous to the original signal.

Analytics. Advanced data analysis and reporting tools that enable the organization to better understand customer trends and business activities.

401

Announcement. A recorded verbal message played to callers. See Delay Announcement.

Answer Supervision. The signal sent by the ACD or other device to the local or long-distance carrier to accept a call. This is when billing for either the caller or the call center will begin, if long-distance charges apply.

Answered Call. When referring to an agent group, a call is counted as answered when it reaches an agent. Related terms: Handled Call, Offered Call, Received Call.

Application Service Provider (ASP). An outsourcing business that enables other organizations to access and use technologies or services for a fee.

Application-Based Routing and Reporting. An ACD capability that enables the system to route and track transactions by type of call, or application (e.g., sales, service, etc.) versus the traditional method of routing and tracking by trunk group and agent group.

Architecture. The basic design of a system. Determines how the components work together, system capacity, ability to upgrade and the ability to integrate with other systems.

Attendant. A person who works at a company switchboard, often called a receptionist or operator. See Agent.

Audio Response Unit (ARU). See Interactive Voice Response.

Audiotex. A voice processing capability that enables callers to automatically access pre-recorded announcements. Related terms: Interactive Voice Response.

Auto Available. An ACD feature whereby the ACD is programmed to automatically put agents into available after they finish talk time and disconnect calls. If they need to go into after-call work, they have to manually put themselves there. Related terms: Auto Wrap-Up, Manual Available.

Auto Wrap-Up. An ACD feature whereby the ACD is programmed to automatically put agents into after-call work after they finish talk time and disconnect calls. When they have completed any after-call work required, they put themselves back into available. See Auto Available.

Automated Attendant. A voice processing capability that automates the attendant (operator or receptionist) function. The system prompts callers to respond to choices (e.g., press one for this, two for that...) and then coordinates with the ACD to send callers to specific destinations. See Interactive Voice Response.

Automated Greeting. An agent's pre-recorded greeting that plays automatically when a call arrives at his or her telephone station.

Automated Reply. A system-generated email that is automatically sent to a customer acknowledging that his or her email was received. See Response Time.

Automatic Answer. See Call Forcing.

Automatic Call Distributor (ACD). The specialized telephone system — or more specifically, a software application — that is used in incoming call centers. Basic ACD capabilities include: route calls; sequence calls; queue calls; encourage callers to wait (by playing delay announcements and, in some cases, predicting and announcing wait times); distribute calls among agents; capture planning and performance data, both real-time and historical; and integrate with other systems.

Automatic Call Sequencer (ACS). A simple system that is less sophisticated than an ACD, but provides some ACD-like functionality. See Automatic Call Distributor.

Automatic Number Identification (ANI). A telephone network feature that passes the number of the phone the caller is using to the call center in real-time. ANI is an American term; Calling Line Identity (CLI) is an alternative term used elsewhere. Related terms: Computer Telephony Integration, Dialed Number Identification Service.

Automatic Speech Recognition (ASR). An IVR capability that enables customers to interact with computers using spoken language.

Auxiliary Work State. An agent work state that is typically not associated with handling telephone calls. When agents are in an auxiliary mode, they will not receive inbound calls.

Availability. The time agents spend handling calls or waiting for calls to arrive. See Adherence to Schedule.

Available State. The work state of agents who are signed on to the ACD and are waiting for calls to arrive. See Occupancy.

Available Time. The total time that an agent or agent group waits for calls to arrive, for a given time period.

Average Call Value. A measure common in revenue-producing call centers. It is total revenue divided by total number of calls for a given period of time.

Average Delay. See Average Speed of Answer.

Average Delay to Abandon. See Average Time to Abandonment.

Average Handling Time (AHT). The sum of average talk time plus average after-call work. Related terms: Talk Time, After-Call Work.

Average Holding Time on Trunks (AHT). The average time inbound transactions occupy the trunks.

Average Speed of Answer (ASA). A measure that reflects the average delay of all calls, including those that receive an immediate answer. Also called average delay.

Average Time to Abandonment (ATA). Also called average delay to abandon. The average time that callers wait in queue before abandoning. The calculation considers only the calls that abandon. Related term: Caller Tolerance.

Average Work Time (AWT). See After-Call Work.

Back Office. Business applications and functions that are "behind the scenes" to a customer, e.g., accounting, finance, inventory control, fulfillment, productions and human resources. See Front Office.

Bandwidth. The transmission capacity of a communications line.

Barge-In. An ACD feature that allows a supervisor or manager to join or "barge-in" on a call being handled by an agent.

Base Staff. Also called seated agents. The minimum number of agents required to achieve service level and response time objectives for a given period of time. Related term: Rostered Staff Factor.

Beep Tone. An audible notification that a call has arrived. Beep tone can also refer to the audible notification that a call is being monitored. Also called zip tone. Related terms: Automated Greeting, Call Forcing.

Benchmarking. In quality terms, benchmarking is comparing products, services and processes with those of other organizations to identify new ideas and improvement opportunities.

Blended Agent. An agent who handles both inbound and outbound calls, or who handles contacts from different channels (e.g., email and phone). See Call Blending.

Blockage. Callers blocked from entering a queue. See Blocked Call.

Blocked Call. A call that cannot be connected immediately because: A) no circuit is available at the time the call arrives, or B) the ACD is programmed to block calls from entering the queue when the queue backs up beyond a defined threshold. See Controlled Busies.

Business Rules. A phrase used to refer to various software (or manual) controls that manage contact routing, handling and follow up. At a basic level, business rules are a sequence of "if-then" statements. Often used interchangeably with workflow.

Business to Business (B-to-B). Refers to business or interactions between businesses. See Business to Consumer.

Business to Consumer (B-to-C). Refers to business or interactions between a business and consumers. See Business to Business.

Busy. In use, or "off hook."

Busy Hour. A telephone traffic engineering term, referring to the hour of time in which a trunk group carries the most traffic during the day.

Busy Season. The busiest time of a year for a call center.

Calibration. In a call center, calibration is the process in which variations in the way performance criteria are interpreted from person to person are minimized. See Monitoring.

Call. Also called contact, interaction or transaction. Although it most often refers to a telephone call, call can also refer to a video call, a Web call and other types of customer contacts.

Call Blending. Traditionally, the ability to dynamically allocate call center agents to both inbound and outbound calling based on conditions in the call center and programmed parameters. More recently, call blending is also used to refer to blending calls with non-phone work or handling contacts from different channels (e.g., email, text chat and phone). See Blended Agent.

Call By Call Routing. The process of routing each call to the optimum destination according to real-time conditions. See Percent Allocation and Network Inter-flow.

Call Center. ICMI defines call center as "A coordinated system of people, processes, technologies and strategies that provides access to organizational resources through appropriate channels of communication to enable interactions that create value for the customer and organization." Essentially, call center has evolved into an umbrella term that generally refers to cross-trained groups of agents handling customer service, sales, technical support or other types of contacts.

Call Center Initiated Assistance. Typically, this refers to a text-chat session initiated by the agent, rather than the customer.

Call Center Management. ICMI's definition is: "The art of having the right number of properly skilled people and supporting resources in place at the right times to handle an accurately forecasted workload, at service level and with quality."

Call Control Variables. The set of criteria the ACD uses to process calls. Examples include routing criteria, overflow parameters, recorded announcements and timing thresholds.

Call Detail Recording (CDR). A telephone system feature that allows the system to record the details of incoming and outgoing calls (e.g., when they occur, how long they last and which extensions they go to). Also called station message detail recording.

Call Forcing. An ACD feature that automatically delivers calls to agents who are available and ready to take calls. Sometimes called automatic answer. See Manual Answer.

Call Load. Also called workload. Call load is volume multiplied by average handling time, for a given period of time.

Call Management System (CMS). Another term for an ACD reporting system.

Call Quality (Contact Quality). Typically, a measure that assigns a value to the quality of individual contacts.

Call Recording. A type of monitoring in which the supervisor or automated system records a sampling of calls. The person conducting the monitoring then randomly selects calls for evaluation of agent performance.

Callback Messaging. A feature that enables callers waiting in queue to leave a message or to enter their telephone numbers for later callback from an agent.

Call-by-Call Routing. The process of routing each call to the optimum destination according to real-time conditions. Related terms: Network, Network Interflow, Percent Allocation.

Caller Entered Digits (CED). The digits a caller enters on his or her telephone keypad. Usually used for auto attendant, voice response and CTI applications. Also referred to as prompted digits.

Caller ID. See Automatic Number Identification.

Caller Tolerance. How patient callers will be when they encounter queues or experience busy signals. Related terms: Abandoned Call, Delay Announcements.

Caller-Entered Digits (CED). Digits callers enter using their telephone keypads. The ACD, IVR, or network can prompt for CEDs.

Calling Line Identity (CLI). See Automatic Number Identification.

Calls in Queue. A real-time report that refers to the number of calls received by the ACD system but not yet connected to an agent.

Career Path. Career paths guide individual employee development through structured advancement opportunities within the call center and/or organization. A typical career path model requires the development of job families, which are comprised of a number of jobs arranged in a hierarchy by grade, pay and responsibility (e.g., agent, team leader, supervisor, manager, senior manager and director). See Skill Path.

Carrier. A company that provides telecommunications circuits. Carriers include both local telephone companies, also called local exchange carriers (LECs), and long-distance providers, also called inter-exchange carriers (IXCs).

Cause-and-Effect Diagram. A chart that illustrates the relationships between causes and a specific effect you want to study.

Central Office (CO). Can refer to either a telephone company switching center or the type of telephone switch used in a telephone company switching center. The local central office receives calls from within the local area and either routes them locally or passes them to an inter-exchange carrier (IXC). On the receiving end, the local central office receives calls that originated in other areas from the IXC.

Centum Call Seconds (CCS). A unit of telephone traffic measurement referring to 100 call seconds. The first C represents the Roman numeral for 100. 1 hour of telephone traffic=1 Erlang=60 minutes=36 CCS. Related terms: Erlang, Erlang B, Erlang C.

Circuit Switching. The traditional method of establishing dedicated, end-to-end connections for voice conversations.

Circuit. A transmission path between two points in a network.

Client/Server Architecture. A network of computers that share capabilities and devices.

Co-Browsing. A term that refers to the capability of both an agent and customer to see a Web page simultaneously and share navigation and data entry.

Collateral Duties. Non-phone tasks (e.g., data entry) that are flexible and can be scheduled for periods when call load is slow. Related term: Schedule.

Completed Call. A general term that refers to an inbound contact that successfully reaches and is handled by an agent. Can also refer to an outbound call that successfully reaches a live person (or answering machine, if leaving a message is acceptable). In an outbound context, also called connected call.

Compliance. See Adherence to Schedule.

Computer-Based Training (CBT). Training programs delivered through software applications without the need for a facilitator.

Computer Simulation. A computer-based simulator program that predicts the outcome of various events in the future, given many variables.

Computer Telephony Integration (CTI). The software, hardware and programming necessary to integrate computer systems and telephone systems so they can work together seamlessly and intelligently.

Concentrated Shift. A scheduling technique that requires agents to work more hours in a day, but fewer days in a week. "Four-by-10" shifts (four days on for 10 hours each, with three days off) are particularly popular with many agents.

Conditional Routing. The capability of the ACD to route calls based on real-time criteria (e.g., calls in queue, time of day and type of call). It is based on "if-then" programming statements. For example, "if the number of calls in agent group one exceeds 10 and there are at least two available agents in group two, then route the calls to group two."

Contacts Handled (Calls Per Agent). The number of contacts an agent handles in a given period of time. Related terms: Occupancy, True Calls Per Agent.

Contacts Per Hour. An outbound term that refers to the number of contacts divided by agent hours on the dialer. See Contacts.

Control Chart. A quality tool that provides information on variation in a process.

Controlled Busies. The capability of the ACD to generate busy signals when the queue backs up beyond a programmable threshold. See Blocked Call.

Conventional Shift. A traditional five-day-a-week shift during "normal business hours" (e.g., 9 a.m. to 5 p.m., Monday through Friday).

Cookie. A small file that identifies a user or provides user-related information to Web servers.

Cost of Delay. The money you pay to queue callers, assuming you have toll-free service.

Cost Per Call. Total costs (fixed and variable) divided by total calls for a given period of time.

Cross-Sell. A suggestive selling technique that offers additional products or services to current customers, usually based on relationships established between the customer's profile and the attributes of customers who have already purchased the products or services being cross-sold. See Upsell.

Cross-Train. To train agents to handle more than one defined mix of calls (e.g., to train technical support agents handling laptop calls to also handle desktop issues).

Customer Access Strategy. The overall strategy that defines how customers will interact with the organization. Specifically, "a set of standards, guidelines and processes defining the means by which customers are enabled to access the information and services they need."

Customer Contact. See Call.

Customer Controlled Routing (CCR). A vendor-specific term (originated by Nortel) that refers to a call routing application that enables calls to be handled (e.g., routed, queued, distributed) based on user-defined criteria.

Customer Expectations. The expectations customers have of a product, service or organization.

Customer Information System (CIS). An information systems that provides data on customers, e.g., what they have purchased, prior contacts, and other customer related information.

Customer Lifetime Value. Expresses the value of a customer to the organization over the entire probable time period that the customer will interact with the organization.

Customer Loyalty. Typically defined in terms of the customer's repurchase behavior, intent to purchase again or intent to recommend the organization.

Customer Premises Equipment (CPE). A telecommunications term referring to equipment installed on the customer's premises and connected to the telecommunications network.

Customer Relationship Management (CRM). The process of holistically developing the customer's relationship with the organization. It takes into account their history as a customer, the depth and breadth of their business with the organization, as well as other factors.

Customer Satisfaction. The level of satisfaction customers have with the organization and the organization's products and services.

Customer Segmentation. The process of grouping customers based on what you know about them, in order to apply differentiated marketing, relationship and contact treatment strategies.

Customer Service Representative (CSR). See Agent.

Data Mining. Generally refers to the use of analytics capabilities to analyze data, e.g., to identify trends and causal factors.

Day-of-Week Routing. A network service that routes calls to alternate locations, based on the day of week. There are also options for day-of-year and time-of-day routing.

Delay. Also called queue time. The time a caller spends in queue waiting for an agent to become available. Average delay is the same thing as average speed of answer. Related term: Average Speed of Answer.

Delay Announcements. Recorded announcements that encourage callers to wait for an agent to become available, remind them to have their account number ready, and provide information on access alternatives.

Delayed Call. A call which cannot be answered immediately and is placed in queue.

Dialed Number (DN). The number that the caller dialed to initiate the call.

Dialed Number Identification Service (DNIS). A string of digits that the telephone network passes to the ACD, IVR or other device to indicate which telephone number the caller dialed. One trunk group can have many DNIS numbers. See Automatic Number Identification.

Dialer. Dialers are technologies (hardware/software) for automating the process of making outbound calls. Dialers may also provide campaign management and scripting functionality, track the disposition of calls and provide detailed real-time and historical reporting. Predictive dialing is an application that instructs the switch to dial multiple simultaneous calls from a preloaded list of phone numbers, then matches completed calls with agents. Related terms: Abandoned Rate (Outbound), Completed Call.

Digital. The use of a binary code — 1s and Os — to represent information.

Direct Call Processing. See Talk Time.

Disaster Recovery Plan. A plan that enables managers to avoid or recover expediently from an interruption in the center's operation. Comprehensive plans should include an approved set of arrangements and procedures for facilities, networks, people and service levels.

Display Board. See Readerboard.

Distributed Call Center. See Virtual Call Center.

Dual-Tone Multifrequency (DTMF). A signaling system that sends pairs of audio frequencies to represent digits on a telephone keypad. It is often used interchangeably with the term Touchtone (an AT&T trademark).

Dynamic Answer. An ACD feature that automatically reconfigures the number of rings before the system answers calls based on real-time queue information. Since costs don't begin until the ACD answers calls, this feature can save callers or the call center money on long-distance charges.

Email Response Management System (ERMS). A system that tracks and manages email contacts, similar to how an ACD tracks and manages inbound calls.

Enterprise Resource Planning (ERP). Generally refers to a system that manages back office functions.

Envelope Strategy. A scheduling approach whereby enough agents are scheduled for the day or week to handle both the inbound call load and other types of work. Priorities are based on the inbound call load. When call load is heavy, all agents handle calls, but when it is light, some agents are reassigned to work that is not as time-sensitive.

Erlang. One hour of telephone traffic in an hour of time. For example, if circuits carry 120 minutes of traffic in an hour, that's two Erlangs. Related terms: Erlang B, Erlang C, A.K. Erlang (listed as Erlang, A.K.), Queue Dynamics.

Erlang B. A formula developed by A.K. Erlang, widely used to determine the number of trunks required to handle a known calling load during a one hour period. The formula assumes that if callers get busy signals, they go away forever, never to retry ("lost calls cleared"). Since some callers retry, Erlang B can underestimate trunks required. However, Erlang B is generally accurate in situations with few busy signals.

Erlang C. Calculates predicted waiting times (delay) based on three things: the number of servers (agents); the number of people waiting to be served (callers); and the average amount of time it takes to serve each person. It can also predict the resources required to keep waiting times within targeted limits. Erlang C assumes no lost calls or busy signals, so it has a tendency to overestimate staff required.

Erlang, A.K. A Danish engineer who worked for the Copenhagen Telephone Company in the early 1900s and developed Erlang B, Erlang C and other telephone traffic engineering formulas.

Error Rate. The number or percentage of defective (e.g., incomplete) transactions or the number or percentage of defective steps in a transaction.

Errors and Rework. As a measurement, the percent (and types) of errors and rework that are occurring.

Escalation Plan. A plan that specifies actions to be taken when the queue begins to build beyond acceptable levels. See Real-Time Management.

Exchange Line. See Trunk.

Explanatory Forecasting. See Forecasting Methodologies.

Fast Clear Down. A caller who hangs up immediately after hearing a delay announcement. Related term: Delay Announcement.

Fiber Optics. Thin filaments of transparent glass or plastic that use light to transmit voice, video or data signals.

First-Call Resolution. The percentage of calls that do not require any further contacts to address the customer's reason for calling. The customer does not need to contact the call center again to seek resolution, nor does anyone within the organization need to follow up. Related term: Errors and Rework.

Flex-Time Scheduling. Several weeks in advance, agents are promised schedules within a window of time (e.g., only Tuesdays through Saturdays or from 8 a.m. to 8 p.m. any day of the week), according to their personal availability. Then, specific work hours, and in some cases, days worked, are determined from week to week as forecasted staff requirements are refined. This approach may involve the entire staff, but usually includes only a subset of employees.

Flow Chart. A flow chart is a "map" of a process that is used to analyze and standardize procedures, identify root causes of problems and plan new processes.

Flushing out the Queue. A real-time management term that refers to changing system thresholds so that calls waiting for an agent group are redirected to another group with a shorter queue or more available agents. Related term: Real-Time Management.

Forecasted Call Load vs. Actual. A performance objective that reflects the percent variance between the call load forecasted and the call load actually received. Related term: Forecasting Methodologies.

Forecasting. The process of predicting call center workload and other activities. See Forecasted Call Load vs. Actual and Forecasting Methodologies.

Forecasting Methodologies. General methods used to predict future events, such as the amount of workload that will come into an incoming call center in future time periods. Methodologies are broadly categorized into quantitative and judgmental approaches. Quantitative forecasts include: time-series forecasts, which assume past data will reflect trends that continue into the future; and explanatory forecasting, which essentially attempts to reveal a linkage between two or more variables. Driver-based and event-driven forecasting approaches are variations of explanatory forecasting. Judgmental forecasts go beyond purely statistical techniques. They involve intuition, interdepartmental committees, market research and executive opinion. See Forecasting.

Front Office. Generally refers to customer-facing applications used in customer interactions. Related term: Back Office.

Full-Time Equivalent (FTE). A term used in scheduling and budgeting, whereby the number of scheduled hours is divided by the hours in a full work week. The hours of several part time agents may add up to one FTE.

Gate. See Agent Group.

Gateway. A server dedicated to providing access to a network.

Grade of Service (GOS). The probability that a call will not be connected to a system because all trunks are busy. Grade of service is often expressed as "p.01" meaning 1 percent of calls will be "blocked." Sometimes, grade of service is used interchangeably with service level, but the two terms have different meanings. Related terms: Erlang B, Service Level, Trunk Load.

Graphical User Interface (GUI). A computer interface that is graphical in nature, and uses menus, icons and a mouse to enable the user to interact with the system. Web browsers and the Windows and Apple operating systems are examples of GUI interfaces.

Handled Call. A call that is received and handled by an agent or peripheral equipment. Related terms: Answered Call, Offered Call, Received Call.

Handling Time. The time an agent spends in talk time and after-call work handling a transaction. Handling time can also refer to the time it takes for a machine to process a transaction. See Average Handling Time.

Headset. A device that consists of an earpiece and a microphone, and replaces a telephone handset. Headsets are designed to fit comfortably on the user's head, freeing both hands.

Help Desk. A term that generally refers to a call center that provides technical support (e.g., queries about product installation, usage or problems). The term is most often used in the context of computer software and hardware support centers.

Historical Forecasting. Any method of call volume forecasting that relies solely on past call volume to determine future projections. See Forecasting Methodologies.

Historical Report. A report that tracks call center and agent performance over a period of time. See Real-Time Report.

Idle Time. The inverse of occupancy. The time agents are available and waiting for contacts to arrive. See Occupancy.

Imaging. A process whereby documents are scanned into a system and stored electronically.

Immutable Law. A law of nature that is fundamental and not changeable (e.g., the law of gravity). In an inbound call center, the fact that occupancy goes up when service level goes down is an immutable law.

Incremental Revenue (Value) Analysis. A methodology that estimates the value (cost and revenue) of adding or subtracting an agent.

Increments. Also called intervals. In call centers, increments are the timeframes used for staffing and reporting. Given the variation in workload throughout the day, staff requirements must be calculated at specific increments (which are generally the smallest units of time reflected in the forecast).

Index Factor. In forecasting, a proportion used as a multiplier to adjust another number.

Information Systems (IS). A generic term for systems that perform data processing.

Information Technology (IT). A generic term that refers either to computer and/or communications systems and technologies, or the profession that develops and manages these systems.

Instant Messaging (IM). A type of text-chat between two or more Internet users.

Integrated Services Digital Network (ISDN). A set of international standards for digital telephone transmission.

Intelligent Routing. The use of information about the caller, current conditions or other parameters to route calls to the appropriate group, individual, automated system, etc.

Inter Exchange Carrier (IXC). A long-distance telephone company.

Interactive Voice Response (IVR). An IVR system responds to caller entered digits or speech recognition in much the same way that a conventional computer responds to keystrokes or clicks of a mouse. When the IVR is integrated with database computers, callers can interact with databases to check current information (e.g., account balances) and complete transactions (e.g. make transfers between accounts).

Inter-Exchange Carrier (IXC). A long-distance telephone company.

Interflow. See Overflow.

Interval. See Increment.

Internet Protocol (IP). The set of communication standards that control communications activity on the Internet. An IP address is assigned to every computer on the Internet.

Intraday Forecast. A short-term forecast that assumes activities early in the day will reflect how the rest of the day will go.

Intraflow. See Overflow.

Intraweek Forecast. A short-term forecast that assumes activities early in the week will reflect how the rest of the week will go.

Invisible Queue. When callers do not know how long the queue is or how fast it is moving. Related terms: Queue, Visible Queue.

Job Role. The function or responsibilities related to a specific position in an organization.

Judgmental Forecasting. Goes beyond purely statistical techniques and encompasses what people believe is going to happen. It is in the realm of intuition, interdepartmental committees, market research and executive opinion. See Forecasting Methodologies.

Key Performance Indicator (KPI). A high-level measure of call center performance. Note, some interpret KPI as the single most important measure in a department or unit; however, in common usage, most call centers have multiple KPIs. See Performance Objective.

Law of Diminishing Returns. The declining marginal improvements in service level that can be attributed to each additional agent, as successive agents are added.

Load Balancing. Balancing traffic between two or more destinations.

Local Area Network (LAN). The connection of multiple computers within a building so that they can share information, applications and peripherals. Related term: Wide Area Network.

Local Exchange Carrier (LEC). Telephone companies responsible for providing local connections and services.

Long Call. For staffing calculations and traffic engineering purposes, calls that approach or exceed thirty minutes.

Longest-Available Agent. Also referred to as most-idle agent. A method of distributing calls to the agent who has been sitting idle the longest. With a queue, longest available agent becomes next available agent. Related term: Next-Available Agent.

Longest Delay (Oldest Call). The longest time a caller has waited in queue, before abandoning or reaching an agent.

Look-Ahead Queuing. The ability for a system or network to examine a secondary queue and evaluate the conditions before overflowing calls from the primary queue.

Look-Back Queuing. The ability for a system or network to look back to the primary queue after the call has been overflowed to a secondary queue and evaluate the conditions. If the congestion clears, the call can be sent back to the initial queue.

Lost Call. See Abandoned Call.

Make Busy. To make a circuit or terminal unavailable.

Manual Answer. The ACD system is set up so that agents must manually answer calls. See Call Forcing.

Manual Available. The ACD system is set up so that agents must put themselves back into the available mode after completing any after call work. See Auto Available.

Measurement. A quantifiable unit.

Metrics. Another word for measurements or, sometimes in usage, objectives. Related terms: Key Performance Indicator, Performance Objective.

Middleware. Software that mediates between different types of hardware and software on a network, so that they can function together.

Monitoring. Monitoring is a call evaluation process that appraises the qualitative aspects of call handling. Monitoring programs include the tracking and analysis of data to identify individual agent and overall call center performance trends, anticipated problems, and training and coaching needs. There are several ways to monitor agents' performance; i.e., silent monitoring, call recording, side-by-side monitoring, peer monitoring, and mystery shoppers. Monitoring is also called position monitoring, quality monitoring or service observing. Related terms: Calibration, Call Quality.

Multimedia. Combining multiple forms of media in the communication of information (e.g, a traditional phone call is "monomedia," and a video call is "multimedia").

Multimedia Routing and Queuing. Systems and processes that handle contacts across media — including voice, text-based and Web transactions — based on business rules that define how any transaction, inquiry or problem is processed.

Mystery Shopper. A type of monitoring in which a person acts as a customer, initiates a call to the center and monitors the skills of the agent. See Monitoring.

Network. In the call center world, the term network is typically used to describe the inter-exchange (IXC) services that route calls into a center or among several centers. The network is the "pipe" between the caller and the call center, or between call centers. Related terms: Call-by-Call Routing, Network Control Center, Network Interflow, Percent Allocation.

Network Control Center (NCC). Also called traffic control center. In a networked call center environment, where people and equipment monitor real-time conditions across sites, change routing thresholds as necessary, and coordinate events that will impact base staffing levels. Related terms: Network, Network Management System.

Network Interflow. A technology used in multisite call center environments to create a more efficient distribution of calls between sites. Related terms: Call-by-Call Routing, Network, Percent Allocation.

Next-Available Agent. A call distribution method that sends calls to the next agent who becomes available. The method seeks to maintain an equal load across skill groups or services. When there is no queue, next-available agent reverts to longest-available agent. Related term: Longest-Available Agent.

Non ACD In Calls. Inbound calls that are directed to an agent's extension rather than to a general group. These may be personal calls or calls from customers who dial the agents' extension numbers.

Normalized Calls Per Agent. See True Calls Per Agent.

Number Portability. A shared database among network providers that enables call centers to keep the same telephone numbers even if they change carriers.

Occupancy. Also referred to as agent utilization or percent utilization. The percentage of time agents handle calls vs. wait for calls to arrive; the inverse of occupancy is idle time. Related terms: Adherence to Schedule, Idle Time.

Offered Call. Offered calls include all of the attempts callers make to reach the call center. There are three possibilities for offered calls: 1) They can get busy signals; 2) they can be answered by the system, but hang up before reaching an agent; or 3) they can be answered by an agent. Offered call reports in ACDs usually refer only to the calls that the ACD receives. Related terms: Answered Call, Handled Call, Received Call.

Off-Peak. Periods of time other than the call center's busiest periods. Also a term to describe periods of time when long-distance carriers provide lower rates.

On-the-Job Training (OJT). A method of training that exposes the employee to realistic job situations through observation, guided practice and while working on the job.

Open Ticket. A customer contact (transaction) that has not been completed or resolved (closed). Related terms: First-Call Resolution, Response Time.

Outsourcing. Contracting some or all call center services and/or technology to an outside company. The company is generally referred to as an outsourcer or service bureau.

Overflow. Calls that flow from one group or site to another. More specifically, intraflow happens when calls flow between agent groups and interflow is when calls flow out of the ACD to another site.

Overlay. See Rostered Staff Factor.

Overstaffing. A scheduling term that refers to situations when the call center has more staff than is required to handle the workload.

Overtime. Time beyond an established limit (e.g., working hours in addition to those of a regular schedule or full work week).

Pareto Chart. Created by economist Vilfredo Pareto, a Pareto chart is simply a bar chart that ranks events in order of importance or frequency.

Payback Period. A capital budgeting method that calculates the length of time required to recover an initial investment.

PBX/ACD. A private branch exchange (PBX) that is equipped with ACD functionality. See Private Branch Exchange and Automatic Call Distributor.

Peaked Call Arrival. A surge of traffic beyond random variation. It is a spike within a short period of time. There are two types of peaked traffic — the type you can plan for, and incidents that are impossible to predict. Related term: Increment.

Peer Monitoring. Call center agents monitor peers' calls and provide feedback on their performance. See Monitoring.

Percent Allocation. A call routing strategy sometimes used in multisite call center environments. Calls received in the network are allocated across sites based on user-defined percentages. Related terms: Call-by-Call Routing, Network, Network Interflow.

Performance Driver. A suspect performance driver that has been validated through statistically sound analysis.

Performance Objective. Usually stated as a quantifiable goal that must be accomplished within a given set of constraints, a specified period of time, or by a given date (e.g., reduce turnover by 20 percent within one year).

Performance Target. An interim improvement point at a specific point in time, when striving to attain a new level of performance. Related terms: Key Performance Indicator, Performance Objective.

Personal Digital Assistant (PDA). A small, lightweight "palmtop" computer often used for personal organization tasks (e.g., calendar, database, calculator and note-taking functions) and communications (e.g., email, wireless Internet access and wireless telephone).

Poisson. A formula sometimes used for calculating trunks. Assumes that if callers get busy signals, they keep trying until they successfully get through. Since some callers won't keep retrying, Poisson can overestimate trunks required. Related terms: Erlang B, Retrial Tables, Trunk Load.

Pooling Principle. The powerful pooling principle states: Any movement in the direction of consolidation of resources will result in improved traffic-carrying efficiency. Conversely, any movement away from consolidation of resources will result in reduced traffic-carrying efficiency. A common call center application is that if you take several small, specialized agent groups, effectively cross train them and put them into a single group, you'll have a more efficient environment (assuming all other things are equal). Related terms: Agent Group, Queue Dynamics, Skills-Based Routing.

Position Monitoring. See Monitoring.

Post-Call Processing (PCP). See After-Call Work.

Predictive Dialer. See Dialer.

Priority Queuing Application. Programming that recognizes and "bumps" higher-value customers up in the queue to ensure that they receive the most efficient service possible.

Private Automatic Branch Exchange (PABX). See Private Branch Exchange.

Private Branch Exchange (PBX). Also called private automatic branch exchange (PABX). A telephone system located at the call center's site that handles incoming and outgoing calls. ACD software can provide PBXs with ACD functionality. Many refer to a PBX as a "switch."

Private Network. A network made up of circuits for the exclusive use of an organization or group of affiliated organizations. Can be regional, national or international in scope and are common in large organizations.

Process. A system of causes. See System of Causes.

Qualitative Analysis. Analysis that interprets descriptive data, and is usually expressed as text. Related term: Quantitative Analysis.

Quantitative Analysis. Analysis that focuses on numerical, mathematical or statistical data. Related term: Qualitative Analysis.

Quantitative Forecasting. Using statistical techniques to forecast future events. Related terms: Forecasting Methodologies, Judgmental Forecasting.

Queue. Queue literally means "line of waiting people." Holds callers until an agent becomes available. Queue can also refer to a line or list of items in a system waiting to be processed (e.g., email messages).

Queue Display. See Readerboard.

Queue Dynamics. Queue dynamics refer to how queues behave; e.g., when service level goes up, occupancy goes down. Related terms: Agent Group, Average Speed of Answer, Occupancy, Service Level, Trunk Load.

Queue Time. See Delay.

Random Call Arrival. The normal, random variation in how incoming calls arrive.

Readerboard. Also called display board, queue display, wallboard or electronic display. A visual display, usually mounted on the wall or ceiling of a call center that provides real-time and historical information on queue conditions, agent status and call center performance.

Real-Time Adherence Software. A function of workforce management software that tracks how closely agents conform to their schedules. See Adherence to Schedule.

Real-Time Management. Making adjustments to staffing and thresholds in the systems and network in response to current queue conditions. Related terms: Queue Dynamics, Real-Time Report, Service Level.

Real-Time Report. Information on current conditions.

Real-Time Threshold. A marker that is identified in advance (e.g., number of calls in queue, longest in queue, etc.) that automatically initiates a certain response in a call center. For example, at a given time, a call center may not react to a queue unless it reaches 25 calls or more.

Received Call. A call detected and seized by a trunk. Received calls will either abandon or be answered by an agent. Related terms: Answered Call, Handled Call, Offered Call.

Recorded Announcement. A general reference to announcements callers hear while waiting in queue. Recorded announcements may remind callers to have certain information ready for the call, include general information about products or services, or provide alternative contact alternatives (e.g., "Visit our Web site at..."), etc. See Delay Announcement.

Recorded Announcement Route (RAN). See Delay Announcement.

Response Time. Defined as "100 percent of contacts handled within N days/hours/minutes" (e.g., all email will be handled within 24 hours). It is the preferred objective for contacts that do not have to be handled when they arrive. See Service Level.

Retention. The opposite of turnover; keeping employees in the call center. See Turnover.

Retrial Tables. Sometimes used to calculate trunks and other system resources required. They assume that some callers will make additional attempts to reach the call center if they get busy signals. Related terms: Erlang B, Poisson.

Retrial. Also called redial. When a person tries again to complete a call after encountering a busy signal.

Ring Delay. Also called delay before answer. An ACD feature that enables the system to adjust the number of rings before the system automatically answers a call.

Root Cause. A primary cause of a problem or outcome. See System of Causes.

Rostered Staff Factor (RSF). Alternatively called overlay, shrink factor or shrinkage. RSF is a numerical factor that leads to the minimum staff needed on schedule over and above base staff required to achieve your service level and response time objectives. It is calculated after base staffing is determined and before schedules are organized, and accounts for things like breaks, absenteeism and ongoing training. Related term: Base Staff.

Round-Robin Distribution. A method of distributing calls to agents according to a predetermined list. Related terms: Next-Available Agent, Longest-Available Agent.

Sales Force Automation (SFA). The use of computer and communications systems to support and boost the productivity of salespeople.

Scatter Diagram. A quality tool that assesses the strength of the relationship between two variables. Is used to test and document possible cause-and-effect scenarios. See System of Causes.

Schedule. A plan that specifies when employees will be on duty, and which may indicate specific activities that they are to handle at specific times. A schedule includes the days worked, start times and stop times, breaks, paid and unpaid status, etc.

Schedule Compliance. See Adherence to Schedule.

Schedule Exception. An activity not planned in an employee's schedule that becomes an "exception" to the plan. Related terms: Adherence to Schedule, Schedule.

Schedule Horizon. How far in advance schedules are determined.

Schedule Preference. A description of the times and days that an employee prefers to work. Related terms: Schedule, Schedule Horizon.

Schedule Trade. When agents are allowed to trade or "swap" schedules.

Scheduled Callback. A specified time that the call center will call a customer, usually based on the customer's preferences.

Scheduled Staff vs. Actual. A performance measure that is a comparison of the number of agents scheduled vs. the number actually in the center, involved in the activities specified by the schedule. Related term: Adherence to Schedule.

Screen Monitoring. A system capability that enables a supervisor or manager to remotely monitor the activity on agents' computer terminals. See Monitoring.

Screen Pop. A CTI application that delivers an incoming call to an agent, along with the data screen pertaining to that call or caller. See Computer Telephony Integration.

Screen Refresh. The rate at which real-time information is updated on a display (e.g., every five to 15 seconds). Screen refresh does not correlate with the timeframe used for real-time calculations.

Seated Agents. See Base Staff.

Self-Service System. A system that enables customers to access the information or services they need without interacting with an agent.

Service Bureau. A service bureau, sometimes referred to as an outsourcer, is a company hired to handle some or all of another organization's contacts. See Outsourcing.

Service Level. Also called telephone service factor (TSF). Service level is defined specifically as: "X percent of contacts answered in Y seconds"; e.g., 90 percent answered in 20 seconds. Contacts that must be handled when they arrive require a service level objective, and those that can be handled at a later time require a response time objective. Related Terms: Response Time, Service Level Agreement.

Service Level Agreement (SLA). An agreement — usually between a client organization and an outsourcer (although they increasingly exist between departments within an organization) — which defines performance objectives and expectations.

Service Observing. See Monitoring.

Shrink Factor. See Rostered Staff Factor.

Shrinkage. See Rostered Staff Factor.

Silent Monitoring. See Monitoring.

Site Selection. The process of choosing a call center location that best meets the needs of the organization.

Six Sigma. Originally developed by Motorola, Six Sigma is a highly disciplined process that focuses on developing and delivering near-perfect products and services. Sigma is a statistical term that measures process variation. See System of Causes.

Skill Group. See Agent Group.

Skill Path. Skill paths focus on the development of specific skills rather than the progression of positions through the call center and/or organization. Skill paths can move laterally (e.g., a printer technical support agent can be cross-trained to handle technical support on fax machines, as well) or upward (e.g., an agent can acquire leadership and coaching skills to add peer coaching responsibilities to his or her current position). See Career Path.

Skills-Based Routing. An ACD capability that matches a caller's specific needs with an agent that has the skills to handle that call, on a real-time basis. Related terms: Agent Group, Pooling Principle.

Smooth Call Arrival. Calls that arrive evenly across a period of time. Virtually non-existent in incoming call center environments.

Span of Control. The number of individuals a manager supervises. A large span of control means that the manager supervises many people. A small span of control means he or she supervisors fewer people.

Speech Recognition. Speech recognition enables IVR systems to interact with databases using spoken language, rather than the telephone keypad. There are two major types of speech recognition used in call centers today: 1) directed dialogue or structured language, which is prompting that coaches the caller through the selections; and 2) natural language, which uses a more open-ended prompt, recognizing what the caller says without as much coaching. See Interactive Voice Response.

Split Shifts. Shifts in which agents work a partial shift, take part of the day off, then return later to finish their shift. Related term: Schedule.

Split. See Agent Group.

Staff Sharing. A staff-sharing relationship is when two or more organizations (or different units of an organization) share a common pool of employees, typically to meet seasonal demands. Related term: Schedule.

Staggered Shifts. Shifts that begin and end at different times. For example, one shift begins at 7 a.m., the next at 7:30 a.m., the next at 8 a.m., until the center is fully staffed for the busy midmorning traffic. Related term: Schedule.

Standard. A quantifiable minimum level of performance; performance below or outside the standard is not acceptable.

Super Agent. See Universal Agent.

Supervisor Monitor. Computer monitors that enable supervisors to monitor the call handling statistics of their supervisory groups or teams.

Supervisor. The person who has frontline responsibility for a group of agents. Generally, supervisors are equipped with special telephones and computer terminals that enable them to monitor agent activities. Related terms: Job Role, Monitoring, Span of Control.

Swat Team. The term some companies use for a team of non call center employees that act as "reservists" to quickly be assigned to call handling duties if the call load soars. Related term: Schedule.

System of Causes. The variables that are part of a process. A call center is a process or system of causes.

Talk Time. Everything from "hello" to "goodbye" in a phone call. In other words, it's the time callers are connected with agents. Anything that happens during talk time, such as placing customers on hold to confer with supervisors, should be included in this measurement. Also called direct call processing. Related terms: After-Call Work, Call Load.

Telemarketing. Generally refers to outbound calls for the purpose of selling products or services, or placing informational calls to customers, prospective customers or constituents.

Telephone Sales or Service Representative (TSR). See Agent.

Telephone Service Factor (TSF). See Service Level.

Text-Chat. Allows customers visiting the corporate Web site to have real-time, text-based conversations with live agents.

Threshold. The point at which an action, change or process takes place.

Toll-Free Service. Enables callers to reach a call center out of the local calling area without incurring charges.

Touchtone. A trademark of AT&T. See Dual-Tone Multifrequency.

Trouble Ticket. The report of a customer's problem with a particular device or system, which is tracked through the workflow process.

True Calls Per Agent. Also called normalized calls per agent. It is actual calls (contacts) an individual or group handled divided by occupancy for that period of time. Related terms: Adherence to Schedule, Call Quality, Contacts Handled (Calls Per Agent).

Trunk. Also called a line, exchange line or circuit. A telephone circuit linking two switching systems. See Trunk Load.

Trunk Group. A collection of trunks associated with a single peripheral and usually used for a common purpose. Related terms: Trunk, Trunk Group.

Trunk Load. The load that trunks carry. Includes both delay and talk time.

Turnover. When a person leaves the call center. Turnover can be categorized as voluntary (when the employee decides to leave the organization or position) or involuntary (when management makes the decision to end the employment relationship).

Unavailable Work State. An agent work state used to identify a mode not associated with handling telephone calls.

Unified Reporting. When data from different channels and systems are included on one reporting tool. This supports better analysis and decision-making in the organization.

Uniform Call Distributor (UCD). A simple system that distributes calls to a group of agents and provides some reports.

Uniform Resource Locator (URL). The address for a Web page that is translated to an IP address.

Universal Agent. Also known as super agent. Refers to either: A) an agent who can handle all types of incoming calls, or B) an agent who can handle all channels of contact (e.g., inbound calls, outbound calls, email, text-chat, etc.).

Upsell. A suggestive selling technique of offering more expensive products or services to current customers during the sales decision. See Cross-sell.

Variance Report. A report illustrating budget/cost objectives that look at the difference between projected and actual expenditures for various budget categories.

Virtual Call Center. A distributed call center that acts as a single site for call handling and reporting purposes.

Visible Queue. When callers know how long the queue that they just entered is, and how fast it is moving (e.g., they hear a system announcement that relays the expected wait time). Related terms: Invisible Queue, Queue.

Wallboard. See Readerboard.

Web Callback. By clicking on a button, the customer lets the company know that he/she wants to be called back either immediately or at a designated time.

Web Call-Through. Using voice over Internet (VoIP) technology, the customer clicks on a button that establishes a voice line directly to the call center.

Web Collaboration. A broad term referring to the ability for an agent and customer to share content by pushing/pulling Web pages and/or whiteboarding and page markup.

Web Self-Service Tools. Tools that enable customers to receive information and answers to questions, place orders and view order status directly from the corporate Web site without contacting the call center for assistance. See Self-Service System.

Wide Area Network (WAN). The connection of multiple computers across a wide area.

Work State. An ACD-produced indicator of the status of a call center agent's activity or status. See Agent Status.

Workforce Management System (WFMS). Software systems that, depending on available modules, forecast call load, calculate staff requirements, organize schedules and track real-time performance of individuals and groups. Related terms: Computer Simulation, Erlang B, Erlang C, Forecasting Methodologies, Queue Dynamics.

Workload. Often used interchangeably with Call Load. Work load can also refer to non-call activities.

Wrap-Up Codes. Codes that agents enter on their phones to identify the types of calls they are handling. The ACD can then generate reports on call types by handling time, time of day, etc. See After-Call Work.

Zip Tone. See Beep Tone.

Index

How to Reach ICMI Press and the Author

We would love to hear from you! How could this book be improved? Has it been helpful? No comments are off limits! You can reach us at:

Mailing Address: ICMI Press
                      P.O. Box 6177
                      Annapolis, MD 21401
Telephone: 410-267-0700, 800-672-6177
Fax: 410-267-0962
Email: icmi@icmi.com
Web site: www.icmi.com
Author email: bradc@icmi.com

About ICMI

The International Customer Management Institute (ICMI) is one of the call center industry's most established and respected organizations. Founded in 1985, ICMI delivered the industry's first management-level conferences, educational programs and publications.

While ICMI's path-breaking work continues, the mission remains much the same: to provide resources and expertise that help individuals and organizations improve operational performance, attain superior business results and increase the strategic value of their customer contact services. Today's ICMI melds the traditional focus on consulting, training, and high-level engagement with CMP's strength in media and events to create a powerful one-stop-shop resource. Through the dedication and experience of its team, uncompromised objectivity and results-oriented vision, ICMI has earned a reputation as the industry's most trusted source for:

- Consulting
- Training
- Publications
- Events
- Professional Membership

Through constant innovation and research, ICMI's consulting and training services have become the industry's gold standard. ICMI publications, such as *Call Center Magazine* and *Call Center Management Review*, and events, including the Annual Call Center Exhibition (ACCE) and Call Center Demo and Exhibition conferences, continue to lead the industry. And ICMI's growing membership community now includes professionals representing organizations in over 50 countries.

Order Form

QTY.	Item	Member Price	Price	Total
	Call Center Management On Fast Forward: Succeeding In Today's Dynamic Customer Contact Environment**	**$33.96**	$39.95	
	A Career for the 21st Century	**$11.01**	$12.95	
	The Voice of Your Company: Conversational Skills for Customer Service Reps	**$11.01**	$12.95	
	Driving Peak Sales Performance in Call Centers**	**$33.96**	$39.95	
	Call Center Technology Demystified: The No-Nonsense Guide to Bridging Customer Contact Technology, Operations and Strategy**	**$33.96**	$39.95	
	ICMI's Call Center Management Dictionary: The Essential Reference for Contact Center, Help Desk and Customer Care Professionals**	**$21.21**	$24.95	
	ICMI's Pocket Guide to Call Center Management Terms*	**$5.12**	$5.95	
	ICMI Handbook and Study Guide Series Module 1: People Management*** Module 2: Operations Management*** Module 3: Customer Relationship Management*** Module 4: Leadership and Business Management***	**$169.15 ea.**	$199.00 ea.	
	Topical Books: **The Best of *Call Center Management Review*** Call Center Recruiting and New Hire Training* Call Center Forecasting and Scheduling* Call Center Agent Motivation and Compensation* Call Center Agent Retention and Turnover*	**$14.41 ea.**	$16.95 ea.	
	Forms Books Call Center Sample Monitoring Forms** Call Center Sample Customer Satisfaction Forms Book**	**$42.46 ea.**	$49.95 ea.	
	Software QueueView: A Staffing Calculator — CD ROM* Easy Start™ Call Center Scheduler Software — CD-ROM*	**$41.65** **$254.15**	$49.95 $299.00	
	Call Center Humor: The Best of *Call Center Management Review* Volume 3*	**$8.45**	$9.95	
	The Call Centertainment Book*	**$7.61**	$8.95	
	Shipping & Handling @ $5.00 per US shipment, plus .50¢ per* item, $1.00 per** item and $2.00 per*** item. Additional charges apply to shipments outside the US.			
	Tax (5% MD residents, 7% GST Canadian residents)			
	TOTAL (US dollars)			

Please contact us for quantity discounts
For more information on our products, please visit **www.icmi.com**

❏ Please send me a free issue of *Call Center Magazine* and information on ICMI's publications, services and membership.

Please ship my order and/or information to:

Name _____

Title _____

Industry_____

Company_____

Address_____

City_____State/Province _____

Country_____Postal Code _____

Telephone (   ) _____

Fax (   ) _____

Email_____

Method of Payment (if applicable)

❏ Check enclosed (Make payable to ICMI Inc.; U.S. Dollars only)

❏ Charge to: ❏ American Express   ❏ MasterCard   ❏ Visa

Account No._____

Expiration Date _____

Name on Card _____

Fax order to: 410-267-0962
call us at: 800-672-6177 or 410-267-0700
order online at: www.icmi.com
or mail order to: ICMI
P.O. Box 6177, Annapolis, MD 21401